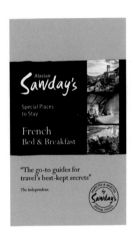

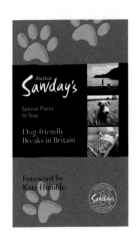

Alastair
## Sawday's

Special Places to Stay

Seventeenth edition
Copyright © 2015
Alastair Sawday Publishing Co. Ltd
Published in September 2015
ISBN-13: 978-1-906136-75-8

Alastair Sawday Publishing Co. Ltd,
Merchants House, Wapping Road,
Bristol BS1 4RW, UK
Tel: +44 (0)117 204 7801
Email: info@sawdays.co.uk
Web: www.sawdays.co.uk

The Globe Pequot Press,
P. O. Box 480, Guilford,
Connecticut 06437, USA
Tel: +1 203 458 4500
Email: info@globepequot.com
Web: www.globepequot.com

Series Editor Alastair Sawday
Editor Tom Bell
Assistant to Editor Lianka Varga
Senior Picture Editor Alec Studerus
Production Coordinators Lianka Varga,
Sarah Frost Mellor
Writing Tom Bell
Inspections Tom Bell

Marketing & PR
0117 204 7801
marketing@sawdays.co.uk

*We have made every effort to ensure the accuracy of the information in this book at the time of going to press. However, we cannot accept any responsibility for any loss, injury or inconvenience resulting from the use of information contained therein.*

Production: Pagebypage Co Ltd
Maps: Maidenhead Cartographic Services
Printing: Pureprint, Uckfield
UK distribution: Travel Alliance, Bath
diane@popoutmaps.com

Cover photo credits.
Front 1. Magdalen Chapter, entry 76  2. Artist Residence Brighton, entry 5 3. The George in Rye, entry 215
Back: 1. Artist Residence Brighton, entry 5   2. At the Chapel, entry 177  3. The Bell Alderminster, entry 218
Spine: Chalk & Cheese, entry 145

# Alastair Sawday's

## Special Places to Stay

# British
## Hotels & Inns

# 4    Contents

I contemplate a hotel landscape that shifts even as I watch it, buffeted by the winds of a change that never lets up. Those delightful, family-run, hotels that reflect the personalities of their owners are still with us, but they have to work hard to survive.

We have always set out to help the best of the independent hotels, yet they have more battles to fight than we can keep up with. The 'heavies' of the online booking world push hotels to come up with very generous offers, then take a sizeable commission. The owner is left with very

Photo above: Tom Germain
Photo right: Castleman Hotel & Restaurant, entry 84

little after paying staff, food, insurance, health and safety. Others find themselves paying hearty tourist taxes, investing in fire systems and meeting all sorts of regulatory demands while watching informal, unregulated challengers set up without having to conform to any of the same rules. How on earth can they make a profit? The temptation to spend as little as possible on your food must be strong; and to cut staff costs too. If you want your favourite hotels to survive, you've got to pay for them — and some of them are within these pages.

I feel protective of the families who have worked their socks off for decades and are now struggling — as I feel protective of London taxi cabs who pay heavily for licences and training only to find unlicensed 'Uber' cars carrying off their passengers.

Given how tough it is for hotels, it's moving to witness so many of them adapting — and flourishing. I have watched as the old Penzance Arts Club was gutted and re-built by a remarkable woman who will throw her considerable energy and personality into running it as a hotel/B&B. She is totally up to date, delights in mixing people together, listens to new ideas and advice and will make a success of it. (I am not sure she knows quite what hard work it will be!) May there be more like her, to encourage the brave survivors we so much admire. This book is full of them.

*Alastair Sawday*

It's simple. There are no rules, no boxes to tick. We choose places that we like and are fiercely subjective in our choices. We also recognise that one person's idea of special is not necessarily someone else's so there is a huge variety of places, and prices, in this book.

Those who are familiar with our Special Places series know that we look for comfort, originality, authenticity, and reject the anonymous and the banal. The way guests are treated comes as high on our list as the setting, the architecture, the atmosphere and the food.

## Inspections

We visit every place in the guide to get a feel for how both hotel and owner tick.

Photo: Tudor Farmhouse Hotel, entry 96

We don't take a clipboard and we don't have a list of what is acceptable and what is not. Instead, we chat for an hour or so with the owner or manager and look round. It's all very informal, but it gives us an excellent idea of who would enjoy staying there. If the visit happens to be the last of the day, we may stay the night. Once in the book, properties are re-inspected regularly, so that we can keep things fresh and accurate.

## Feedback

In between inspections we rely on feedback from our army of readers, as well as from staff members who are encouraged to visit properties across the series. This feedback is invaluable to us and we always follow up on comments.

So do tell us whether your stay has been a joy or not, if the atmosphere was great or stuffy, the owners and staff cheery or bored. The accuracy of the book depends on what you, and our inspectors, tell us. A lot of the new entries in each edition are recommended by our readers, so keep telling us about new places you've discovered too. Please use the forms on our website at www.sawdays.co.uk.

However, please do not tell us if your starter was cold, or the bedside light broken. Tell the owner, immediately, and get them to do something about it. Most owners, or staff, are more than happy to correct problems and will bend over backwards to help. Far better than bottling it up and then writing to us a week later!

## Subscriptions

Owners pay to appear in this guide. Their fee goes towards the high costs of inspecting, of producing an illustrated book and of developing our website. We only include places that we find special: it is not possible for anyone to buy their way onto these pages. Nor is it possible for the owner to write their own description. We will say if the bedrooms are small, or if a main road is near. We do our best to avoid misleading people.

## Disclaimer

We make no claims to pure objectivity in choosing these places. They are here simply because we like them. Our opinions and tastes are ours alone and this book is a statement of them; we hope you will share them. We have done our utmost to get our facts right but apologise unreservedly for any mistakes that may have crept in.

You should know that we don't check such things as fire alarms, swimming pool security or any other regulation with which owners of properties receiving paying guests should comply. This is the responsibility of the owners. At some of our smaller places – particularly our inns – you should request a contact number for emergencies if staff are not present overnight.

Do remember that the information in this book is a snapshot in time and may have changed since we published it; do call ahead to avoid being disappointed.

Photo: The Horn of Plenty, entry 61

## Finding the right place for you

All these places are special in one way or another. All have been visited and then written about honestly so that you can take what you want and leave the rest. Those of you who swear by Sawday's trust our write-ups precisely because we don't have a blanket standard; we include places simply because we like them. But we all have different priorities, so do read the descriptions carefully and pick out the places where you will be comfortable.

## Maps

Each property is flagged with its entry number on the maps at the front. These maps are a great starting point for planning your trip, but please don't use them as anything other than a general guide — use a decent road map for real navigation. Most places will send you detailed instructions once you have booked your stay.

## Symbols

These are explained at the very back of the book. They are based on the information given to us by the owners. However, things do change: bikes may be under repair or a new pool may have been put in. Please use the symbols as a guide rather than an absolute statement of fact and double-check anything that is important to you — owners occasionally bend their own rules, so it's worth asking if you may take your child or dog even if they don't have the symbol.

Wheelchair access &#x267F; — Some hotels are keen to accept wheelchair users into their

hotels and have made provision for them. However, this does not mean that wheelchair users will always be met with a perfect landscape. You may encounter ramps, a shallow step, gravelled paths, alternative routes into some rooms, a bathroom (not a wet room), perhaps even a lift. In short, there may be the odd hindrance and we urge you to call and make sure you will get what you need.

Limited mobility — The limited mobility symbol &#x1F6B6; shows those places where at least one bedroom and bathroom is accessible without using stairs. The symbol is designed to satisfy those who walk slowly, with difficulty, or with the aid of a stick. A wheelchair may be able to navigate some areas, but in our opinion these places are not fully wheelchair friendly. If you use a chair for longer distances, but are not too bad over shorter distances, you'll probably be OK; again, please ring and ask. There may be a step or two, a bath

Photo left: Langar Hall, entry 160
Photo: Cley Windmill, entry 153

or a shower with a tray in a cubicle, a good distance between the car park and your room, slippery flagstones or a tight turn.

Children – The 🚸 symbol shows places which are happy to accept children of all ages. This does not mean that they will necessarily have cots, high chairs, etc. If an owner welcomes children but only those above a certain age, we have put these details at the end of their write-up. These houses do not have the child symbol, but even these folk may accept your younger child at quiet times. If you want to get out and about in the evenings, check when you book whether there are any babysitting services. Even very small places can sometimes organise this for you.

Pets – Our 🐕 symbol shows places which are happy to accept pets. Do let the owners know when booking that you'd like to bring your pet – particularly if it is not the usual dog! Be realistic about your pet – if it is nervous or excitable or doesn't like the company of other dogs, people, chickens, children, then say so.

Owners' pets – The 🐈 symbol is given when the owners have their own pet on the premises. It may not be a cat! But it is there to warn you that you may be greeted by a dog, serenaded by a parrot, or indeed sat upon by a cat.

## Hotel Awards

We have picked those places that deserve a special mention. Our categories are:

Hotels of the Year
(England, Scotland, Wales);
Favourite newcomers;
Old favourites;
Nicely priced;
Fabulous food.

More details are given on pages 16-21 and all the award winners have been stamped.

Photo: Brocco on the Park, entry 225

## Types of places

Hotels can vary from huge, humming and slick to those with only a few rooms that are run by owners at their own pace. In some you may not get room service or have your bags carried in and out. In smaller hotels there may be a fixed menu for dinner with very little choice, so if you have dishes that leave you cold, it's important to say so when you book your meal. If you decide to stay at an inn remember that they can be noisy, especially at weekends. If these things are important to you, then do check when you book.

## Rooms

Bedrooms – These are described as double, twin, single, family or suite. A double may contain a bed which is anything from 135cm wide to 180cm wide. A twin will contain two single beds (usually 90cm wide). A suite will have a separate sitting area, but it may not be in a different room. Family rooms can vary in size, as can the number of beds they hold, so do ask. And do not assume that every bedroom has a TV.

Bathrooms – All bedrooms have their own bathrooms unless we say that they don't. If you have your own bathroom but you have to leave the room to get to it we describe it as 'separate'. There are very few places in the book that have shared bathrooms and they are usually reserved for members of the same party. Again, we state this clearly.

Photo: Hever Castle Luxury Bed & Breakfast, entry 118

## Meals

Breakfast is included in the room price unless otherwise stated. If only a continental breakfast is offered, we let you know.

Some places serve lunch, most do Sunday lunch (often very well-priced), the vast majority offer dinner. In some places you can content yourself with bar meals, in others you can feast on five courses. Most offer three courses for £25-£35, either table d'hôte or à la carte. Some have tasting menus, very occasionally you eat communally. Some large hotels (and some posh private houses) will bring dinner to your room if you prefer, or let you eat in the garden by candlelight. Always ask for what you want and sometimes, magically, it happens.

## Prices and minimum stays

We quote the lowest price per night for two people in low season to the highest price in high season. Only a few places have designated single rooms; if no single

rooms are listed, the price we quote refers to single occupancy of a double room. In many places prices rise even higher when local events bring people flooding to the area, a point worth remembering when heading to Cheltenham for the racing or Glyndebourne for the opera.

The half-board price quoted is per person per night and includes dinner, usually three courses. Mostly you're offered a table d'hôte menu. Occasionally you eat à la carte and may find some dishes carry a small supplement. There are often great deals to be had, mostly mid-week in low season.

Most hotels do not accept one-night bookings at weekends. Small country hotels are rarely full during the week and the weekend trade keeps them going. If you ring in March for a Saturday night in July, you won't get it. If you ring at the last moment you may. Some places insist on three-night stays on bank holidays.

Photo above: Cnapan Restaurant & Hotel, entry 308
Photo right: Saracens Head, entry 154

### Booking and cancellation

Most places ask for a deposit at the time of booking, either by cheque or card. If you cancel – depending on how much notice you give – you can lose all or part of this deposit unless your room is re-let.

It is reasonable for hotels to take a deposit to secure a booking; they have learnt that if they don't, the commitment of the guest wanes and they may fail to turn up.

Some cancellation policies are more stringent than others. It is also worth noting that some owners will take the money directly from your credit/debit card without contacting you to discuss it. So ask them to explain their cancellation policy clearly before booking so you understand exactly where you stand; it may well avoid a nasty surprise. And consider taking out travel insurance (with a cancellation clause) if you're concerned.

### Arrivals and departures

Housekeeping is usually done by 2pm, and your room will usually be available by mid-afternoon. Normally you will have to wave goodbye to it between 10am and 11am. Sometimes one can pay to linger. Some inns are closed between 3pm and 6pm, so do try and agree an arrival time in advance or you may find nobody there.

### Closed

When given in months this means for the whole of the month stated. So, 'Closed: November–March' means closed from 1 November to 31 March.

## Sawday's British Hotel Awards 2016

This is the time of year we throw a gong or two at some of our hotels, so here are 15 very special places that typify the Sawday ethos.

**Award categories**

Hotels of the Year

Favourite newcomers

Old favourites

Nicely priced

Fabulous food

**Plas Bodegroes**            Entry 295
WALES
Pwllheli, Gwynedd

## Hotels of the Year

We love small, intimate hotels and inns where the art of hospitality is practiced with flair – these three wonders of our world have mastered that art in spades.

**Tiroran House**            Entry 248
SCOTLAND
Isle of Mull, Argyll & Bute

**Tudor Farmhouse Hotel**     Entry 96
ENGLAND
Clearwell, Gloucestershire

**Brocco on the Park**     Entry 225
Sheffield, Yorkshire

## Favourite newcomers

New hotels are hard to find in tough economic times, but that hasn't stopped creative owners bursting onto the scene with beautiful new places that delight us.

**The Pierhouse**     Entry 244
Appin, Argyll & Bute

**The Coach House
at Middleton Lodge**     Entry 234
Richmond, Yorkshire

**Pen-y-Dyffryn Country Hotel**
Entry 172     Oswestry, Shropshire

**The Old Rectory Hotel**     Entry 56
Barnstable, Devon

## Old favourites

Like a good red wine, some hotels get better with age – these places have a clear instinct for great hospitality and have been delighting guests for years.

**The Traddock**     Entry 239
Settle, Yorkshire

**The Henley Hotel**     Entry 64
Bigbury-on-Sea, Devon

## Nicely priced

There's nothing like washing up at a lovely small hotel and finding it has a lovely small price, too – here are three that do that with ease.

**Penbontbren**     Entry 289
Llandysul, Ceredigion

**The Black Swan**     Entry 34
Ravenstonedale, Cumbria

**The Olive Branch**  Entry 169
Oakham, Rutland

**Read's Restaurant with Rooms**
Entry 127 Faversham, Kent

## Fabulous food

From hot kitchens come small miracles to delight our tastebuds – here are three places where your pleasure receptors will delight in ambrosial food.

**BridgeHouse Hotel**  Entry 80
Beaminster, Dorset

Photo: Idle Rocks Hotel, entry 26

### Alastair
# Sawday's

'More than a bed
for the night…'

Britain
France
Ireland
Italy
Portugal
Spain

www.sawdays.co.uk

Self-Catering | B&B | Hotel | Pub | Treehouses, Cabins, Yurts & More

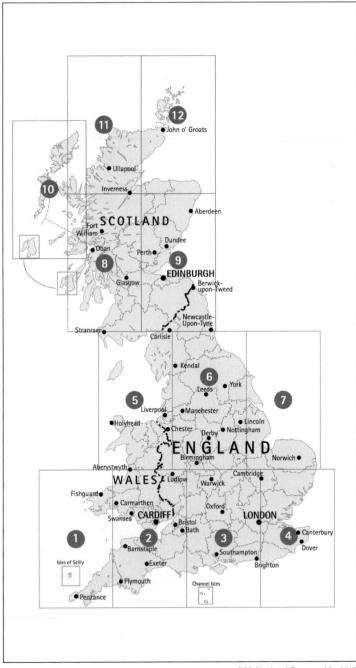

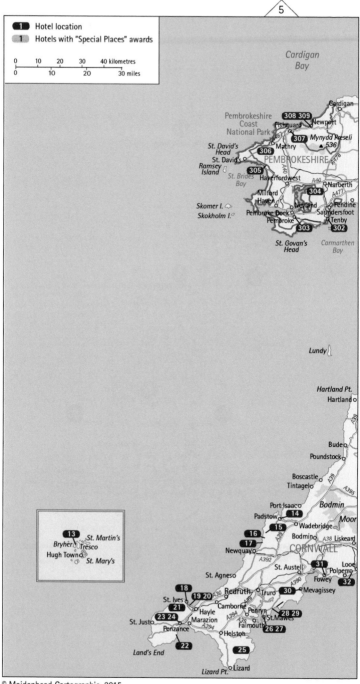

Map 2                                                                                    27

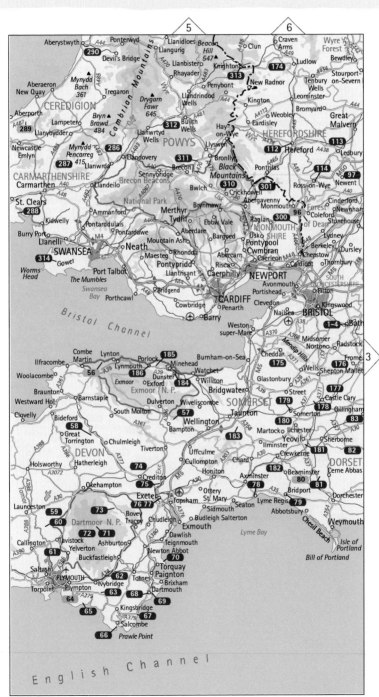

© Maidenhead Cartographic, 2015

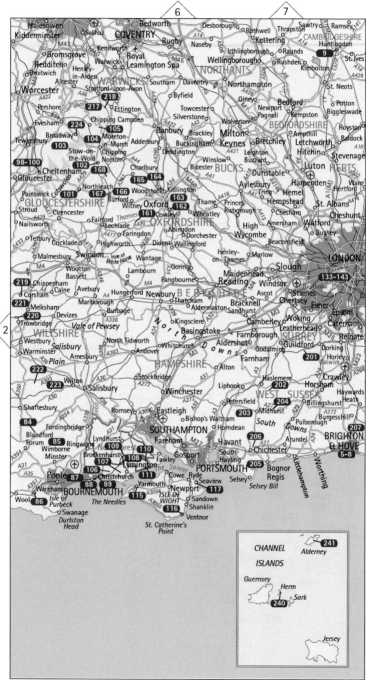

# Map 4

29

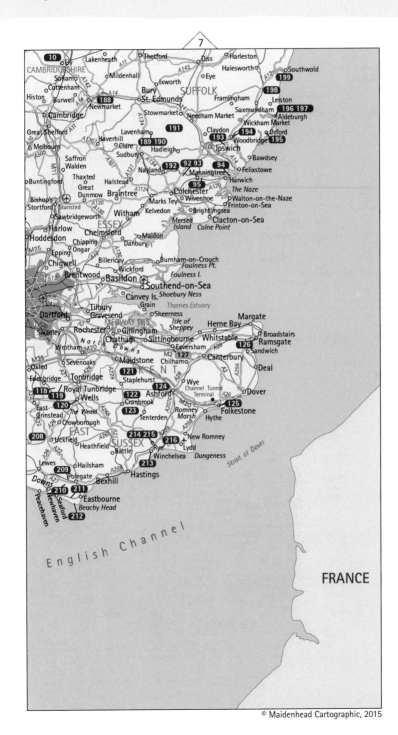

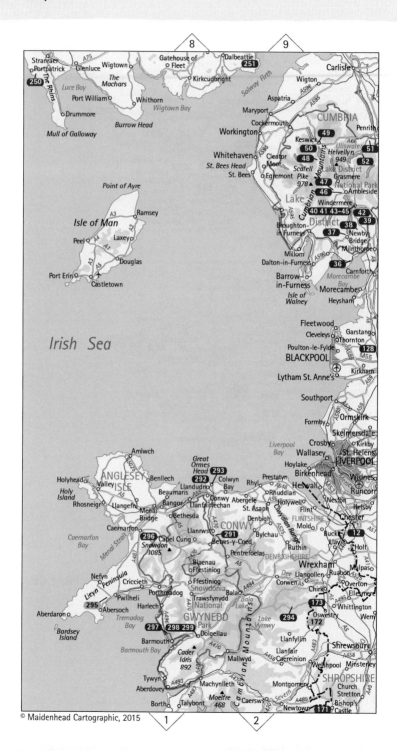

© Maidenhead Cartographic, 2015

# Map 6

31

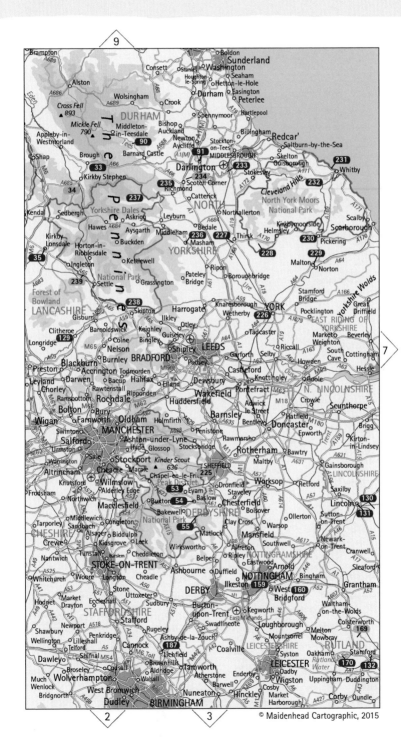

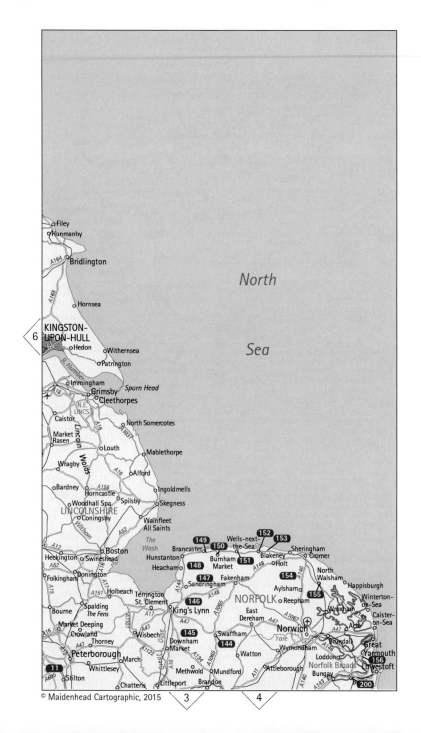

North

Sea

Filey
Hunmanby
A164 Bridlington
A165
Hornsea
KINGSTON-
UPON-HULL
6
Hedon
Withernsea
Patrington
R. Humber
Immingham
A18
Grimsby
Spurn Head
Cleethorpes
N.E.
LINCS
Caistor
North Somercotes
A16
Market
Rasen
A1031
Lincoln
Louth
Mablethorpe
Wolds
Wragby
A16
Alford
Bardney
A158
Ingoldmells
Horncastle
Woodhall Spa
Spilsby
Skegness
LINCOLNSHIRE
Coningsby
Wainfleet
All Saints
Witham
A52
152 153
Wells-next-
149
the-Sea
The
150
Sheringham
A12
Wash
Brancaster
Cromer
Heckington
Swineshead
Boston
Hunstanton
Burnham
151
Blakeney
A149
Holt
A52
Market
Donington
148
North
Folkingham
Heacham
Walsham
Happisburgh
A15
A17
Holbeach
147
Fakenham
154
Winterton-
Spalding
Terrington
A146
Sandringham
Aylsham
on-Sea
Bourne
St. Clement
A148
155
A151
The Fens
146
Reepham
Wroxham
Caister-
A12
NORFOLK
on-Sea
Market Deeping
A1101
King's Lynn
A1065
East
A47
Acle
Crowland
A41
Dereham
Ouse
A10
Wisbech
145
A16
Thorney
Norwich
A47
Brundall
Downham
Swaffham
Great
Peterborough
A1122
Market
144
Yare
Loddon
Yarmouth
11
March
A134
A1065
Watton
Wymondham
Norfolk Broads
156
Whittlesey
Methwold
A11
A140
Lowestoft
A605
Stilton
Mundford
Attleborough
Bungay
200
Chatteris
Littleport
Brandon
A143

3        4

# Map 8

33

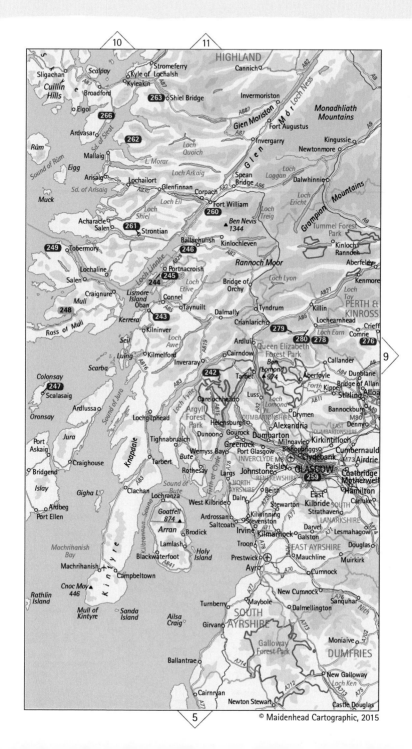

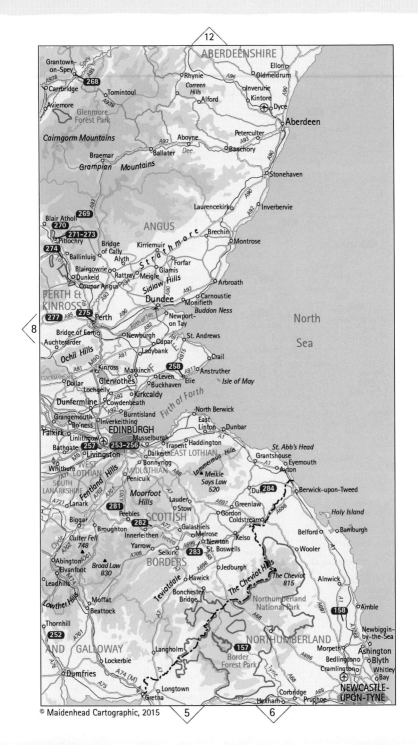

© Maidenhead Cartographic, 2015

Map 10                                                        35

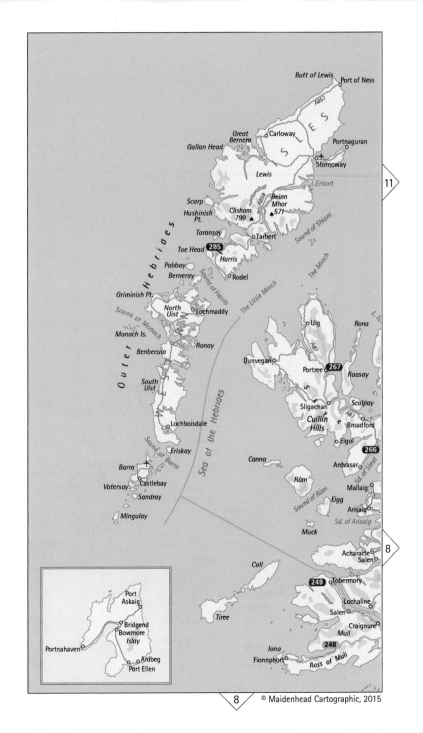

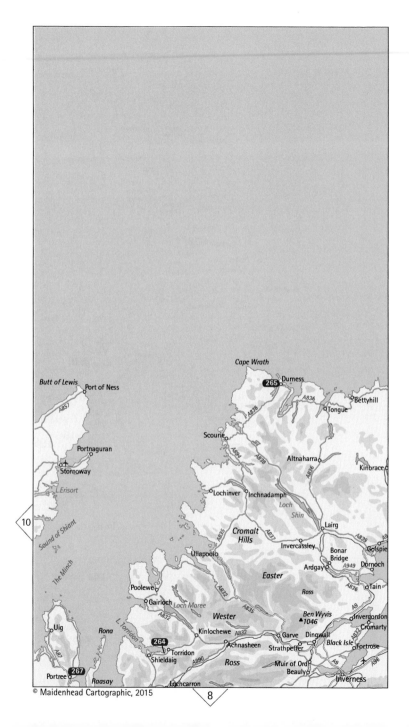

Cape Wrath
Durness
265
A836
Bettyhill
Butt of Lewis
Port of Ness
Tongue
A857
A838
Scourie
A894
A836
Portnaguran
Altnaharra
Kinbrace
Stornoway
A838
L.Erisort
Lochinver
Inchnadamph
Loch Shin
10
A835
Lairg
A839
A9
Cromalt Hills
A837
Invercassley
Bonar Bridge
Golspie
Sound of Shiant
Ullapool
Ardgay
A949
Dornoch
The Minch
Easter
A836
Tain
Poolewe
Ross
A9
Gairloch
Loch Maree
A832
Wester
Ben Wyvis
▲1046
Invergordon
Uig
Rona
A835
Cromarty
L. Torridon
A832
Kinlochewe
A832
Garve
Dingwall
Black Isle
Fortrose
264
Torridon
Achnasheen
Strathpeffer
Shieldaig
A890
Ross
Muir of Ord
A9
267
Beauly
A96
Portree
Raasay
Inverness
Lochcarron
8

© Maidenhead Cartographic, 2015

# Map 12

37

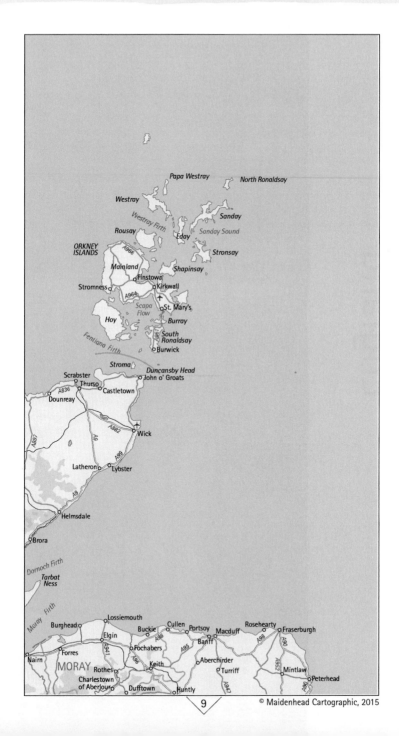

© Maidenhead Cartographic, 2015

# England

## Abbey Hotel

You're in the epicentre of Bath, just behind the abbey, in one of the prettiest quarters in town. Parade Gardens waits across the road, the river Avon pours over the weir at Pulteney Bridge, Bath rugby club stands on the far bank. As for the hotel, in summer you take to the terrace café for coffee and watch the world go by; in winter it turns into an après-ski bar for mince pies and mulled wine. Inside, you find contemporary art in the sitting room, wine glasses hanging from the ceiling in the stylish bar, then Chris Staines's lovely food in the theatrical restaurant, perhaps Thai mussels with lemongrass and ginger, whole roast spring chicken with herb gnocchi, salted peanut parfait with caramel popcorn and vanilla yogurt. Smart rooms wait upstairs, where deeply comfy beds have woollen throws and colourful headboards. Some are small, others are big, all have iPads for room service, sparkling new bathrooms are beginning to emerge. Bath waits on your doorstep: rugby at the Rec, the Christmas market, all things Jane Austen. You're close to the station, too, so leave your car at home. *Minimum stay: 2 nights at weekends.*

| | |
|---|---|
| Rooms | 46 doubles, 14 twin/doubles: £105–£330. |
| Meals | Breakfast £15. Lunch from £7.50. Dinner, 3 courses, £30–£35. Sunday lunch from £16. |
| Closed | Never. |
| Directions | In central Bath, 100m south of the abbey, 100m west of the river Avon. Parking in Southgate car park £13 a day. |

Ian & Christa Taylor
Abbey Hotel
North Parade, Bath, BA1 1LF
Tel     +44 (0)1225 805615
Email   reception@abbeyhotelbath.co.uk
Web     www.abbeyhotelbath.co.uk

## Villa Magdala

Villa Magdala is one of those lovely places that scores top marks across the board. You're pretty much in the middle of town, but hidden away on a quiet side street opposite a park. Then, there's a batch of smart bedrooms, which have style and comfort in equal measure. Add to this lovely staff on hand to book restaurants, balloon flights or day trips to Stonehenge and you have a perfect base. You're a five-minute stroll from magnificent Pulteney Bridge; the station isn't much further, so leave your car at home. You can hire bikes in town, then follow a towpath along the river out into the country. Back home, there's tea and cake on arrival, buck's fizz for breakfast, even bats and balls for children who want to go to the park. Breakfast – served in an airy dining room – is exceptional: smoked salmon and free-range scrambled eggs, buttermilk pancakes, the full cooked works. Rooms vary in size, but all have excellent beds, pretty wallpaper and sparkling bathrooms. Good restaurants wait close by. Don't miss the Roman Baths or the Fashion Museum. There's off-street parking, too – a real boon. *Minimum stay: 2 nights at weekends.*

| | |
|---|---|
| Rooms | 9 doubles, 11 twin/doubles: £99-£325. Singles from £89. Extra bed/sofabed available £45 per person per night. |
| Meals | Restaurant within 500m. |
| Closed | Christmas. |
| Directions | West into Bath on A4. Left into Cleveland Place (signed Through Traffic & University). Over bridge, 2nd right and on right opposite park. |

**Michael Hamilton**
Villa Magdala
Henrietta Street, Bath, BA2 6LX

| | |
|---|---|
| Tel | +44 (0)1225 466329 |
| Email | enquiries@villamagdala.co.uk |
| Web | www.villamagdala.co.uk |

## Grays Boutique Bed & Breakfast Hotel

Welcome to Grays, a Victorian villa on Bath's southern slopes, with 12 luscious bedrooms and the city a skip down the hill. The moment you enter the hall – high ceilings, gilded mirrors, sweet sofa – you feel you've arrived somewhere special. It's family run and the service is second to none: a mix of impeccable and warm-hearted. Smart coir carpeting brings you up to serene bedrooms with harmonious colours, beds (some French-retro, one modern four-poster) with sumptuous mattresses and heaps of pillows, fresh flowers, lavender bags, sweets, treats and chandeliers, limestone touches in the bathrooms and drenching showers. Rooms with the best views are at the front, the most peaceful at the back, and the most fun up in the attic – slopey-ceilinged but spacious. Saunter into town to take a guided dusk stroll around 'Bizarre Bath', swim, steam and soak at Britain's only natural spa. Then wake to breakfasts at gingham tables in the peaceful conservatory at the back, where eggs from Benedict to Florentine are announced on the board and the vegetarian option sounds delicious. *Minimum stay: 2 nights at weekends. Over 12s welcome.*

| | |
|---|---|
| Rooms | 10 doubles, 2 twin/doubles: £85–£200. |
| Meals | Pubs/restaurants 15-minute walk. |
| Closed | Rarely. |
| Directions | A36 into Bath, then A367 south for Wells. Up hill and first right at sharp left hand bend. On left after 200m. |

Jamie Grundy
Grays Boutique Bed & Breakfast Hotel
9 Upper Oldfield Park,
Bath, BA2 3JX

| | |
|---|---|
| Tel | +44 (0)1225 403020 |
| Email | hello@graysbath.co.uk |
| Web | www.graysbath.com |

## Bath Paradise House Hotel

The view here is sublime, a wide sweep across the city that's best observed on a sunny afternoon while tucking into afternoon tea in the garden. Not that you will spend your time looking out of the windows, even if most of the rooms do have the view: what you find inside is just as special. This is a hugely welcoming house with owners and staff who go out of their way to help you make the most of Bath. Downstairs, a smart sitting room has three arched windows framing the city and an airy breakfast room with Lloyd Loom furniture. Bedrooms are lovely, even the smallest, coveted by returning guests for its doors onto the terrace. Others are more substantial, especially those with bay windows that look the right way. You'll find four-posters, beautiful fabrics, warm colours, no clutter at all. Some have vast bedheads, others travertine bathrooms; bigger rooms have sitting areas, perhaps a claw-foot bath. Menu Gordon Jones, a very short stroll, is a top spot for dinner, while the occasional peal of bells comes from a nearby church. The Thermae Spa with its rooftop pool is a must. *Minimum stay: 2 nights at weekends.*

| | |
|---|---|
| Rooms | 3 doubles, 3 twins, 4 four-posters: £120–£175.<br>1 family room for 3: £130–£185.<br>Singles £75–£120. |
| Meals | Restaurants in Bath within half a mile. |
| Closed | 24 & 25 December. |
| Directions | From train station one-way system to Churchill Bridge. A367 exit from r'bout up hill; 0.75 miles, left at Andrews estate agents. Left down hill into cul-de-sac; on left. |

David & Annie Lanz
Bath Paradise House Hotel
86–88 Holloway,
Bath, BA2 4PX

Tel       +44 (0)1225 317723
Web     www.paradise-house.co.uk

## Artist Residence Brighton

At the top of a square, looking down to the sea, a cute hotel with an arty vibe. You're bang in the middle of Brighton with all the stuff you'd want on your doorstep: galleries, bars, the pier and the Brighton Pavilion. As for the hotel, good food, great staff, relaxed informality and a playful style are the hallmarks here. You get stripped boards, exposed brick walls, then an old garage door that slides back to reveal a chic new restaurant with an open kitchen on display. In typical AR style, it's now one of the best places to eat in Brighton – delicious tasting menus that get you talking as well as eating. You'll find cool art, the odd wall clad in corrugated iron, even an ornamental drainpipe! Bedrooms come in different styles. Some have Pop Art murals, others come in Regency colours, a new batch are super-cool with baths in the room. Most have small, stylish shower rooms, one has a decked terrace. There's a hip bar for cocktails, a ping pong table that doubles as a boardroom, then lunch in the front restaurant with views through big windows down to the sea. The beach waits below. *Minimum stay: 2 nights at weekends.*

| | |
|---|---|
| Rooms | 12 doubles, 5 twins: £75-£350. 1 suite for 6: £125-£360. 5 triples: £120-£210. |
| Meals | Breakfast £2.50-£8. Lunch from £7. Dinner, 4 courses, about £30. Restaurants within 500m. |
| Closed | Never. |
| Directions | A23 south into Brighton. Right at pier along seafront. Right after 1 mile into Regency Square. Hotel in northeast corner. Car park below square. |

Charlie Newey & Justin Salisbury
Artist Residence Brighton
33 Regency Square,
Brighton, BN1 2GG
Tel        +44 (0)1273 324302
Email      brighton@artistresidence.co.uk
Web        www.artistresidence.co.uk

## Drakes

Drakes has the lot: cool rooms, a funky bar, big sea views, one of the best restaurants in town. It stands across the road from the beach, with the famous pier a three-minute walk and the big wheel even closer. Inside, a chic style has conquered all corners. Bedrooms are exemplary. Eleven have free-standing baths in the room, all have waffle bathrobes and White Company lotions, but what impresses most is the detail and workmanship. Handmade beds rest on carpets that are changed every year, contemporary plaster mouldings curl around ceilings like mountain terraces, Vi-Spring mattresses, wrapped in the crispest linen, are piled high with pillows. Don't worry if you can't afford the best rooms; others may be smaller and those at the back have city views, but all are fantastic and the attic rooms are as cute as could be. As for the food, it's some of the best in town, perhaps cauliflower soup with a smoked quail egg, honey-glazed duck with cassis sauce, pears poached in sweet wine with a chocolate and hazelnut mousse. The Lanes are close and packed with hip shops. Don't miss the Royal Pavilion.

| | |
|---|---|
| Rooms | 16 doubles, 1 twin/double: £120–£290. |
| | 1 suite for 2: £300–£360. |
| | 2 singles: £120–£160. |
| | Dinner, B&B from £92.50 per person. |
| | Extra bed/sofabed available £25 p.p.p.n. |
| Meals | Breakfast £7.50–£15. |
| | Lunch, 2-3 courses, £20–£25. |
| | Dinner, 2-3 courses, £32.50–£45. |
| | Chef's Taster Menu, 5 courses, £60. |
| Closed | Never. |
| Directions | M23 & A23 into Brighton. At seafront, with pier in front, turn left up the hill. Drakes on left after 300 yds. |

**Richard Hayes**
Drakes
43-44 Marine Parade,
Brighton, BN2 1PE

| | |
|---|---|
| Tel | +44 (0)1273 696934 |
| Email | info@drakesofbrighton.com |
| Web | www.drakesofbrighton.com |

## Kemp Townhouse

This smart Regency townhouse stands on a street that runs down to the beach. Brighton Pier is a breezy stroll and the cool restaurants and bars of Kemptown are around the corner. Inside, stylish interiors come as standard, making this a cool and comfortable base in one of England's greenest cities. You'll find period colours, charcoal carpets and an Art Deco-style chandelier in the elegant first-floor breakfast room/bar. Bedrooms come in different shapes and sizes, all with the same graceful restraint: padded headboards, lovely linen, incredibly comfortable beds, cool, but compact wet rooms. You can glimpse the sea from front-facing rooms; one has a contemporary four-poster with a free-standing bath in the room. Spin down to the dining room for an excellent breakfast: freshly squeezed orange juice, baskets of pâtisserie, then freshly made pancakes, boiled eggs and soldiers, eggs Benedict, the full cooked works. Brighton's colourful cornucopia waits on the doorstep; the Kemp Town carnival takes place in June, there's an open-air cinema on the beach in summer. Excellent restaurants wait, too. *Minimum stay: 2 nights at weekends.*

| | |
|---|---|
| Rooms | 6 doubles, 1 twin/double: £145–£215. 2 singles: £75–£115. |
| Meals | Pubs/restaurants nearby. |
| Closed | Rarely. |
| Directions | South to seafront, then left at r'bout in front of pier. Uphill, past New Steine, then left at lights into Lower Rock Gardens. Right at lights; 1st right into Atlingworth. On left. |

**Paul Lantsbury & Robert Philpot**
Kemp Townhouse
21 Atlingworth Street,
Brighton, BN2 1PL
Tel +44 (0)1273 681400
Email reservations@kemptownhouse.com
Web www.kemptownhouse.com

## brightonwave

A small, friendly, boutique B&B hotel in the epicentre of trendy Brighton. The beach and the pier are a two-minute walk, the bars and restaurants of St James Street are around the corner. An open-plan sitting room/dining room comes in cool colours with big suede sofas, fairy lights in the fireplace and ever-changing art on the walls. Bedrooms at the front are big and fancy, with huge padded headboards that fill the wall and deluge showers in sandstone bathrooms. Those at the back may be smaller, but so is their price and they come with spotless compact showers; if you're out more than in, why worry? All rooms have fat duvets, white linen, flat-screen TVs and DVD/CD players; the lower-ground king-size has its own whirlpool bath and garden. Richard and Simon are easy-going and happy for guests to chill drinks in the kitchen (there are corkscrews in all the rooms). Breakfast, served late at weekends, offers pancakes, the full English or sautéed tarragon mushrooms on toast. Good food waits on your doorstep: Riddle and Finns, The Salt Rooms, an Italian restaurant up the road. Fabulous Brighton waits. *Minimum stay: 2 nights.*

| | |
|---|---|
| Rooms | 3 doubles, 4 twin/doubles, 1 four-poster: £95–£185. Singles from £65. |
| Meals | Restaurants nearby. |
| Closed | 1 week over Christmas & 2 weeks in January. |
| Directions | A23 to Brighton Pier roundabout at seafront; left towards Marina; 5th street on left. On-street parking vouchers £9 for 24 hours. |

**Richard Adams & Simon Throp**
brightonwave
10 Madeira Place,
Brighton, BN2 1TN

Tel      +44 (0)1273 676794
Email    info@brightonwave.co.uk
Web      www.brightonwave.co.uk

## The Old Bridge Hotel

This lovely hotel, the best in town, mixes old-fashioned hospitality with contemporary flair, a template of excellence for others to follow. It's a big hit with the locals, who come for the food (delicious), the wines (exceptional) and the stylish interiors. Ladies lunch, businessmen chatter, kind staff weave through the throng. You can eat wherever you want: in the muralled restaurant; from a sofa in the lounge; or sitting in a winged armchair in front of the fire in the bar. You feast on anything from homemade soups to rack of lamb (starters are available all day), while breakfast is served in a panelled morning room with Buddha in the fireplace. It's all the work of owners John and Julia Hoskins. Julia's beautiful bedrooms have warm colours, fine fabrics, crisp linen and padded bedheads. One has a mirrored four-poster, several have vast bathrooms, others overlook the river Ouse. All have posh TVs, power showers and bathrobes. John, a Master of Wine, has a wine shop in reception, where you can taste before you buy. The A14 passes at the back, but it doesn't matter a jot. Cambridge is close.

| Rooms | 18 doubles, 1 twin, 3 four-posters: £120-£230. 2 singles: £89. Dinner, B&B £90-£130 per person. |
|---|---|
| Meals | Lunch & dinner £5-£35. |
| Closed | Never. |
| Directions | A1, then A14 into Huntingdon. Hotel on southwest flank of one-way system that circles town. |

Nina Rhodes
The Old Bridge Hotel
1 High Street, Huntingdon, PE29 3TQ
Tel       +44 (0)1480 424300
Email   oldbridge@huntsbridge.co.uk
Web     www.huntsbridge.com

## The Anchor Inn

A 1650 ale house on Chatteris Fen. The New Bedford river streams past outside. It was cut from the soil by the pub's first residents, Scottish prisoners of war brought in by Cromwell to dig the dykes that drain the fens. These days, cosy comforts infuse every corner. Inside, you find low ceilings, timber-framed walls, dark panelling and terracotta-tiled floors. A wood-burner warms the bar, so stop for a pint of cask ale, then feast on fresh local produce served by charming staff, perhaps king scallops with chorizo jam, Denham venison with red cabbage, chocolate fondant with beetroot sorbet and marshmallow sauce. Four rooms above the shop fit the mood nicely – very comfy, not too posh. Expect trim carpets, wicker chairs, crisp white duvets and Indian cotton throws. One room gets a little noise from the restaurant below. The suites have sofabeds, three rooms have river views. Footpaths flank the water; stroll down and you might see mallards or Hooper swans, even a seal (the river is tidal to the Wash). Don't miss Ely (the bishop comes to eat), Cambridge, or the nesting swans at Welney.

| Rooms | 1 double, 1 twin/double: £80–£99. 2 suites for 2: £115–£155. Singles from £59.50. Extra bed £20. |
| --- | --- |
| Meals | Lunch, 2 courses, £13.95. Dinner, 3 courses, £25–£30. Sunday lunch from £12.95. |
| Closed | Never. |
| Directions | From Ely A142 west. In Sutton left on B1381 for Earith. Right in southern Sutton, signed Sutton Gault. 1 mile north on left at bridge. |

Jeanene Flack & Mike Connolly
The Anchor Inn
Bury Lane, Sutton Gault, Ely, CB6 2BD

Tel     +44 (0)1353 778537
Email   anchorinn@popmail.bta.com
Web     www.anchorsuttongault.co.uk

## The Crown Inn

A thatched inn built of mellow stone that stands on the green in this pretty village. Paths lead out into open country and you can follow the river up to Fotheringhay, where Mary Queen of Scots lost her head. Back at the pub, warm interiors mix style and tradition to great effect. The bar has stone walls, ancient beams, flagstone floors and a roaring fire; in summer you decant onto the terrace and sip a pint of Black Sheep while watching village life pass by. Back inside, a beautiful new restaurant has recently appeared with golden stone walls, pale olive panelling and some very good food, anything from glazed ham and local eggs to oxtail lasagne, saddle of venison, sticky toffee tart with toffee sauce. You can also eat in the sitting-room bar on smart armchairs in front of another fire. Stylish bedrooms — some in the main house, others off the courtyard — are all different. You'll find smart colours, chic wallpapers, excellent bathrooms and good art. The bar hosts quiz nights, live music and the odd game of rugby on the telly, while on May Day there's a hog roast for the village fête.

| | |
|---|---|
| Rooms | 6 doubles with sofabeds, 2 twin/doubles: £120–£180. Singles from £55. Sofabed for 2, £30 per child. |
| Meals | Lunch & dinner £5–£25 (not Sun night or Mon lunch). Restaurant closed first week January. |
| Closed | Rarely. |
| Directions | A1(M), junc. 17, then A605 west for 3 miles. Right on B671 for Elton. In village left, signed Nassington. |

**Marcus Lamb**
The Crown Inn
8 Duck Street, Elton,
Peterborough, PE8 6RQ

| | |
|---|---|
| Tel | +44 (0)1832 280232 |
| Email | inncrown@googlemail.com |
| Web | www.thecrowninn.org |

## Edgar House

Edgar House, a super-cool bolthole, has a position that's hard to beat, with a garden that runs down to the city's Roman wall and the river Dee pouring past beyond. It's one of those lovely places that mixes the informality of a small B&B with the luxury of a five-star hotel. Downstairs, there's a breakfast room that doubles as a library, a sitting room with a smouldering fire, then doors onto a pretty garden – Chester's equivalent of the royal box – where you tuck into afternoon tea while watching the river pass. Back inside, an honesty bar, a mini-cinema, then a smart staircase that sweeps you up to flawless bedrooms. You get beautiful art, lots of colour, gorgeous beds wrapped in crisp white linen, and sofas and interactive TVs. Two rooms have balconies, all but one have river views and magnificent bathrooms with walk-in showers or a double-ended bath; the suite has a copper bath in the bedroom. Drop down to the river, feed the ducks, then check out the cathedral and the mediaeval quarter with its excellent shopping. Good restaurants wait around the corner, breakfast is a treat. *Over 14s welcome.*

| | |
|---|---|
| Rooms | 3 doubles, 1 twin/double: £149–£249. 1 suite for 2: £159–£225. |
| Meals | Lunch from £8. Sunday lunch from £13.95. Afternoon tea £17.75. Dinner (Thur–Sat) about £30. |
| Closed | Never. |
| Directions | North into Chester on A483. Over bridge, then right with main flow at r'bout. 2nd right onto Lower Bridge Street. 1st left into Duke Road. Right into car park after Recorder's Office. keep right and on left. |

Tim Mills & Mike Stephen
Edgar House
22 City Walls,
Chester, CH1 1SB

| | |
|---|---|
| Tel | +44 (0)1244 347007 |
| Email | hello@edgarhouse.co.uk |
| Web | www.edgarhouse.co.uk |

## Hell Bay

This must be one of the most inaccurately named hotels in Britain – Hell Bay is heaven!
It sits on Bryher, one of the smaller islands of the Scillies. You can walk around it in a couple
of hours, one sandy beach after another. As for the hotel, it's lovely from top to toe.
Bedrooms have a smart beach-house feel with airy colours, wicker sofas and robes in
excellent bathrooms, but best of all is your terrace or balcony for fabulous watery views.
Elsewhere, there's a heated swimming pool flanked by sun loungers and a treatment room
that looks the right way. It's very family friendly, too; children can gather eggs from the
coop and have them cooked for breakfast, and there's a playroom with games galore.
The hotel lazes on the west coast. There's nothing between you and America, so grab a
drink and wander onto the terrace for sunset. Back inside, there's great local food –
scallops with chilli and honey, lamb with a rosemary jus, chocolate fondant with pistachio
ice-cream. Also, boat trips, babysitters, lovely staff and other islands to explore.
Honeymooners love it. Dogs are very welcome, too. *Under 2s free.*

| | |
|---|---|
| Rooms | 25 suites for 2: £240–£640. Price includes dinner for 2. Child in parents' room £60 (incl. high tea). Dogs £12 a night. |
| Meals | Lunch from £6.95. Dinner included; non-residents £42.50. |
| Closed | November to mid-March. |
| Directions | Ship from Penzance, or fly to St Mary's from Exeter, Newquay or Land's End; boat transfer to Bryher. |

|  |  |
|---|---|
|  | **Philip Callan** |
|  | Hell Bay |
|  | Bryher, Isles of Scilly, TR23 0PR |
| Tel | +44 (0)1720 422947 |
| Email | contactus@hellbay.co.uk |
| Web | www.hellbay.co.uk |

## The Seafood Restaurant

In 1975 a young chef called Rick Stein opened a restaurant in Padstow. These days he has four more as well as a deli, a pâtisserie, a seafood cookery school and 40 beautiful bedrooms. Despite this success, his homespun philosophy has never wavered: buy the freshest seafood from fisherman on the quay, then cook it simply and eat it with friends. It is a viewpoint half the country seems to share – the Seafood Restaurant is now a place of pilgrimage – so come to discover the Cornish coast, walk on the cliffs, paddle in the estuary, then drop into this lively restaurant for a fabulous meal, perhaps hot shellfish with garlic and lemon juice, Dover sole with sea salt and lime, apple and quince tartlet with vanilla ice-cream. Book in for the night and a table in the restaurant is yours, though flawless bedrooms are so seductive you may find them hard to leave. They are scattered about town, some above the restaurant, others at the bistro or just around the corner. All are immaculate. Expect the best fabrics, stunning bathrooms, the odd terrace with estuary views. *Minimum stay: 2 nights at weekends.*

|  |  |
|---|---|
| Rooms | 32 doubles, 8 twin/doubles: £110-£330. |
| Meals | Lunch £38.50. Dinner £58.50. |
| Closed | 25-26 December. |
| Directions | A39, then A389 to Padstow. Follow signs to centre; restaurant on left opposite harbour car park. |

Jill & Rick Stein
The Seafood Restaurant
Riverside, Padstow, PL28 8BY

Tel       +44 (0)1841 532700
Email     reservations@rickstein.com
Web       www.rickstein.com

## Bedruthan Hotel & Spa

A family friendly hotel that delights adults and children alike. It has beautiful interiors, delicious food, sea views and an inexhaustible supply of distractions. There's a football pitch, a surf school, a zip wire, then a cool spa with a couple of pools. If you can think of it, it's probably here, and younger children can be supervised by lovely, qualified staff. There's lots for adults, too, who get the run of the place during school time: a sitting room that hogs the view, a wood-burner to keep things cosy, a terrace in good weather for sea views. There are three restaurants (one for children's parties). Younger children have early suppers, adults return later for a slap-up meal, perhaps hand-picked crab, chargrilled steak, hazelnut tart with pistachio ice-cream. There's a beach below, but you may spurn it for the indoor pool or a game of tennis. Lovely bedrooms have warm retro colours, blond wood, sparkling bathrooms, then separate rooms for children. Some open onto private terraces, lots have sea views, a few overlook the car park. Impeccable eco credentials and fantastic staff, too.

| | |
|---|---|
| Rooms | 38 twin/doubles: £135–£270. |
| | 27 suites for 4: £205–£490. |
| | 30 family rooms for 4: £175–£305. |
| | 6 singles: £75–£125. |
| | Dinner, B&B from £95 per person. |
| Meals | Lunch from £7. Dinner £30–£35. |
| | Sunday lunch from £15. |
| Closed | Christmas & 3 weeks in January. |
| Directions | On B3276 in Mawgan Porth. |

Janie White
Bedruthan Hotel & Spa
Mawgan Porth,
Newquay, TR8 4BU

| | |
|---|---|
| Tel | +44 (0)1637 860860 |
| Email | stay@bedruthan.com |
| Web | www.bedruthan.com |

## The Scarlet

A super-cool design hotel which overlooks the sea; a vast wall of glass in reception frames the view perfectly. The Scarlet does nothing by halves – this is a serious contender for Britain's funkiest bolthole – but it also offers a guilt-free destination as it's green to its core. Cutting-edge technology includes a biomass boiler, solar panels and state-of-the-art insulation. You'll find a couple of indoor swimming pools to ensure against the weather, then hot tubs in a garden from which you can stargaze at night. There's a cool bar, a pool table in the library, a restaurant that opens onto a decked terrace, where you eat fabulous Cornish food while gazing out to sea. Exceptional bedrooms come with huge views: all have balconies or terraces, private gardens or viewing pods. Expect oak floors from sustainable forests, organic cotton, perhaps a free-standing bath in your room. Some are enormous, one has a dual-aspect balcony, another comes with a rooftop lounge. If that's not enough, there's an ayurvedic-inspired spa, where tented treatment rooms are lit by lanterns. Amazing. *Minimum stay: 2 nights at weekends.*

| | |
|---|---|
| Rooms | 21 doubles, 8 twin/doubles: £195–£405. |
| | 8 suites for 2: £270–£460. |
| | Dinner, B&B from £127.50 p.p. |
| Meals | Lunch, 3 courses, £22.50. |
| | Dinner, 3 courses, £42.50. |
| Closed | 4 January to 12 February. |
| Directions | North from Newquay on B3276 to Mawgan Porth. Signed left in village halfway up hill. |

Meeche Hood
The Scarlet
Tredragon Road,
Mawgan Porth, TR8 4DQ

Tel      +44 (0)1637 861800
Email    stay@scarlethotel.co.uk
Web     www.scarlethotel.co.uk

## Watergate Bay Hotel

Watergate Bay is one of those lovely Cornish landscapes where nature rules the roost, a world of sand, sea and sky and nothing but. The few buildings that have taken root here don't qualify as a village and have no name, they're just chattels of the sandy beach that runs for a mile and is one of the best in Cornwall. The hotel sits directly above it, making the most of the view, with walls of glass in the café/bar, a smart terrace strewn with sun loungers, a swimming pool that looks out to sea. Outside, the hotel's surf school will kit you out to ride the waves and you can kite surf and paddle board, too, while beach polo and music festivals come in summer. As for the hotel, it mixes cool design with an informal vibe. Coastal light floods the café, there's a cute sitting room with an open fire, then a cool pool with treatment rooms and a hot tub. Airy bedrooms — some with sea views, others with balconies — have seaside colours and fancy bathrooms. As for the food, you can eat in the café or the grill, or walk 50 paces to the Beach Hut for a burger, or head for Jamie Oliver's Fifteen.

| Rooms | 47 twin/doubles: £145-£345. |
| | 2 suites for 2, 20 suites for 4: £230-£405. |
| | Singles £109-£259. |
| Meals | Lunch from £5.75. |
| | Dinner, 3 courses, about £35. |
| Closed | Never. |
| Directions | Leave A30 at Indian Queens and follow signs past Newquay Airport. Left at the T-junction and hotel in village. |

Mark Williams
Watergate Bay Hotel
On the Beach,
Watergate Bay, TR8 4AA

| Tel | +44 (0)1637 860543 |
| Email | reservations@watergatebay.co.uk |
| Web | www.watergatebay.co.uk |

## Blue Hayes Private Hotel

The view from the terrace is magical, a clean sweep across the bay to St Ives. You breakfast here in good weather in the shade of a Monterey pine, as if transported back to the French Riviera circa 1950. As for the hotel, it's an unadulterated treat, mostly due to Malcolm, whose limitless generosity is stamped over every square inch. Few hotels close for four months to redecorate every winter, but that's the way things are done here – this may explain why so many guests book for the following year when checking out. The house shines in ivory white with the occasional dash of colour from carpets and curtains. A wall of glass in the bar weatherproofs the view. Big rooms are gorgeous, two with balconies, one with a terrace, all with sparkling bathrooms. Light suppers are on hand, though a short stroll into town leads to dozens of restaurants; Alfresco on the harbour is excellent and torches are provided for the journey back. Penzance, Zennor, Tate St Ives and a host of beaches are all close. There's folk and jazz for the September festival, a great time to visit. A true one-off. *Children over 10 welcome.*

| | |
|---|---|
| Rooms | 4 doubles: £180-£220.<br>1 suite for 2: £240-£260.<br>1 triple: £190-£220.<br>Singles £120-£140. |
| Meals | Packed lunch by arrangement.<br>Light suppers from £12.<br>Restaurants within walking distance. |
| Closed | November to February. |
| Directions | A30, then A3074 to St Ives. Through Lelant & Carbis Bay, over mini-r'bout (Tesco on left) and down hill. On right immed. after garage on right. |

Malcolm Herring
Blue Hayes Private Hotel
Trelyon Avenue,
St Ives, TR26 2AD
Tel    +44 (0)1736 797129
Email  info@bluehayes.co.uk
Web   www.bluehayes.co.uk

## Headland House

A super-chic B&B hotel that stands above Carbis Bay with big views across the water to St Ives. Mark and Fenella refurbished from top to toe, turning their home into a small-scale pleasure dome that's run with infectious informality. Outside, sun loungers and a hammock wait on the lawn; inside, there's a snug bar with leather sofas, then a stylish breakfast room that opens onto a terrace in summer. Breakfast is exceptional: lavender-scented yogurt, freshly pressed smoothies, perhaps smoked salmon and scrambled eggs or the full Cornish works. Nine gorgeous rooms wait (a couple are small). Expect white walls to soak up the light, pretty fabrics, lovely beds, gorgeous bathrooms. Some have sea views, a couple have claw-foot baths, one has its own small garden. A vast sandy beach waits below so bring your bucket and spade. There's tea and cake 'on the house' in the afternoon, then a glass of sherry before heading out for dinner. You can follow the coastal path into St Ives, or jump on the tiny train. Good restaurants wait: don't miss the Porthmeor Beach Café opposite Tate St Ives.

| Rooms | 9 doubles: £135–£160. |
| | Singles from £125. Extra beds £25. |
| Meals | Pubs/restaurants 5-minute walk. |
| Closed | November to March. |
| Directions | A30, then A3074 for St Ives. After 2 miles, right, signed station and Carbis Bay Beach. On right at junction with Headland Road. |

**Mark & Fenella Thomas**
Headland House
Headland Road, Carbis Bay,
St Ives, TR26 2NS

Tel       +44 (0)1736 796647
Email    info@headlandhousehotel.co.uk
Web      www.headlandhousehotel.co.uk

## Boskerris Hotel

A lovely little hotel with big views of ocean and headland. In summer, sofas appear on the decked terrace so you can gaze out on the water in comfort. Godrevy Lighthouse twinkles to the right, St Ives slips into the sea on the left, the wide sands of Carbis Bay and Lelant shimmer between. Back inside, white walls and big mirrors soak up the light. You get painted floorboards and smart sofas in the sitting room, fresh flowers and big views with your bacon and eggs in the dining room. Airy bedrooms are nicely uncluttered, with silky throws, padded headboards, seaside colours and crisp linen. Eleven rooms have the view, all have fancy bathrooms, some with deep baths and deluge showers. You'll find White Company lotions, Designers Guild fabrics; in one room you can soak in the bath whilst gazing out to sea. Staff are kind, nothing is too much trouble, breakfasts are exceptional. A coastal path leads down to St Ives (20 mins), mazy streets snake up to the Tate. There's good food on your return, perhaps Newlyn crab salad, Trevaskis Farm steak, pear and almond tarte tatin with vanilla ice-cream. *Children over 7 welcome.*

| | |
|---|---|
| Rooms | 10 doubles, 3 twins: £125–£255. |
| | 1 family room for 4: £190–£240. |
| | 1 triple: £165–£200. |
| | Singles from £93.50. |
| Meals | Dinner, 3 courses, about £30. |
| Closed | Mid-November to late February. |
| Directions | A30 past Hayle, then A3074 for St Ives. After 3 miles pass sign for Carbis Bay, then third right into Boskerris Road. Down hill, on left. |

Jonathan & Marianne Bassett
Boskerris Hotel
Boskerris Road, Carbis Bay,
St Ives, TR26 2NQ

| | |
|---|---|
| Tel | +44 (0)1736 795295 |
| Email | reservations@boskerrishotel.co.uk |
| Web | www.boskerrishotel.co.uk |

## The Gurnard's Head

The coastline here is utterly magical and the walk to St Ives is full of surprises. Secret beaches appear at low tide, cliffs tumble down to the water and wild flowers streak the land pink in summer. As for this inn, you couldn't hope for a better base. It's earthy, warm, stylish and friendly, with airy interiors, colour-washed walls, stripped wooden floors and fires at both ends of the bar. Logs are piled up in an alcove, maps and art hang on the walls, books fill every shelf; if you pick one up and don't finish it, take it home and post it back. Rooms are warm, cosy and spotless, with Vi-Spring mattresses, crisp white linen, throws over armchairs, Roberts radios. Downstairs, super food, all homemade, can be eaten wherever you want: in the bar, in the restaurant or out in the garden in good weather. Snack on rustic delights – pork pies, crab claws, half a pint of Atlantic prawns – or tuck into more substantial treats, maybe salt and pepper squid, braised shoulder of lamb, pineapple tarte tatin. Picnics are easily arranged, there's bluegrass folk music in the bar most weeks. Dogs are very welcome.

| | |
|---|---|
| Rooms | 3 doubles, 4 twin/doubles: £110-£175. Dinner, B&B from £80 per person. |
| Meals | Lunch from £12. Dinner, 3 courses, £25-£35. Sunday lunch from £13. |
| Closed | Christmas. |
| Directions | On B3306 between St Ives & St Just, 2 miles west of Zennor, at head of village of Treen. |

Charles & Edmund Inkin
The Gurnard's Head
Zennor, St Ives, TR26 3DE
Tel      +44 (0)1736 796928
Email    enquiries@gurnardshead.co.uk
Web      www.gurnardshead.co.uk

## The Old Coastguard

The Old Coastguard stands bang on the water in one of Cornwall's loveliest coastal villages. It's a super spot and rather peaceful – little has happened here since 1595, when the Spanish sacked the place. Recently, the hotel fell into the benign hands of Edmund and Charles, past masters at reinvigorating lovely small hotels; warm colours, attractive prices, great food and a happy vibe are their hallmarks. Downstairs, the airy bar and the dining room come together as one, the informality of open plan creating a great space to hang out. There are smart rustic tables, earthy colours, local ales and local art, then a crackling fire in the restaurant. Drop down a few steps to find a bank of sofas and a wall of glass framing sea views; in summer, doors open onto a decked terrace, a lush lawn, then the coastal path weaving down to the small harbour. Bedrooms are lovely: sand-coloured walls, excellent beds, robes in fine bathrooms, books everywhere. Most have the view, eight have balconies. Don't miss dinner: crab rarebit, fish stew, chocolate fondant and marmalade ice-cream. Dogs are very welcome.

| | |
|---|---|
| Rooms | 10 doubles, 3 twin/doubles: £130–£220. |
| | 1 suite for 2: £185–£235. |
| | 1 family room for 4: £170–£200. |
| | Dinner, B&B from £90 per person. |
| Meals | Lunch from £6. |
| | Dinner, 3 courses, about £30. |
| | Sunday lunch from £12.50. |
| Closed | 1 week in early January. |
| Directions | Take coastal road west from Penzance, through Newlyn and on to Mousehole. Hotel on left after car park. |

Charles & Edmund Inkin
The Old Coastguard
The Parade, Mousehole,
Penzance, TR19 6PR

| | |
|---|---|
| Tel | +44 (0)1736 731222 |
| Email | bookings@oldcoastguardhotel.co.uk |
| Web | www.oldcoastguardhotel.co.uk |

## Artist Residence Penzance

Distinctly hip, deliciously quirky and overflowing with colour and style, this groovy little bolthole is hard to beat. The house dates to 1600 and stands on the ley line that connects St Michael's Mount to Stonehenge. You're in the old quarter of town, a stone's throw from the harbour. Inside, Charlie, Justin and their lovely staff potter about, stopping for a chat. Inside, a new bar/café/restaurant has recently taken shape. They've done it all with huge originality and flair: corrugated iron, walls of wood and contemporary art all feature. There's a beach-hut bar in the garden, too, where you'll find table football, ping pong and barbecues on sunny days. Back inside, lovely bedrooms wait, many with brightly coloured murals, so expect art everywhere. Most have compact shower rooms, one has a claw-foot bath, all have smart beds, white linen and toppers for a good night's sleep. Family rooms have fridges, too, while five new apartments are spacious and stylish and come with fully equipped kitchens. Lovely breakfasts offer American pancakes, local eggs, homemade granola. Don't miss St Michael's Mount. *Minimum stay: 2 nights at weekends in summer.*

| | |
|---|---|
| Rooms | 8 doubles, 2 twins: £75–£180. |
| | 1 family room for 4: £110–£235. |
| | 2 triples: £125–£170. |
| | 3 apartments for 4, 2 apartments for 2: £110–£320. |
| Meals | Lunch & dinner from £6; |
| | 3 courses £20–£25. |
| | Pub/restaurant across the road. |
| Closed | 24–26 December. |
| Directions | A30 into Penzance. Follow signs to town centre; up main street; left at top; keep left and on right after 200m. |

**Charlie Newey & Justin Salisbury**
Artist Residence Penzance
20 Chapel Street, Penzance, TR18 4AW

| | |
|---|---|
| Tel | +44 (0)1736 365664 |
| Email | penzance@artistresidence.co.uk |
| Web | www.arthotelcornwall.co.uk |

## Chapel House

Everything here is beautiful – a stunning Georgian house; views over town that stretch out to sea; bedrooms and bathrooms to rival those in the best design hotels. All of which would be blossom in the wind without Susan, whose instinct to go the extra mile knows no restraint – this is not only a lovely house, but a happy one, too. Outside, smart red bricks give some idea of the grandeur within, but step inside and find a contemporary wonderland that took two years to refurbish from top to toe. The hall is home to works from the Newlyn School of Art, the double sitting room has high ceilings, an open fire and a baby grand piano, then doors that lead down to a courtyard garden, a peaceful retreat in summer. Uncluttered bedrooms elate: white walls soak up the light; handmade beds give a fine night's sleep; super-chic wet rooms have fabulous showers. One has a bath in the room, another a bath under a glass roof you can slide open. There's much more: delicious kitchen suppers at weekends; cooking demonstrations with local chefs; great restaurants along the road. The magical west coast waits. Perfect.

| | |
|---|---|
| Rooms | 6 doubles: £120–£180. Singles from £100. Extra beds for babies to 12-year-olds free; 12+ £10. |
| Meals | Kitchen suppers on Fri/Sat £22–£25 (or on request during the week). Sunday lunch from £14.50. |
| Closed | Rarely. |
| Directions | Along seafront with sea on left. Right before bridge, then left up hill and left onto Chapel Street. Opposite church. |

Susan Stuart
Chapel House
Chapel Street,
Penzance, TR18 4AQ
Tel        +44 (0)1736 362024
Email     hello@chapelhousepz.co.uk

## Bay Hotel

The Bay Hotel sits beneath a vast Cornish sky with views to the front of nothing but sea – unless you count the beach at low tide, where buckets and spades are mandatory. Outside, the lawn rolls down to the water, sprinkled with deckchairs and loungers in summer, so grab a book, snooze in the sun or listen to the sounds of the English seaside. Stylish interiors are just the ticket, but you can't escape the view: dining room, conservatory and sitting room all look the right way, with big windows to keep your eyes glued to the horizon. Warm colours fit the mood, there are flowers everywhere, cavernous sofas, a small bar for pre-dinner drinks. Bedrooms vary in size, some smaller, suites bigger; one has its own balcony, all have sea views (some from the side). Expect a Cape Cod feel – tongue-and-groove, airy colours, super bathrooms. As for Ric's delicious food, fish comes straight from the sea, though his steak and kidney pie is every bit as good. Try potted brown shrimps, salmon en croute, poached pears with vanilla ice-cream. The coastal path passes directly outside. Don't miss afternoon tea.

| | |
|---|---|
| Rooms | 5 doubles, 5 twin/doubles £150–£260. 3 suites £260–£290. Price includes dinner for two. |
| Meals | Lunch from £6. Dinner included; non-residents £34.95. |
| Closed | New Year. |
| Directions | A3083 south from Helston, then left onto B3293 for St Keverne. Right for Coverack after 8 miles. Down hill, right at sea, second on right. |

|  | Ric, Gina & Zoe House |
|---|---|
| | Bay Hotel |
| | North Corner, Coverack, |
| | Helston, TR12 6TF |
| Tel | +44 (0)1326 280464 |
| Email | enquiries@thebayhotel.co.uk |
| Web | www.thebayhotel.co.uk |

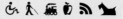

## The Idle Rocks Hotel

A stunning hotel, bang on the water, in one of Cornwall's prettiest seaside towns. The terrace is gorgeous, a place to linger in the sun, with waves lapping directly below and sail boats cruising beyond. Fisherman land their lobsters at the quay, water taxis whizz you off to sandy beaches, you can hire kayaks and explore the bay. As for Idle Rocks, a recent renovation has turned it into Cornwall's coolest bolthole. Chic interiors flood with light, pristine rooms have flawless bathrooms, delicious food comes from the hills and the water around you. Seaside elegance abounds: sofas in front of the sitting room fire, lamps that hang above the bar, walls of glass in the restaurant that open onto the terrace. Uncluttered bedrooms, most with sea views, have whitewashed walls, fine local art, padded window seats, then the best beds and crisp white linen. Bathrooms are just as good, some with claw-foot baths, others with walk-in power showers, all with robes and aromatherapy oils. Don't miss dinner, perhaps Cornish crab with mango, black bream with chorizo, chocolate and ale ganache. Magical.

| | |
|---|---|
| Rooms | 10 doubles, 5 twin/doubles, 1 twin: £150–£335. 3 suites for 2: £280–£395. 1 family room for 4: £325–£395. Cots £10. Extra beds from £35. |
| Meals | Lunch from £7. Dinner: set menu £21–£25; à la carte £35–£45. |
| Closed | 5 January to 5 February. |
| Directions | Leave A390 between St Austell and Truro for St Mawes on A3078. Drop into village and on left on water. |

Anthony Chapman
The Idle Rocks Hotel
Harbourside, Tredenham Road,
St Mawes, TR2 5AN

| | |
|---|---|
| Tel | +44 (0)1326 270270 |
| Email | info@idlerocks.com |
| Web | www.idlerocks.com |

## The St Mawes Hotel

Seaside chic, a relaxed feel and some lovely rooms are the hallmarks of this small hotel that stands on the water with big views out to sea. Outside, pavement tables are popular with people watchers, though those in the know head upstairs to the balcony, an unbeatable spot on a good day. Inside, you'll find sofas in front of the fire in the bar, then rugs on stripped boards in the first-floor dining room. The food is delicious, the best local produce cooked simply, perhaps squid with a red onion salsa, a crispy goats' cheese pizza, chocolate mousse with salted caramel. Beautiful bedrooms are scattered about. Those at the front have watery views, all have smart fabrics, colourful art, the best beds, then robes and walk-in showers; a couple have baths, too. You'll find driftwood art scattered about too and well-kept ales waiting at the bar, while a small cinema is coming in October 2015 in case it rains. The harbour stands directly outside and you can hire kayaks and explore the bay. Don't miss the castle or cricket on the beach. The coastal path starts at the front door. *Minimum stay: 2 nights at summer weekends.*

| | |
|---|---|
| Rooms | 7 twin/doubles: £155–£225. |
| Meals | Breakfast: continental included, full English £8. Lunch from £6.50. Dinner, 3 courses, £25–£30. |
| Closed | January. |
| Directions | Hotel on the seafront in town. Parking available in nearby car park (£4.50 a day). |

Anthony Chapman
The St Mawes Hotel
Harbourside,
St Mawes, TR2 5DW
Tel      +44 (0)1326 270266
Email   stay@stmaweshotel.com
Web     www.stmaweshotel.co.uk

## The Rosevine

A perfect family bolthole on the Roseland Peninsula with views that tumble across trim lawns and splash into the sea. Tim and Hazel welcome children with open arms and have created a small oasis where guests of all ages can have great fun. There's a playroom for kids (Xbox, plasma screen, DVDs, toys), an indoor pool, and a beach at the bottom of the hill. High teas are on hand, there are cots and highchairs, babysitters can be arranged. Parents don't fare badly either: an elegant sitting room with sofas in front of the wood-burner; sea views and Lloyd Loom furniture in a light-filled restaurant; sun loungers dotted about a semi-tropical garden. Suites and apartments come with small kitchens (fridge, sink, dishwasher, microwave/oven); you can self-cater, eat in the restaurant or mix and match (there's a deli menu for posh takeaways). Some rooms are open-plan while others have separate bedrooms. Expect airy, uncluttered interiors, flat-screen TVs, top-notch bed linen and robes in good bathrooms. Eight have a balcony or terrace. St Mawes is close.

| | |
|---|---|
| Rooms | 4 family rooms for 2-4 with kitchenette, 4 apartments for 2-5 with kitchenette: £185-£415<br>4 studios for 2 with kitchenette: £165-£220. |
| Meals | Breakfast £3-£12. Lunch from £8. Dinner, 3 courses, about £30. |
| Closed | January. |
| Directions | From A390 south for St Mawes on A3078. Signed left after 8 miles. Right at bottom of road; just above beach. |

Hazel & Tim Brocklebank
The Rosevine
Rosevine, Portscatho,
Truro, TR2 5EW

| | |
|---|---|
| Tel | +44 (0)1872 580206 |
| Email | robert@rosevine.co.uk |
| Web | www.rosevine.co.uk |

## Driftwood Hotel

A faultless position, one of the best. Six acres of gardens drop down to a private beach, coastal paths lead off for cliff-top walks. At Driftwood, Cape Cod meets Cape Cornwall with smart, airy interiors at every turn. The sitting room is stuffed with beautiful things – fat armchairs, deep sofas, driftwood lamps, a smouldering fire. Best of all are walls of glass that pull in the view. In summer, doors open onto a decked terrace for breakfast and lunch in the sun. Bedrooms are gorgeous (all but one have sea views), some big, others smaller, one in a cabin halfway down the cliff with its own terrace. All have the same clipped elegance: warm colours, big beds, white linen, wicker chairs. There are Roberts radios on bedside tables, cotton robes in excellent bathrooms. Drop down to the dining room for your Michelin-starred dinner: cuttlefish consommé, loin of Fallow venison, spiced pineapple with coconut meringue. There are high teas for children, hampers for beach picnics and rucksacks for walkers. On clear nights the sky is full of stars. Brilliant.
*Minimum stay: 2 nights at weekends.*

| Rooms | 13 doubles, 1 twin: £180-£270. 1 cabin for 4: £225-£255. Dinner, B&B from £122.50 per person. |
|---|---|
| Meals | Dinner £50 (inc. in room price in low season). Tasting menu £80. |
| Closed | Early December to early February. |
| Directions | From St Austell, A390 west. Left on B3287 for St Mawes; left at Tregony on A3078 for approx. 7 miles. Signed left down lane. |

Paul & Fiona Robinson
Driftwood Hotel
Rosevine, Portscatho,
Truro, TR2 5EW

Tel    +44 (0)1872 580644
Email    info@driftwoodhotel.co.uk
Web    www.driftwoodhotel.co.uk

## Trevalsa Court Hotel

Trevalsa stands at the top of the cliff with rather good sea views. In summer, the sitting room decants into the garden, with deckchairs and sun loungers sprinkled about. You can nip down to a sandy beach or pick up Cornwall's coastal path, which passes at the end of the garden; turn left for cliff walks or right for Mevagissey, a cute old fishing village. Don't dally too long. Trevalsa is a seaside treat: friendly, stylish, gently spoiling. Inside, the view is weatherproofed by an enormous mullioned window in the beautiful sitting room, a great place to watch the weather spin by. Elsewhere, you'll find a small bar with colourful art, then a panelled dining room for tasty food, perhaps mussels steamed in Cornish cider, lamb cutlets with root vegetables, chocolate fondant with basil ice-cream. Lovely bedrooms have warm colours, pretty fabrics, padded headboards and the odd wall of paper. Most have sea views, bigger rooms have sofas, the family suite is getting a terrace, all have excellent bathrooms. Breakfast is served on the terrace in summer, the Lost Gardens of Heligan are close. *Minimum stay: 2 nights in high season.*

| | |
|---|---|
| Rooms | 7 doubles, 3 twin/doubles, 2 twins: £110–£250. |
| | 1 family suite for 4: £185–£250. |
| | 2 singles: £60–£105. |
| Meals | Dinner £30. |
| Closed | December/January. |
| Directions | B3273 from St Austell signed Mevagissey, through Pentewan to top of the hill, left at the x-roads, over mini r'bout. Hotel on left, signed. |

**Susan & John Gladwin**
Trevalsa Court Hotel
School Hill, Mevagissey,
St Austell, PL26 6TH

Tel     +44 (0)1726 842468
Email   stay@trevalsa-hotel.co.uk
Web    www.trevalsa-hotel.co.uk

## The Old Quay House Hotel

You drop down the hill, weave through narrow lanes, then pull up at this boutique hotel which started life as a seaman's mission. It's a perfect spot, with the estuary lapping behind the house and a waterside terrace for summer dining, a good spot to watch the boats zip past. Inside, stylish bedrooms have goose down duvets, beautiful fabrics and smart wicker furniture, then spoiling bathrooms that come replete with bathrobes, the odd claw-foot tub, perhaps a separate shower. Most rooms look the right way, eight have balconies (some tiny), the view from the penthouse suite is hard to beat. Downstairs great food waits, so slink onto the terrace for a cocktail, then dig into excellent food prepared from a wealth of local ingredients, perhaps crab ravioli with shellfish bisque, roast bream with a clam broth, passion fruit parfait with mango curd. Fowey is enchanting, bustles with life and fills with sailors for the August Regatta. If you want to escape, take the ferry across to Polruan where Daphne du Maurier lived or potter over to spectacular Lantic Bay for a picnic lunch on the beach. *Minimum stay: 2 nights at weekends in high season.*

| | |
|---|---|
| Rooms | 5 doubles, 5 twin/doubles: £190–£285. 1 suite for 2: £335. Singles from £130. |
| Meals | Lunch (April–September) about £15. Dinner £30–£37.50. |
| Closed | Rarely. |
| Directions | Entering Fowey, follow one-way system past church. Hotel on right where road at narrowest point, next to Lloyds Bank. Nearest car park 800 yds. |

Jane Carson
The Old Quay House Hotel
28 Fore Street,
Fowey, PL23 1AQ

Tel      +44 (0)1726 833302
Email    info@theoldquayhouse.com
Web      www.theoldquayhouse.com

## Talland Bay Hotel

The position here is magical. First you plunge down rollercoaster lanes, then you arrive at this lovely hotel. Directly in front, the sea sparkles through pine trees, an old church crowns the hill and two acres of lawns end in a ha-ha, then the land drops down to the bay. In summer, sun loungers and croquet hoops appear on the lawn and you can nip down to a beach café for lunch by the water. Back at the hotel there's a conservatory brasserie, a sitting room bar, and a roaring fire in the half-panelled dining room. Masses of art hangs on the walls, there are vast sofas, polished flagstones, a terrace for afternoon tea. Follow the coastal path over the hill, then return for a good dinner, perhaps John Dory and squid, Bodmin lamb with black olives, carrot cake with candied walnuts and cinnamon ice cream. As for the bedrooms, they've been nicely refurbished and pamper you rotten. Expect rich colours, vast beds, beautiful linen, the odd panelled wall. One has a balcony, a couple open onto terraces, all have lovely bathrooms. Gardens, beaches, pretty villages and the coastal path all wait.

| | |
|---|---|
| Rooms | 15 twin/doubles: £100–£240. |
| | 4 suites for 2: £180–£260. |
| | 3 cottages for 2: £140–£230. |
| | Dinner, B&B £95–£155 per person. |
| Meals | Lunch from £5.95. Dinner £32–£38. |
| Closed | Never. |
| Directions | From Looe A387 for Polperro. Ignore 1st sign to Talland. After 2 miles, left at x-roads; follow signs. |

Vanessa Rees
Talland Bay Hotel
Porthallow,
Looe, PL13 2JB

| | |
|---|---|
| Tel | +44 (0)1503 272667 |
| Email | info@tallandbayhotel.co.uk |
| Web | www.tallandbayhotel.co.uk |

Entry 32   Map 1

## Augill Castle

Simon and Wendy's folly castle may look rather grand, but inside is a wonderfully informal world – no uniforms, no rules, just a place to kick off your shoes and relax. Follow your nose and find sofas in front of the fire in the hall, a grand piano in the music room, an honesty bar that opens onto a terrace. Fancy getting married in a castle? They'll do that too. Breakfast is served communally in a vast dining room under a wildly ornate ceiling – local bacon, eggs from resident hens, homemade breads and jams. Elsewhere, panelled walls, roaring fires, books, art and antiques. Bedrooms are deliciously different. Some are enormous, one has a wardrobe in the turret, you'll find big bathrooms, bold colours and vintage luggage. Cottage suites have extra space for families. If you decide to bring the children, there's lots for them to do too – dressing up boxes, five acres of gardens with a treehouse and a playground, even a cinema in the old potting shed. The Dales and the Lakes are close for spectacular walking and cycling, but sybarites may just want to stay put. *Minimum stay: 2 nights at weekends.*

| | |
|---|---|
| Rooms | 8 doubles, 2 four-posters: £130–£180. 1 suite for 2: £240. 6 family rooms for 4: £200–£280. Singles from £100. |
| Meals | Dinner, 3 courses, £30 (booking essential). Supper platter £15. Afternoon tea £18. Children's high tea £10. |
| Closed | Never. |
| Directions | M6 junc. 38; A685 thro' Kirkby Stephen. Before Brough right for South Stainmore; signed on left in 1 mile. Kirkby Stephen station 3 miles. |

Simon & Wendy Bennett
Augill Castle
South Stainmore,
Kirkby Stephen, CA17 4DE

| | |
|---|---|
| Tel | +44 (0)17683 41937 |
| Email | enquiries@stayinacastle.com |
| Web | www.stayinacastle.com |

Inn

## The Black Swan

A lovely small hotel in the middle of a pretty village that's surrounded by blistering country. It's all things to all men: a smart restaurant, a lively bar, a village shop; they even hold a music festival here in September. A stream runs through the big garden, where you can eat in good weather; free-range hens live in one corner. Inside, chic country interiors fit the mood perfectly. You get fresh flowers, tartan carpets, games and books galore. There's a bar for local ales, a sitting-room bar with an open fire, but the hub of the hotel is the bar in the middle, where village life gathers. You can eat wherever you want – there's an airy restaurant, too – so dig into delicious country fare, with meat from the hills around you, perhaps a tasty home-made soup, Galloway beef and root vegetable stew, sticky toffee pudding with vanilla ice cream. Pretty bedrooms are fantastic for the money. Expect warm colours, beautiful linen, smart furniture, super bathrooms; one suite has a wood-burner. Stunning walking waits, the Lakes and Dales are close, children and dogs are welcome. A very happy place.

| Rooms | 10 twin/doubles: £80–£100. 5 suites for 2: £115–£130. Singles from £65. |
|---|---|
| Meals | Lunch from £4.50. Dinner, 3 courses, £25–£30. |
| Closed | Never. |
| Directions | Off A685 between M6 junc. 38 & A66 at Brough. |

Alan & Louise Dinnes
The Black Swan
Ravenstonedale,
Kirkby Stephen, CA17 4NG

| Tel | +44 (0)15396 23204 |
| Email | enquiries@blackswanhotel.com |
| Web | www.blackswanhotel.com |

AWARD WINNER

Nicely priced

## The Sun Inn

This lovely old inn sits between the Dales and the Lakes in an ancient market town, one of the prettiest in the north. It backs onto St Mary's churchyard, where wild flowers flourish, and on the far side you'll find 'the fairest view in England,' to quote John Ruskin. Herons fish the river Lune, lambs graze the fells, a vast sky hangs above. Turner came to paint it in 1825 and benches wait for those who want to gaze upon it. As for the Sun, it does what good inns do – looks after you in style. There's lots of pretty old stuff – stone walls, rosewood panelling, wood-burners working overtime – and it's all kept spic and span, with warm colours, fresh flowers and the daily papers on hand. You find leather banquettes, local art and chairs in the dining room from Cunard's Mauretania, so eat in style, perhaps mussels with cider, saddle of venison, Yorkshire rhubarb and ginger sponge trifle. Bedrooms upstairs are stylishly uncluttered with Cumbrian wool carpets, robes in smart bathrooms and earplugs to ward off the church bells. Car-park permits come with your room and can be used far and wide. Brilliant. *Minimum stay: 2 nights at weekends.*

| | |
|---|---|
| Rooms | 8 doubles, 2 twin/doubles: £110–£183. 1 family room for 4: £170–£203. Singles from £80. Dinner, B&B from £86 per person. Extra bed/sofabed available £20 per person per night. |
| Meals | Bar snacks & lunch from £5.95. Dinner, 4 courses, £32.95. Sunday lunch from £13.95. |
| Closed | Never. |
| Directions | M6 junc. 36, then A65 for 5 miles following signs for Kirkby Lonsdale. In town centre. |

**Mark & Lucy Fuller**
The Sun Inn
6 Market Street, Kirkby Lonsdale,
Carnforth, LA6 2AU

| | |
|---|---|
| Tel | +44 (0)15242 71965 |
| Email | email@sun-inn.info |
| Web | www.sun-inn.info |

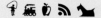

## Aynsome Manor Hotel

A small country house with a big heart. It may not be the grandest place in the book but the welcome is genuine, the peace is intoxicating and the value unmistakable. From the front, a long sweep across open meadows leads south to Cartmel and its priory, a view that has changed little in 800 years. The house, a mere pup by comparison, dates to 1512. Step in to find red armchairs, a grandfather clock and a coal fire in the hall. There's a small bar for a dram at the front and a cantilever staircase with cupola dome that sweeps you up to a first-floor drawing room, where panelled windows frame the view. Downstairs, you eat under a wildly ornate ceiling with Georgian colours and old portraits on the walls. You get lovely country cooking, too: French onion soup, roast leg of Cumbrian lamb, rich chocolate mousse served with white chocolate sauce. Bedrooms are simple, spotless, cosy and colourful. Some have views over the fields, one may be haunted, all have good bathrooms. Staff are lovely, nothing is too much trouble, kippers with lemon at breakfast are a treat. Windermere and Coniston are close.

| | |
|---|---|
| Rooms | 5 doubles, 4 twins, 1 four-poster: £90-£125. 2 family rooms for 4: £90-£150. Dinner, B&B £75 from per person. |
| Meals | Packed lunches by arrangement £9.50. Dinner, 4 courses, £33. |
| Closed | Christmas. |
| Directions | From M6 junc. 36 take A590 for Barrow. At top of Lindale Hill follow signs left to Cartmel. Hotel on right 3 miles from A590. |

Christopher & Andrea Varley
Aynsome Manor Hotel
Aynsome Lane, Cartmel,
Grange-over-Sands, LA11 6HH

| | |
|---|---|
| Tel | +44 (0)15395 36653 |
| Email | aynsomemanor@btconnect.com |
| Web | www.aynsomemanorhotel.co.uk |

## The Swan Hotel & Spa

This lovely hotel, originally a 17th-century monastic farmhouse, stands on the river Leven, a wide sweep of water that pours out of Windermere on its way to Morecambe Bay. It's a fabulous spot and the Swan makes the most of it, with a terrace that runs along to an ancient packhorse bridge. Interiors are just as good – this is a happy hotel with a relaxed vibe and lots of style. Pretty sitting rooms come dressed in Designers Guild fabrics, there's a lively bar for a pint of local ale, then a stylish brasserie for good food. Potter about and find cool colours, beautiful wallpapers, then sofas in front of open fires. There's also a spa – hard to miss as the swimming pool shimmers behind a wall of glass in reception. Treatment rooms, sauna, steam room and gym all wait. Pretty bedrooms have the same crisp style: comfy beds, smart white linen, a wall of paper, a sofa if there's room. Those at the front have river views, family suites have doll's houses and PlayStations. Back downstairs, dig into tasty food in the bar or brasserie, perhaps crispy squid, Cartmel venison, damson Bakewell tart.

| | |
|---|---|
| Rooms | 13 doubles, 30 twin/doubles: £99–£234. 8 suites for 4: £189–£329. |
| Meals | Lunch from £5.95. Bar meals from £9.95. Dinner, 3 courses, £25–£35. Sunday lunch from £13.95. |
| Closed | Never. |
| Directions | M6 junc. 36, then A590 west. Into Newby Bridge. Over roundabout, then 1st right for hotel. |

Sarah Gibbs
The Swan Hotel & Spa
Newby Bridge, LA12 8NB

| | |
|---|---|
| Tel | +44 (0)15395 31681 |
| Email | reservations@swanhotel.com |
| Web | www.swanhotel.com |

## Mason's Arms

A perfect Lakeland inn tucked away two miles inland from Windermere. You're on the side of a hill with huge views across ancient fields to Scout Scar in the distance. In summer, all pub life decants onto a spectacular terrace – a sitting room in the sun – where window boxes and flowerbeds tumble with colour. The inn dates from the 16th century and is impossibly pretty. The bar is wonderfully traditional with roaring fires, flagged floors, wavy beams and some good local ales to quench your thirst. Rustic elegance upstairs comes courtesy of stripped floors, country rugs and red walls in the first-floor dining room – so grab a window seat for fabulous views and dig into devilled crab cakes, Cartmel lamb shank, warm fudge sundae with Lakes ice-cream. Apartments (in the pub, nicely cosy) and cottages (off the courtyard, great for families) are a steal. All come with good kitchens to cook your own breakfast (hampers can be arranged). You get cool colours and comfy beds; several have private terraces. There's jazz on Sundays in summer and Cartmel Priory is close. *Minimum stay: 2 nights at weekends.*

| | |
|---|---|
| Rooms | 5 apartments for 2: £75–£140. 1 self-catering cottage for 2-4, 1 self-catering cottage for 2-6: £110–£165. |
| Meals | Breakfast hampers £15–£25 (or BYO). Lunch from £4.95. Bar meals from £9.95. Dinner, 3 courses, £25–£30. |
| Closed | Never. |
| Directions | M6 junc. 36; A590 west, then A592 north. 1st right after Fell Foot Park. Straight ahead for 2.5 miles. On left after sharp right-hand turn. |

**John & Diane Taylor**
Mason's Arms
Strawberry Bank, Cartmel,
Grange-over-Sands, LA11 6NW

| | |
|---|---|
| Tel | +44 (0)15395 68486 |
| Email | info@masonsarmsstrawberrybank.co.uk |
| Web | www.masonsarmsstrawberrybank.co.uk |

## The Punch Bowl Inn

You're in the hills above Windermere in a pretty village encircled by lanes that defeat most tourists. It's a lovely spot, deeply rural, with ten-mile views down the valley and a church that stands next door; bell ringers practise on Friday mornings, the occasional bride glides out in summer. Yet while the Punch Bowl sits lost to the world, it is actually a deliciously funky inn. Rescued from neglect and renovated in great style, it now sparkles with a stylish mix of old and new. Outside, honeysuckle and roses ramble on stone walls. Inside, a clipped elegance runs throughout, with Farrow & Ball colours, rugs on wood floors and sofas in front of the wood-burner. Scott Fairweather's ambrosial food is a big draw, perhaps Lancashire cheese soufflé, loin of rabbit with crayfish mousse, pear soufflé and pecan ice-cream. Chic bedrooms are lovely, too, all with beautiful linen, pretty fabrics and Roberts radios, while fabulous bathrooms have double-ended baths, separate showers and white robes. Four have the view, the suite is enormous, weekday prices are tempting. There's a terrace for lunch in the sun, too.

| | |
|---|---|
| Rooms | 5 doubles, 1 twin/double, 2 four-posters: £105–£235. 1 suite for 2: £180–£305. Singles from £80. |
| Meals | Lunch from £5. Dinner, 3 courses, £30–£35. |
| Closed | Never. |
| Directions | M6 junc. 36, then A590 for Newby Bridge. Right onto A5074, then right for Crosthwaite after 3 miles. Pub on southern flank of village, next to church. |

Lorraine Stanton
The Punch Bowl Inn
Crosthwaite,
Kendal, LA8 8HR

| | |
|---|---|
| Tel | +44 (0)15395 68237 |
| Email | info@the-punchbowl.co.uk |
| Web | www.the-punchbowl.co.uk |

## Linthwaite House Hotel & Restaurant

It's not just the view that makes Linthwaite so special, though Windermere sparkling half a mile below with a chain of peaks rising beyond does grab your attention. There's loads to enjoy here — 15 acres of gardens and grounds, a fantastic terrace for sunny days and interiors that go out of their way to pamper your pleasure receptors. The house itself is beautiful, one of those grand Lakeland Arts & Crafts wonders, with original woodwork and windows in all the right places. Logs are piled high by the front door, fires smoulder, sofas wait in the conservatory sitting room, where big views loom. Gorgeous country-house bedrooms are coolly uncluttered with warm colours, chic fabrics, hi-tech gadgetry, fabulous bathrooms. Those at the front have lake views, a couple have hot tubs, you can stargaze from one of the suites. Downstairs, ambrosial food waits in the dining rooms (one is decorated with nothing but mirrors), perhaps seared tuna with pickled ginger, chargrilled pigeon with beetroot purée, caramelised banana tart with peanut butter. Sunbeds wait on the terrace. Fabulous. *Minimum stay: 2 nights at weekends.*

| | |
|---|---|
| Rooms | 22 doubles, 5 twin/doubles: £202–£490. 3 suites for 2: £410–£630. Singles from £136. Dinner, B&B from £135 per person. |
| Meals | Lunch from £6.95. Dinner for non-residents £52. |
| Closed | Rarely. |
| Directions | M6 junc. 36. Take A590 north, then A591 for Windermere. Left at roundabout onto B5284. Past golf course and hotel signed left after 1 mile. |

Mike Bevans
Linthwaite House Hotel & Restaurant
Crook Road, Bowness-on-Windermere,
Windermere, LA23 3JA

| | |
|---|---|
| Tel | +44 (0)15394 88600 |
| Email | stay@linthwaite.com |
| Web | www.linthwaite.com |

## Gilpin Hotel

Gilpin is one of the loveliest places to stay in the country, simple as that. Run by two generations of the same family, it delivers at every turn, its staff delightful, its food divine – a treasure trove of beautiful things. It is a country house that has moved with the times, its chic interiors a beautiful fusion of contemporary and traditional styles. Cool elegance flows throughout – smouldering coals, Zoffany wallpaper, gilded mirrors, flowers everywhere. Afternoon tea is served every day, the wine cellar is on display in the bar, there's a beautiful sitting room in golden hues that overflows with art. Doors open onto a pretty terrace, perfect for Pimm's in the sun; magnolia trees, cherry blossom and a copper beech wait in the beautiful 20-acre garden. Bedrooms are divine: crisp linen, exquisite fabrics, delicious art, fabulous bathrooms; garden suites have contemporary flair and hot tubs on private terraces. As for the food, it's marvellous stuff, perhaps poached pear with blue cheese mousse, Cartmel venison with liquorice and brambles, chocolate tart with orange sherbet and fennel ice. Unbeatable. *Minimum stay: 2 nights at weekends.*

| | |
|---|---|
| Rooms | 8 doubles, 12 twin/doubles: £335-£385. 6 suites for 2: £385-£485. Price includes dinner for 2. Special rates for 3 or more nights. |
| Meals | Lunch £10-£35. Dinner included; non-residents £58. |
| Closed | Never. |
| Directions | M6 junc 36, A591 north, then B5284 west for Bowness. On right after 5 miles. |

John, Christine, Barnaby & Zoe Cunliffe
Gilpin Hotel
Crook Road,
Windermere, LA23 3NE

| | |
|---|---|
| Tel | +44 (0)15394 88818 |
| Email | hotel@thegilpin.co.uk |
| Web | www.thegilpin.co.uk |

## Gilpin Lake House & Spa

Every now and then you bump into a hotel that knocks your socks off, and Gilpin Lake House does just that. This is an extraordinary little place – a tiny spa hotel with only six rooms, luxury and intimacy entwined. It sits away from the crowds, lost in the hills, surrounded by acres of peaceful woodland, with a private lake in front and a hot tub on the terrace. Sun loungers are sprinkled about, beautiful gardens and sun-dappled trees, a rowing boat for fun on the water. Best of all is the cabin above the lake that's a treatment room – pure heaven. There's an indoor pool and sauna, too, while the house itself is coolly elegant at every turn. You'll find sofas, a wood-burner and lake views in the sitting room, books galore and beautiful art. Bedrooms above are luxurious – sofas and armchairs, fabulous beds and fabrics, bathrooms that don't hold back. Breakfast is served wherever you want: in your room, on the terrace, in the conservatory. There's a chauffeur to take you to dinner, too. Come with friends and take the whole place. Out of this world.
*Minimum stay: 2 nights at weekends, 3 nights bank holidays & Easter. Children over 7 welcome.*

| | |
|---|---|
| Rooms | 6 twin/doubles: £495-£605. Price includes dinner for 2 at Gilpin Hotel with a chauffeured car to and fro. |
| Meals | Dinner included; non-residents £58. |
| Closed | Never. |
| Directions | B5284 west for Bowness. Left at Wild Boar pub, right through village and straight ahead for 2 miles. Keep right at fork and on left. |

John, Christine, Barnaby & Zoe Cunliffe
Gilpin Lake House & Spa
Crook,
Windermere, LA8 8LN
Tel       +44 (0)15394 88818
Email     hotel@thegilpin.co.uk
Web       www.thegilpin.co.uk/lake-house

## Cedar Manor Hotel

A small country house on the edge of Windermere with good prices, pretty interiors and delicious food. Jonathan and Caroline love their world and can't stop spending money on it. They recently added a smart terrace at the front, turned the office into another sitting room, and put in a couple of fancy bathrooms. This 17th-century house was once home to a retired vicar, hence the ecclesiastic windows. Outside, an ancient cedar of Lebanon shades the lawn. Inside, cool colours and an easy style flow throughout. The big sitting room doubles as the bar and comes in browns and creams with sofas and local art. Bedrooms — some warmly traditional, others nicely contemporary — have Zoffany fabrics, Lloyd Loom wicker and flat-screen TVs; most have fancy bathrooms, some have big views, the bathroom in the coach-house suite is out of this world. You eat in a pretty dining room with views to the front or on the terrace in good weather, perhaps goat's cheese with a red pepper mousse, local lamb with tarragon gnocchi, warm chocolate fudge cake with real-ale ice cream. All things Windermere are on your doorstep. *Minimum stay: 2 nights at weekends.*

| | |
|---|---|
| Rooms | 7 doubles, 1 twin: £135-£185. 2 suites for 2: £225-£385. Singles from £100. Dinner, B&B £102 per person. Extra bed/sofabed available £40-£70 per person per night. |
| Meals | Dinner £32.95-£39.95. |
| Closed | Rarely. |
| Directions | From Windermere A591 east out of town for Kendal; hotel on right, next to church, before railway station. |

Jonathan & Caroline Kaye
Cedar Manor Hotel
Ambleside Road,
Windermere, LA23 1AX

| | |
|---|---|
| Tel | +44 (0)15394 43192 |
| Email | info@cedarmanor.co.uk |
| Web | www.cedarmanor.co.uk |

## Jerichos

A friendly B&B hotel with attractive prices in the middle of Windermere. Step inside and find airy interiors with stripped wood floors and a splash of colour on the walls. There's a sitting room with a couple of baby chesterfields, then a pretty dining room where you breakfast on homemade bread and local eggs, perhaps a grilled kipper or smoked salmon and scrambled eggs. Spotless bedrooms offer a night or two of affordable luxury. Those on the first floor have high ceilings, you get leather bedheads, comfy armchairs, white duvets and excellent bathrooms. Most have fancy showers, all come with iPod docks, a wall of paper and Lakeland art. Good restaurants wait on your doorstep – Hooked for fish. Francine's for tasty bistro fare, Wild & Co. for a good steak – the sort of stuff you want after a day in the hills. As for Windermere, the Lake is a short stroll, a good way to round off breakfast. You can hire kayaks, learn to sail, take a cruise. There are mountain bike trails and the odd hill to climb, too. The station is close, so come by train; from London it's faster than by car. *Minimum stay: 2 nights at weekends, 3 nights on bank holiday weekends.*

| | |
|---|---|
| Rooms | 8 doubles: £105–£135. |
| | 2 singles: £55–£65. |
| Meals | Restaurants nearby. |
| Closed | Last 3 weeks in January. |
| Directions | A591 from Kendal to Windermere. Pass train station, don't turn left into town, rather next left 200 yards on. First right and on right after 500m. |

Chris & Jo Blaydes
Jerichos
College Road,
Windermere, LA23 1BX

| | |
|---|---|
| Tel | +44 (0)15394 42522 |
| Email | info@jerichos.co.uk |
| Web | www.jerichos.co.uk |

## Miller Howe Hotel & Restaurant

The view is breathtaking, a clean sweep over Windermere to the majestic Langdale Pikes. As for Miller Howe, this Edwardian country house was made famous by TV chef John Tovey in the 1970s. These days the atmosphere is nicely relaxed. Interiors flood with light, contemporary art mixes with period features, and you can grab the daily papers, then sink into a sofa and roast away in front of the fire. You'll find vintage wallpapers, the odd bust, beautiful fabrics, original wood floors. There's a cute little bar, a conservatory for afternoon tea, then a terrace for drinks in summer, with five acres of beautiful gardens rolling down towards the lake. Back inside, spin into the dining room, where walls of glass frame the view. Menus offer local delights, perhaps Cartmel venison, Cumbrian pork with a cider jus, ginger panna cotta with roast pineapple. Bedrooms vary in size, but all are individually designed with smart fabrics, period furniture and posh TVs. Some have balconies with big lake views, cottage suites in the garden offer sublime peace. Don't miss sunset. *Minimum stay: 2 nights at weekends. Pets are allowed in 2 bedrooms.*

| | |
|---|---|
| Rooms | 5 doubles, 7 twin/doubles: £170–£240. 3 suites for 2: £170–£270. Dinner, B&B from £105 per person. |
| Meals | Lunch from £8.95. Sunday lunch £30. Dinner £47.50. |
| Closed | Rarely. |
| Directions | From Kendal A591 to Windermere. Left at mini-r'bout onto A592 for Bowness; 0.25 miles on right. |

Helen & Martin Ainscough
Miller Howe Hotel & Restaurant
Rayrigg Road,
Windermere, LA23 1EY
Tel    +44 (0)15394 42536
Email  info@millerhowe.com
Web    www.millerhowe.com

## Nanny Brow

This Lakeland Arts & Crafts house dates to 1904 and sits peacefully in seven beautiful acres on the side of a hill. Views sweep up the valley as the river Brathay runs off towards Wrynose Pass. Interiors are just as good: elegant, colourful, deeply comfy. Sue and Peter refurbished from top to bottom when they arrived. All the lovely old stuff has been restored, but the feel is fresh with airy rooms that bask in the light and an easy elegance flowing throughout. The half-panelled drawing room is gorgeous: smart sofas, original windows, an open fire, vases of flowers. Bedrooms are a treat. Some have arched windows that frame the view, all have comfy beds, crisp colours, the odd wall of paper; gorgeous bathrooms have double-ended baths or walk-in power showers or both. New rooms in the garden wing have sofas, and doors onto a terrace. Cumbrian breakfasts set you up for the day, paths through ancient woodlands lead onto the fells. There's a sitting-room bar, a drying room for walkers, secure storage for bikes. The Lake Road Kitchen serves great food in Ambleside, a mile up the road. *Minimum stay: 2 nights at weekends.*

|  |  |
|---|---|
| Rooms | 7 doubles: £130–£200. |
|  | 6 suites for 2: £190–£300. |
|  | Singles £115–£265. |
| Meals | Restaurants 1 mile. |
| Closed | Never. |
| Directions | West from Ambleside on A593. |
|  | On right after a mile. |

Peter & Susan Robinson
Nanny Brow
Clappersgate,
Ambleside, LA22 9NF

| Tel | +44 (0)15394 33232 |
|---|---|
| Email | unwind@nannybrow.co.uk |
| Web | www.nannybrow.co.uk |

Entry 46   Map 5

## The Eltermere Inn

This gorgeous Lakeland inn seems lost to the world, yet it's only a couple of miles from Grasmere. In summer you sit in the garden with local sheep for company and dig into afternoon tea; in winter you order a pint at the bar, then roast away in front of the fire. You're in an unblemished village that stands back from the water in the shade of forested hills. Inside, beautifully refurbished interiors are part country house, part village pub. There's a grand piano in the dining room, ancient slate floors in the bar, then big sofas and lovely art in the airy sitting rooms. Upstairs, stylish rooms have warm colours, local wool carpets, big beds and Mulberry fabrics. Some have padded window seats, others are open to the eaves, all have excellent bathrooms, those at the front have views of lake and mountain. Downstairs, you find the sort of food you crave after a day in the hills, perhaps mussels with white wine and garlic, rack of Cumbrian lamb, banana gingerbread with toffee sauce. Walks start from the front door, there's croquet on the lawn, they even grow their own vegetables. *Minimum stay: 2 nights at weekends.*

| | |
|---|---|
| Rooms | 12 twin/doubles: £140-£275. Singles £125-£250. Extra bed/sofabed available £40 per person per night. |
| Meals | Lunch from £6.95. Dinner, 3 courses, £30-£35. |
| Closed | Christmas. |
| Directions | West from Ambleside for 3 miles on A593, then right for Eltermere. On right in village. |

**Mark & Ruth Jones**
The Eltermere Inn
Elterwater,
Ambleside, LA22 9HY
Tel        +44 (0)15394 37207
Email    info@eltermere.co.uk
Web      www.eltermere.co.uk

## Borrowdale Gates

If you want deep peace, spectacular landscapes and a slice of luxury in a stylish hotel, you'll find it here. This is Borrowdale, an unchanged corner of the rural idyll, 'the loveliest square mile in Lakeland' to quote Alfred Wainwright. High peaks encircle you, sheep graze the fields, the river Derwent potters past. The view from the top of High Seat is one of the best in the Lakes, with Derwentwater sparkling under a vast sky. Lowland walking is equally impressive: long or short, high or low, Borrowdale delivers. At the end of the day roll back to this lovely hotel. Big windows downstairs frame majestic views. You get binoculars, the daily papers, afternoon tea in front of roaring fires or out on the terrace in summer. Bedrooms are great value for money, with warm colours, super beds, smart bathrooms, a sofa if there's room. Some open onto terraces, several have small balconies, all have the view. As for the restaurant, a wall of glass looks out over the village and beyond, a fine spot for a good meal, perhaps hand-dived scallops, fell-bred lamb, lemon tart with cassis sorbet.
*Minimum stay: 2 nights at weekends. Pets by arrangement.*

| | |
|---|---|
| Rooms | 18 twin/doubles: £186–£216. 3 suites for 2: £220–£310. 4 singles: £93–£108. Price includes dinner for 2. Non-residents £30–£41 p.p. |
| Meals | Light lunches from £8. Price includes dinner for 2. |
| Closed | Rarely. |
| Directions | M6 to Penrith, A66 to Keswick, then B5289 south for 4 miles. Right at humpback bridge, through Grange, hotel on right. |

Colin Harrison
Borrowdale Gates
Grange-in-Borrowdale,
Keswick, CA12 5UQ

| | |
|---|---|
| Tel | +44 (0)17687 77204 |
| Email | hotel@borrowdale-gates.com |
| Web | www.borrowdale-gates.com |

## Swinside Lodge Hotel

This small, intimate country house sits in silence at the foot of Catbells. Pheasants strut across the lawn, fells rise all around, Derwentwater, Queen of the Lakes, is a short stroll through the woods. Kathy and Mike – the real stars of the show – came back from France to take up the reins of this ever-popular hotel and refurbished from top to toe: warm colours, new sash windows, smart bedrooms and fancy new bathrooms all come as standard. Downstairs, you'll find fresh flowers and comfy sofas in the yellow drawing room, shelves of books and a jukebox in the sitting room, red walls and gilt-framed mirrors in the dining room, where windows frame views of Skiddaw. There's super food here, too, just what you want after a day on the fells, perhaps smoked salmon with a beetroot dressing, carrot and ginger soup, roast duck with a red wine jus, a warm apple sponge with a calvados syrup. Lovely bedrooms have a cool country elegance with crisp linen, golden throws and super comfy beds. Outside, a host of characters visit the garden: a woodpecker, red squirrels, roe deer. Wonderful. *Over 12s welcome.*

| | |
|---|---|
| Rooms | 5 doubles, 2 twins: £184–£304. Price includes dinner for 2. |
| Meals | Dinner, 4 courses, included; non-residents £38. Packed lunches £9. |
| Closed | 13 December to 12 February. |
| Directions | M6 junc. 40. A66 west past Keswick, over r'bout, then 2nd left for Portinscale & Grange. Follow signs to Grange for 2 miles (not right-hand turns). House signed on right. |

**Mike & Kathy Bilton**
Swinside Lodge Hotel
Newlands,
Keswick, CA12 5UE

| | |
|---|---|
| Tel | +44 (0)17687 72948 |
| Email | info@swinsidelodge-hotel.co.uk |
| Web | www.swinsidelodge-hotel.co.uk |

## The Cottage in the Wood

A great little base for the northern Lakes with lots of style, super food and owners who go the extra mile. You're on the side of Whinlatter Pass with big views east to a chain of Lakeland peaks. Outside, the terrace looks the right way, a great spot for a drink in summer. Inside, chic interiors are just the ticket: an airy sitting room, a fire that burns on both sides, books and games to keep you amused, windows galore in the restaurant. Nicely priced bedrooms have white walls to soak up the light and sparkling bathrooms for a good wallow. One in the eaves has a claw-foot bath, four have mountain views, one has a fabulous bathroom and opens onto its own terrace. There's lots to do – lakes to visit, hills to climb, cycle trails to follow. Whatever you do, come home to some lovely local food, perhaps Curthwaite goat curd with beetroot and rocket, Herdwick hogget with garlic dumplings, passion fruit soufflé with mango ice-cream. There's a drying room for walkers, secure storage for bikes, a burn that tumbles down the hill. Starry skies on clear nights will amaze you. Brilliant. *Minimum stay: 2 nights at weekends.*

| | |
|---|---|
| Rooms | 6 doubles, 2 twin/doubles: £110-£175. 1 suite for 2: £190-£215. Singles from £88. |
| Meals | Lunch from £14.95. Sunday lunch £25. Dinner £36-£55. Not Sun night. |
| Closed | January. Mondays. |
| Directions | M6 junc. 40, A66 west to Braithwaite, then B5292 for Lorton. On right after 2.5 miles (before visitor centre). |

Kath & Liam Berney
The Cottage in the Wood
Braithwaite,
Keswick, CA12 5TW

| | |
|---|---|
| Tel | +44 (0)17687 78409 |
| Email | relax@thecottageinthewood.co.uk |
| Web | www.thecottageinthewood.co.uk |

## Askham Hall

Despite its grandeur – this is a Grade I-listed manor house with a 12th-century peel tower – Charlie runs Askham with huge informality and you're encouraged to kick off your shoes and treat the place as home. It's not a hotel, more a restaurant with fancy rooms, but there's lots to keep you amused: contemporary art and open fires, a beautiful drawing room with an honesty bar, a small spa with an outdoor pool, then gardens that open to the public and a café for pizza at lunch. The hall sits in 40 acres of prime Cumbrian grazing land between Ullswater and the Eden Valley with paths that follow the river below into glorious parkland. It's all part of the Lowther estate, where Charlie rears his own meat for Richard Swale's kitchen. And the restaurant lies at the heart of Askham, its seasonal food a big draw, perhaps slow-cooked duck with fig and walnut, Lowther venison with parmesan gnocchi, buttermilk panna cotta with sorrel sorbet. Chic bedrooms have a contemporary country-house style: some vast, one with a tented bathroom, others have views to Knipe Scar. Home-laid duck eggs wait at breakfast, too.

| | |
|---|---|
| Rooms | 8 twin/doubles: £150–£260. 4 suites for 2: £250–£320. Singles from £138. Extra bed/sofabed available £30 per person per night. |
| Meals | Lunch from £9. Dinner, 3 courses, £50. 5-course tasting menu £65. |
| Closed | Sun and Mon. January & early February. |
| Directions | M6, junc. 39, then A6 north. Askham signed left after 7 miles. In village. |

Charlie Lowther
Askham Hall
Askham, CA10 2PF

| | |
|---|---|
| Tel | +44 (0)1931 712350 |
| Email | enquiries@askhamhall.co.uk |
| Web | www.askhamhall.co.uk |

## Howtown Hotel

Welcome to Howtown, a world lost in time on a lane that goes nowhere on the quiet side of Ullswater. The position here is heavenly — water, mountain, field and sky — one of the best in the Lakes. The house sits in its own hamlet, dates to 1640, and has been welcoming guests for 114 years, a licensed farmhouse that has passed though five generations of the same family, who still run sheep and cattle on 400 acres of Lakeland fell. Inside, the past lives on: a panelled bar, William Morris wallpaper, smouldering coal fires, wall clocks and lots of brass. Homely bedrooms upstairs have simple pleasures: good beds, sheets and blankets, toile throws, fabulous views. Most are en suite, three have bathrooms one step across the landing. Dinner is old-school — you're summonsed by a gong — then served at oak tables with a beautiful dresser at one end of the dining room. There's a set menu, perhaps vegetable soup, roast lamb, then Howtown's famous sherry trifle; delicious sandwiches are available at lunch. David has an amphibious car for the odd lake cruise. Walking starts from the front door. Matchless. *No email — phone enquiries only.*

| | |
|---|---|
| Rooms | 8 doubles; 3 twin/doubles, each with separate bathroom: £178.<br>1 single sharing shower room: £89.<br>(All room prices include dinner.)<br>2 self-catering cottages for 7,<br>2 for 5: £450-£700 per week. |
| Meals | Lunch (cold table) £14.<br>Dinner included; non-residents £25.<br>Sunday lunch £16. |
| Closed | 1st Sunday in November to mid-March. |
| Directions | South from Pooley Bridge with Ullswater on right. Hotel on left after 4 miles. |

Jacquie & David Baldry
Howtown Hotel
Ullswater,
Penrith, CA10 2ND

| | |
|---|---|
| Tel | +44 (0)17684 86514 |
| Web | www.howtown-hotel.co.uk |

## The George

Charlotte Brontë set part of *Jane Eyre* here. She called the village Morton, referred to this hotel as The Feathers and stole the name of an old landlord for her heroine. A copy of her famous novel sits on the shelves of 'the smallest library in the world', which occupies a turret in the sitting room. The bigger turret, equally well employed, is now the bar. The George, a 500-year-old coaching inn on the Manchester to Sheffield road, has grown in stature over time. These days wood floors, stone walls and heavy beams mix with purple sofas, fancy wallpaper and Lloyd Loom furniture. It all works rather well, making this small hotel a good base in the northern Peak District. It's part of its community, too, with a couple of rooms for family celebrations, small weddings and the odd board meeting. Airy bedrooms hit the spot. Expect warm colours, the odd sofa and fine bathrooms. Comfy beds have padded heads and crisp linen; those at the back are quietest. Good food waits in the restaurant, perhaps smoked salmon, venison pudding, chocolate pavé. The Crucible Theatre in Sheffield is within easy reach.

| | |
|---|---|
| Rooms | 17 doubles, 4 twin/doubles: £95-£198. 3 singles: £70. |
| Meals | Lunch from £4.75. Dinner, 3 courses, £36.50. |
| Closed | Never. |
| Directions | In village at junction of A6187 and B6001, 10 miles west of M1 at Sheffield. |

James Fair
The George
Main Road, Hathersage,
Hope Valley, S32 1BB

| | |
|---|---|
| Tel | +44 (0)1433 650436 |
| Email | info@george-hotel.net |
| Web | www.george-hotel.net |

## Cavendish Hotel

The Cavendish has impeccable credentials. It stands on the Chatsworth Estate, is owned by the Duke and Duchess of Devonshire, and Chatsworth House itself stands a mile or two across the fields from this smart hotel. All of which means you can rise leisurely, have a good breakfast, then follow paths across to one of Britain's loveliest houses; fine gardens and a jaw-dropping art collection wait. As for the hotel, it has a warm country-house feel: sofas in front of the fire in the sitting room; art from the 'big house' on the walls; afternoon tea served on the lawn in summer. Bedrooms mix pretty florals with period colours and smart fabrics. None are small, all but one have country views, some are rather swanky. You get robes in excellent bathrooms, a sofa if there's room, crisp linen on comfy beds. Downstairs you can eat in the Garden Room or out on its terrace (more informal, lovely views) or in the elegant restaurant, perhaps hand-dived scallops, haunch of venison, Granny Smith apple crumble. Outside, the Peak District waits for walkers, while fishing can be arranged.

| | |
|---|---|
| Rooms | 20 doubles, 2 twins: £189–£219. 1 suite for 2: £300. 1 family room for 4: £169–£219. Singles from £133. |
| Meals | Continental breakfast £9.70; full English £18.90. Lunch from £6. Dinner £30–£45. |
| Closed | Never. |
| Directions | M1 junc. 29, A617 to Chesterfield, A619 to Baslow. On left in village. |

Philip Joseph
Cavendish Hotel
Church Lane, Baslow,
Bakewell, DE45 1SP

| | |
|---|---|
| Tel | +44 (0)1246 582311 |
| Email | info@cavendish-hotel.net |
| Web | www.cavendish-hotel.net |

## The Peacock at Rowsley

The Peacock sits between two fine houses, Haddon Hall and Chatsworth House. You can follow rivers up to each – the Derwent to Chatsworth, the Wye to the Hall – both a stroll through beautiful parkland. As for the hotel, it was built in 1652 and was home to the steward of Haddon. Inside, old and new mix gracefully: mullioned windows, hessian rugs, aristocratic art, then striking colours that give a contemporary feel. You'll find Mouseman tables and chairs in the restaurant, where French windows open onto the terrace. Elsewhere, a fire smoulders in the bar every day, the daily papers wait in the sitting room, the garden lawn runs down to the river. Stylish bedrooms have crisp linen, good beds, Farrow & Ball colours, the odd antique; one has a bed from Belvoir Castle. Good food waits in the restaurant, with meat and game from the estate, perhaps venison terrine, roast partridge, Bakewell Tart with buttermilk ice cream. There's afternoon tea in the garden in summer and you can fish both rivers, with day tickets available from reception. Guests also receive a discount on entry to Haddon Hall. *Minimum stay: 2 nights at weekends.*

| | |
|---|---|
| Rooms | 10 doubles, 2 four-posters: £180–£280. 1 suite for 2: £220–£280. 2 singles: £110–£125. Dinner, B&B from £125 per person. Extra beds £40. Dogs £10. |
| Meals | Lunch from £4.50. Sunday lunch £22.50–£29.50. Dinner £60. |
| Closed | Rarely. |
| Directions | A6 north through Matlock, then to Rowsley. On right in village. |

Laura Ball
The Peacock at Rowsley
Bakewell Road, Rowsley,
Matlock, DE4 2EB

Tel       +44 (0)1629 733518
Email     reception@thepeacockatrowsley.com
Web       www.thepeacockatrowsley.com

## The Old Rectory Hotel Exmoor

A gorgeous small hotel in the hills above the Exmoor coast. The road from Lynton is a great way in, through woods that cling to a hill with the sea below. As for the Old Rectory, it's a mini Gidleigh Park, charming from top to toe. Three acres of spectacular gardens wrap around you, only birdsong disturbs you, though Exmoor deer occasionally come to drink from the pond. Inside, Huw and Sam continue to lavish love and money in all the right places. Their most recent addition is a beautiful orangery with smart sofas and warm colours then doors onto the garden for afternoon tea in the sun. Interiors are lovely: Farrow & Ball colours, the odd stone wall, a cute little sitting room, fresh flowers and books everywhere. Bedrooms are just as good with big beds, crisp linen, cool colours and beautiful bathrooms. You'll find digital radios, flat-screen TVs and the odd leather sofa, too. Spin into the restaurant for an excellent meal, perhaps Ilfracombe crab, Exmoor duck, strawberry champagne trifle. Afternoon tea 'on the house' is served in the garden in good weather.

| | |
|---|---|
| Rooms | 3 doubles, 4 twin/doubles: £185-£230. 4 suites for 2: £245-£270. Price includes dinner for 2. |
| Meals | 4-course dinner included in price; non-residents £35. |
| Closed | November-March. |
| Directions | M5 junc. 27, A361 to South Molton, then A399 north. Right at Blackmoor Gate onto A39 for Lynton. Left after 3 miles, signed Martinhoe. In village, next to church. |

Huw Rees & Sam Prosser
The Old Rectory Hotel Exmoor
Martinhoe, Parracombe,
Barnstable, EX31 4QT

| | |
|---|---|
| Tel | +44 (0)1598 763368 |
| Email | info@oldrectoryhotel.co.uk |
| Web | www.oldrectoryhotel.co.uk |

AWARD WINNER

Old favourite

## Loyton Lodge

You get the impression the tiny lanes that wrap around this small estate act as a sort of fortification, one designed to confuse invaders and protect this patch of heaven. And heaven it is – 280 acres of rolling hills and ancient woodland, with wild flowers, pristine rivers, strutting pheasants and the odd red deer commuting across the fields. It's England circa 1964 with nothing but birdsong to break the peace and glorious walks that start at the front door. As for Loyton, it's a great little base for a night or two deep in the hills. It mixes contemporary interiors with an old-school feel – roaring fires, comfy sofas, wonderful art, even a snooker room. Bedrooms have warm colours and smart fabrics, perhaps a sleigh bed or a claw-foot bath, then books and robes and crisp white linen. Breakfast is a treat – bacon and sausages from home-reared pigs, eggs from estate hens – and there's dinner by arrangement, perhaps local asparagus, lemon sole, walnut and fruit crumble. Take the whole house and bring the family or come for the odd night of live jazz. Exmoor waits, as do good local restaurants.

| | |
|---|---|
| Rooms | 7 doubles, 2 twin/doubles, 1 twin: £95-£130. Singles from £80. Extra beds £20 (under 12s free). |
| Meals | Dinner, 3 courses, about £30 by arrangement. |
| Closed | Rarely. |
| Directions | A396 north from Tiverton to Bampton, then right onto B3227. After 1 mile, left for Loyton. Over x-roads, left at hill. Lodge on right after 0.5 mile. |

Isobel, Sally & Angus Barnes
Loyton Lodge
Morebath,
Tiverton, EX16 9AS
Tel +44 (0)1398 331051
Email thelodge@loyton.com
Web www.loyton.com

## Northcote Manor

A small country-house hotel built on the site of a 15th-century monastery. Those who want peace in deep country will find it here. You wind up a one-mile drive, through a wood that bursts with colour in spring, then emerge onto a lush plateau of rolling hills; the view from the croquet lawn drifts east for ten miles. As for the house, wisteria wanders along old stone walls, while the odd open fire smoulders within. There's an airy hall that doubles as the bar, a country-house drawing room that floods with light, and a sitting room where you gather for pre-dinner drinks. Super food waits in a lovely dining room, steps lead down to a pretty conservatory, doors open onto a gravelled terrace for summer breakfasts with lovely views. Bedrooms are no less appealing – more traditional in the main house, more contemporary in the garden rooms. Expect padded bedheads, mahogany dressers, flat-screen TVs, silky throws. You can walk your socks off, then come home for a good meal, perhaps white Cornish crab, local lamb, strawberry soufflé with vanilla ice-cream. Exmoor and North Devon's coasts are close.

| | |
|---|---|
| Rooms | 9 twin/doubles, 7 suites for 2: £170–£280. Singles from £120. Dinner, B&B from £155 per person. Extra bed/sofabed available £15–£25 per person per night. |
| Meals | Light dishes from £6.50. Lunch £22.50–£25.50. Dinner, 3 courses, £45. Tasting menu £90. Sunday lunch from £28.50. |
| Closed | Never. |
| Directions | M5 junc. 27, A361 to S. Molton. Fork left onto B3227; left on A377 for Exeter. Entrance 4.1 miles on right, signed. |

Richie Herkes
Northcote Manor
Burrington,
Umberleigh, EX37 9LZ

| | |
|---|---|
| Tel | +44 (0)1769 560501 |
| Email | rest@northcotemanor.co.uk |
| Web | www.northcotemanor.co.uk |

## Lewtrenchard Manor

A magnificent Jacobean mansion, a wormhole back to the 16th century. Inside, the full aristocratic monty is on display: a spectacular hall with a cavernous fireplace, a dazzling ballroom with extraordinary plasterwork. There are priest holes, oak panelling, oils by the score. Best of all is the 1602 gallery with its stunning ceiling and grand piano, while *Onward Christian Soldiers* was written in the library. Bedrooms are large. Some are grandly traditional (the four-poster belonged to Queen Henrietta Maria, wife of Charles I); others are more contemporary with airy colours and modern bathrooms. All have jugs of iced water, garden flowers and bathrobes. Delicious food waits downstairs – perhaps smoked haddock risotto, thyme-roasted Lewdown venison, salted caramel and chocolate delice with banana ice cream; there's a chef's table, too, where you watch the kitchen at work on a bank of TVs. Outside, a beautiful courtyard that's home to an ancient wisteria, a Gertrude Jekyll parterre garden, and an avenue of beech trees that makes you feel you're in a Hardy novel. Dartmoor is close. *Minimum stay: 2 nights at weekends.*

| | |
|---|---|
| Rooms | 4 doubles, 6 twin/doubles: £175–£230. 4 suites for 2: £230–£245. Singles from £120. Dinner, B&B from £132.50 per person. |
| Meals | Lunch: bar meals from £5.50; restaurant from £19.50. Dinner, 3 courses, £49.50. Children over seven welcome in restaurant. |
| Closed | Rarely. |
| Directions | From Exeter, exit A30 for A386. At T-junc., right, then 1st left for Lewdown. After 6 miles, left for Lewtrenchard. Keep left, house on left after 0.5 miles. |

Sue, James, Duncan & Joan Murray
Lewtrenchard Manor
Lewdown,
Okehampton, EX20 4PN

| | |
|---|---|
| Tel | +44 (0)1566 783222 |
| Email | info@lewtrenchard.co.uk |
| Web | www.lewtrenchard.co.uk |

## Tor Cottage

A rural idyll at the end of a track in a pretty valley lost to the world. It's a fabulous hideaway wrapped up in 28 acres of majestic country and those who seek peace and a place to unwind will love it here. Hills rise, cows sleep, streams run, birds sing. Bridle paths lead onto the hill, wild flowers carpet the hay meadow. Big rooms in converted outbuildings are the lap of old-school, rustic luxury. Each comes with a wood-burner and private terrace, one is straight out of *House and Garden*, another has ceilings open to the rafters. Most romantic of all is the cabin in its own valley – a wonderland in the woods – with a hammock in the trees, a stream passing below, the odd deer pottering past. Maureen's magnificent breakfasts are served in the conservatory or on the terrace in good weather: homemade muesli, local sausages, farm-fresh eggs. You can have smoked salmon sandwiches by the pool for lunch or spark up the barbecue and cook your own dinner; all rooms have fridges and microwaves, so you don't have to go out. Maureen is the star of the show, her staff couldn't be nicer. Wonderful. *Minimum stay: 2 nights.*

| | |
|---|---|
| Rooms | 2 doubles, 1 twin/double, 1 suite for 2: £150. 1 cabin for 2: £155. Singles from £98. |
| Meals | Picnic platters £16. Pubs/restaurants 3 miles. |
| Closed | Mid-December to end of January. |
| Directions | In Chillaton keep pub & Post Office on left, up hill towards Tavistock. After 300 yards right down bridleway (ignore 'No Access' signs). |

Maureen Rowlatt
Tor Cottage
Chillaton,
Lifton, PL16 0JE

| | |
|---|---|
| Tel | +44 (0)1822 860248 |
| Email | info@torcottage.co.uk |
| Web | www.torcottage.co.uk |

## The Horn of Plenty

The Horn of Plenty is one of those clever hotels that has survived the test of time by constantly improving itself. This year's contribution is six gorgeous new rooms, four of which have terraces or balconies that give 40-mile views over the Tamar Valley. Potter about outside and find six acres of gardens, then a path that leads down through bluebell woods to the river. Inside, beautiful simplicity abounds: stripped floors, gilt mirrors, fine art, fresh flowers everywhere. Bedrooms in the main house come in country-house style, those in the garden have a contemporary feel. All have smart colours, big comfy beds, perhaps a claw-foot bath or a ceiling open to the rafters; ten have a terrace or a balcony. Despite all this, the food remains the big draw, so come to eat well, perhaps beetroot mousse with goat's cheese parfait, grilled duck with chicory and orange, chocolate cannelloni with banana sorbet; views of the Tamar snaking through the hills are included in the price. Afternoon tea is served in the shade of a magnolia tree in summer. Tavistock, Dartmoor and The Eden Project are close.

| | |
|---|---|
| Rooms | 16 twin/doubles: £110–£245. Singles from £100. Dinner, B&B from £135 per person. Extra bed/sofabed available £25 per person per night. |
| Meals | Lunch from £19.50. Dinner, 3 courses, £49.50. Tasting menu £65. |
| Closed | Never. |
| Directions | West from Tavistock on A390 following signs to Callington. Right after 3 miles at Gulworthy Cross. Signed left after 0.75 miles. |

Julie Leivers & Damien Pease
The Horn of Plenty
Gulworthy,
Tavistock, PL19 8JD

| | |
|---|---|
| Tel | +44 (0)1822 832528 |
| Email | enquiries@thehornofplenty.co.uk |
| Web | www.thehornofplenty.co.uk |

## Glazebrook House Hotel

The front door at Glazebrook House could well be a rip in the space-time continuum. Outside, English decorum reigns; inside, a wonderland for your senses waits. You don't really find a hotel, more a contemporary art installation that you get to live in for a day or two. It's a reinvention of a 19th-century collector's house and it overflows with beautiful things: pink flamingos, enormous chandeliers, ancient maps, a bust of the queen with a halo instead of a crown. Downstairs, there's a dinosaur in the library, a tasting room for wine and whisky, a red-marbled bar with sofas and armchairs, then doors onto a terrace for afternoon tea. Bedrooms come fully loaded: vast beds, the loveliest linen, bold colours, quirky art. You get iPads, smart TVs and bulging minibars 'on the house'. Black marble bathrooms are faultless: expect walk-in showers, fluffy robes, perhaps a free-standing bath. Tasty bistro food waits downstairs, maybe goats' cheese fritters, fillet of brill, rhubarb and blueberry crumble. The A38 passes close by; you only hear it outside, you won't know it's there at night. Dartmoor waits.

| | |
|---|---|
| Rooms | 6 doubles, 1 twin: £179–£239.<br>1 single: £139–£159. |
| Meals | Lunch from £6.<br>Dinner, 3 courses, about £35. |
| Closed | Rarely. |
| Directions | Leave A38 for South Brent. At west end of village follow brown signs to hotel west out of village. Hotel signed on right after 1 mile. |

Pieter & Fran Hamman
Glazebrook House Hotel
South Brent, TQ10 9JE

| | |
|---|---|
| Tel | +44 (0)1364 73322 |
| Email | enquiries@glazebrookhouse.com |
| Web | www.glazebrookhouse.com |

## Plantation House

This lovely small hotel delivers what so many of us want: a warm welcome, lovely food, rooms that spoil us rotten. Downstairs, a fire smoulders in the sitting-room bar; upstairs, fine Georgian windows frame views of hill and forest. Stylish bedrooms are full of comforts. They come with excellent bathrooms, lovely beds, crisp linen and warm colours. You get padded bedheads, sound systems, bowls of fruit, white robes to pad about in. Back downstairs, you'll succumb to a pre-dinner drink – in front of the fire in the bar in winter, out on the pretty terrace in summer. As for Richard's food, it bursts with flavour, so expect to eat well, perhaps Thai-style sea bass with ginger and lemongrass, local lamb with a Merlot jus, chocolate terrine with hazelnut ice cream. Soft fruits, vegetables and potatoes come from the garden in summer, as do home-laid eggs at breakfast. The river Erme passes across the road – follow it down to the sea and discover wonderful Wonwell Beach. There's lots to see around you: Dartmoor to the north, Totnes, Dartmouth, Salcombe and Slapton Sands to the south. Brilliant.

| | |
|---|---|
| Rooms | 5 doubles, 1 twin: £125–£185. |
| | 1 suite for 2: £195–£230. |
| | 1 single: £75–£80. |
| Meals | Dinner, 5 courses, from £36. |
| Closed | Never. |
| Directions | A38, then A3121 for Ermington. |
| | In village on western fringe. |

Richard Hendey
Plantation House
Totnes Road, Ermington,
Ivybridge, PL21 9NS
Tel       +44 (0)1548 831100
Email     info@plantationhousehotel.co.uk
Web       www.plantationhousehotel.co.uk

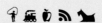

## The Henley Hotel

A small house above the sea with fabulous views, super bedrooms and some of the loveliest food in Devon. Despite these credentials, it's Martyn and Petra who shine most brightly, their kind, generous approach making this a memorable place to stay. Warm interiors have wooden floors, Lloyd Loom furniture, the odd potted palm, then big windows to frame the view. Below, the Avon estuary slips gracefully out to sea. At high tide surfers ride the waves, at low tide you can walk on the sands. There's a pretty garden with a path tumbling down to the beach, binoculars in each room, a wood-burner in the snug and good books everywhere. Bedrooms are a steal (one is huge). Expect warm colours, crisp linen, tongue-and-groove panelling and robes in super little bathrooms. As for Martyn's table d'hôte dinners, expect to eat very well. Fish comes daily from Kingsbridge market, you might find grilled figs with goat's cheese and Parma ham, roast monkfish with a lobster sauce, then hot chocolate soufflé with fresh raspberries. Gorgeous Devon is all around. Better than the Ritz! *Minimum stay: 2 nights at weekends.*

| | |
|---|---|
| Rooms | 2 doubles, 2 twin/doubles: £120–£137. 1 suite for 2: £150. Singles from £85. Dinner, B&B £87–£97 per person (2 night minimum). |
| Meals | Dinner £36. |
| Closed | November – March. |
| Directions | From A38, A3121 to Modbury, then B3392 to Bigbury-on-Sea. Hotel on left as road slopes down to sea. |

Martyn Scarterfield & Petra Lampe
The Henley Hotel
Folly Hill, Bigbury-on-Sea,
Kingsbridge, TQ7 4AR
Tel      +44 (0)1548 810240
Email    thehenleyhotel@btconnect.com
Web      www.thehenleyhotel.co.uk

Nicely priced

## Burgh Island Hotel

Burgh is unique – grand English Art Deco trapped in aspic. Noël Coward loved it, Agatha Christie wrote here. It's much more than a hotel – you come to join a cast of players – so bring your pearls and come for cocktails under a stained-glass dome. By day you lie on steamers in the garden, watch gulls wheeling above, dip your toes into Mermaid's pool or try your hand at a game of croquet. At night you dress for dinner, sip vermouth in a palm-fringed bar, then shuffle off to the ballroom and dine on delicious organic food while the sounds of swing and jazz fill the air. Follow your nose and find flowers in vases four-feet high, bronze ladies thrusting globes into the sky, walls clad in vitrolite, a 14th-century smugglers inn. Art Deco bedrooms are the real thing: Bakelite telephones, ancient radios, bowls of fruit, panelled walls. Some have claw-foot baths, others have balconies, the Beach House suite juts out over rocks. There's snooker, tennis, massage, a sauna. You're on an island, so sweep across the sands at low tide or hitch a ride on the sea tractor. *Minimum stay: 2 nights at weekends.*

| | |
|---|---|
| Rooms | 10 doubles, 3 twin/doubles: £400–£430. 12 suites for 2: £485–£640. Price includes dinner for 2. |
| Meals | Lunch from £13.50. Sunday lunch £48. Dinner included; non-residents £60. 24–hour residents' menu from £10.50. |
| Closed | Rarely. |
| Directions | Drive to Bigbury-on-Sea. At high tide you are transported by sea tractor, at low tide by Landrover. Walking over the beach takes 3 minutes. Eco-taxis can be arranged. |

Deborah Clark & Tony Orchard
Burgh Island Hotel
Burgh Island, Bigbury-on-Sea,
Kingsbridge, TQ7 4BG

| | |
|---|---|
| Tel | +44 (0)1548 810514 |
| Email | reception@burghisland.com |
| Web | www.burghisland.com |

## South Sands Hotel

Two coves west from the bustle of town, this super-smart hotel stands above the beach with views of water, hill and sky. Interiors have a New England feel – seaside colours, softly painted wood, walls of glass for views you can't escape. Doors in the restaurant open onto a decked terrace, where at high tide the beach disappears and the sea laps against the wall below. Pull yourself away to walk in the hills, sail on the water, hire a kayak or try your hand at paddleboarding. Alternatively, just drop down to the beach for family fun. Children are very welcome and you'll find beach towels, buckets and spades, even crabbing nets for excursions to rock pools. Back at the hotel, lovely food waits, perhaps duck liver brûlée, seafood spaghetti, chocolate sundae drenched in chocolate sauce. As for the rooms, those at the front have sublime views, a couple get terraces, all have fabulous bathrooms, cool colours and super-comfy beds. One has 'his and hers' claw-foot baths that look out to sea; the family suites have kitchens, dining tables and separate bedrooms for kids. Brilliant.
*Minimum stay: 2 nights at weekends.*

| Rooms | 16 doubles, 6 twin/doubles: £150–£375. 5 suites for 4: £320–£435. Extra beds £35. Cots £12.50 per stay. Dogs £12.50 per night. |
| Meals | Lunch from £17.95. Dinner £15.95–£40. |
| Closed | Rarely. |
| Directions | A381 to Salcombe, then signed right to South Sands. Follow road down hill, then along water. On left. |

Charles Erleigh
South Sands Hotel
Bolt Head,
Salcombe, TQ8 8LL
Tel +44 (0)1548 859000
Email enquiries@southsands.com
Web www.southsands.com

## Seabreeze

A 16th-century teahouse with rooms on Slapton Sands: only in England. The sea laps ten paces from the front door, the hills of Devon soar behind, three miles of beach shoot off before your eyes. Seabreeze is a treat: cute, relaxed, a slice of old-world magic. Inside, you find Carol and Bonni baking the old-fashioned way, and it's all delicious: hot scones, Victoria sponge, banana and chocolate chip brownies. The tearoom itself — white walls, pretty art, tables topped with maps -- is warmed by a wood-burner in winter. In summer you decamp onto the terrace, where sea and sky fuse. Bedrooms are lovely with seaside colours, jars of driftwood and a warm, cosy feel; you can lie in bed and look out to sea from those at the front. Outside, there's lots to do: buckets and spades on the beach, cliff-top walks to local pubs, a huge lake for migratory birds, kayaks for intrepid adventures. Breakfast sets you up for the day (the bacon sandwich is a thing of rare beauty). Local restaurants wait at night: Start Bay Inn in the village, Church House Inn up the road. *Minimum stay: 2 nights at weekends in high season.*

| | |
|---|---|
| Rooms | 2 doubles, 1 twin/double: £80–£140. Singles from £70. |
| Meals | Lunch from £5. Restaurants in village. |
| Closed | Never. |
| Directions | A379 south from Dartmouth to Torcross. House on seafront in village. |

Carol Simmons & Bonni Lincoln
Seabreeze
Torcross,
Kingsbridge, TQ7 2TQ

| | |
|---|---|
| Tel | +44 (0)1548 580697 |
| Email | info@seabreezebreaks.com |
| Web | www.seabreezebreaks.com |

## Bayards Cove Inn

In 1620 the Mayflower stopped in Bayards Cove before sailing for America. It docked just outside this gorgeous little inn, one of the oldest buildings in Dartmouth. But if its timber frames are ancient, then its jaunty interiors are the polar opposite with a warm contemporary feel that spreads itself far and wide. Once inside you realise you're really in a café/tapas bar that does a good line in world wines and local ales. You also realise you've landed in heaven and soon you're trying to muscle your way onto one of the sofas in the bay windows, from which you can survey life inside and out. Interiors have warm colours, low beams, white stone walls and ancient wood everywhere; there are fairy lights, too, a bar weighed down by freshly baked cakes, and cool tunes afloat in the air. Upstairs, lovely rooms have timber frames, padded bedheads, pretty fabrics, comfy beds. Most have compact shower rooms, but you won't mind for a minute; others have views of the water or wildly wonky floors. There's great food, too, and live flamenco on Sunday nights. Dartmouth waits at the front door. *Minimum stay: 2 nights at weekends.*

| | |
|---|---|
| Rooms | 4 doubles, 1 twin/double: £90–£155. 1 suite for 2: £130–£180. 1 family room for 4: £110–£160. Singles from £95. |
| Meals | Lunch from £5.95. Dinner from £9.95 (not Mon-Wed off season). |
| Closed | Never. |
| Directions | In Dartmouth south along sea front for lower ferry. Follow road right for 200m and on left at T-junction. |

Charlie & Zuzana Deuchar
Bayards Cove Inn
Lower Street,
Dartmouth, TQ6 9AN

| | |
|---|---|
| Tel | +44 (0)1803 839278 |
| Email | bayardscove@gmail.com |
| Web | www.bayardscoveinn.co.uk |

## Nonsuch House

You're halfway up the hill with unbeatable views over the Dart estuary. Yachts zip about, ferries cross to Dartmouth, big boats glide past out at sea. Wherever you go, the view follows you around – the terrace for tea in summer, the conservatory for lovely food, the four big bedrooms that spoil you rotten. One opens onto a small terrace, all have binoculars to scan the high seas. You'll find big comfy beds, Sanderson fabrics, warm colours and seaside art. There are robes in good bathrooms and Bramley oils, too. Kit and Penny are great fun and look after you in style. Kit, an ex-hotelier, cooks lovely dinners four nights a week (BYO). The best local produce makes it to your plate, perhaps hand-dived scallops, Blackawton lamb, Dartmouth lobster, homemade truffles; in winter you retire to the sitting room for coffee in front of an open fire. There's lots to do in the area. Ferries whizz you across to Dartmouth, you can walk to the castle, learn to paddleboard, take boat trips up to Totnes, or follow the coastal path. Mitch Tonks at the Seahorse is a great spot for dinner on Kit's nights off. *Minimum stay: 2 nights at weekends. Children over 10 welcome.*

| | |
|---|---|
| Rooms | 1 double, 3 twin/doubles: £130–£175. Singles from £90. Extra beds £40. |
| Meals | Dinner, 3 courses, £39.50. (not Tues/Wed/Sat.) BYO. Pub/restaurant 5-minute walk & short boat trip. |
| Closed | Rarely. |
| Directions | 2 miles before Brixham on A3022, A379. Right at r'bout, 100yds on fork left (B3205) downhill, through woods, left up Higher Contour Rd, down Ridley Hill. At hairpin bend. Parking nearby. |

Kit & Penny Noble
Nonsuch House
Church Hill, Kingswear,
Dartmouth, TQ6 0BX

| | |
|---|---|
| Tel | +44 (0)1803 752829 |
| Email | enquiries@nonsuch-house.co.uk |
| Web | www.nonsuch-house.co.uk |

## The Cary Arms at Babbacombe Bay

The Cary Arms hovers above Babbacombe Bay with huge views of water and sky that shoot off to Dorset's Jurassic coast. It's a cool little place — half seaside pub, half dreamy hotel — and it makes the most of its spectacular position: five beautiful terraces drop downhill towards a small jetty, where locals fish. The pub has six moorings in the bay, you can charter a boat and explore the coast. Back on dry land the bar comes with stone walls, wooden floors and a fire that burns every day. In good weather you eat on the terraces, perhaps a pint of prawns, fillet of sea bass, lavender panna cotta; groups of friends can hold their own barbecues, too. Dazzling bedrooms come in New England style. All but one opens onto a private terrace or balcony, you get decanters of sloe gin, flat-screen TVs, fabulous beds, super bathrooms (one has a claw-foot bath that looks out to sea). Back outside, you can snorkel on mackerel reefs or hug the coastline in a kayak. If that sounds too energetic, either head to the treatment room or sink into a deck chair on the residents' sun terrace.

| | |
|---|---|
| Rooms | 6 doubles, 1 twin/double: £225-£295. 1 family room for 4: £395. 4 self-catering cottages for 2-8: £1,750-£2,970 per week. Extra bed/sofabed available £25 per person per night. Dogs £20 per night. |
| Meals | Lunch from £7.95. Dinner £25-£35. |
| Closed | Never. |
| Directions | From Teignmouth south on A379; 5 miles to St Marychurch, thro' lights, left into Babbacombe Downs Rd. Follow road right; left downhill. |

Felicia Crosby
The Cary Arms at Babbacombe Bay
Beach Road, Babbacombe,
Torquay, TQ1 3LX

| | |
|---|---|
| Tel | +44 (0)1803 327110 |
| Email | enquiries@caryarms.co.uk |
| Web | www.caryarms.co.uk |

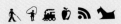

## Lydgate House Hotel

You're in 36 acres of heaven, so come for the wonder of Dartmoor: deer and badger, fox and pheasant, kingfisher and woodpecker all live here. A 30-minute circular walk takes you over the East Dart river, up to a meadow where rare orchids flourish, then back down to a 12th-century clapper bridge. Herons dive in the river, you may spot them from the conservatory as you dig into your locally cured bacon and eggs. The house is a nourishing stream of homely comforts: a drying room for walkers, deep white sofas, walls of books, a wood-burner in the sitting room. Karen cooks the sort of food you'd hope for after a day on the moors, perhaps mushroom and ricotta ravioli, roast partridge with a port and damson jus, plum and almond tart with clotted cream. Homely bedrooms are warm and cosseting with crisp florals and comfy beds. Two are big and have claw-foot baths, all have a nice price. There's breakfast on the terrace in good weather and a stone cottage for six if you want to look after yourselves. Fabulous walks start from the front door, while Castle Drogo and Buckland Abbey are close. *Discounts for stays of 3 or more nights.*

| | |
|---|---|
| Rooms | 5 doubles: £95–£132. |
| | 2 singles: £49–£60. |
| | 1 cottage for 2–6 £400–£1,000. |
| Meals | Dinner, 2–3 courses, £22.95–£27.50 |
| | (not Sun & Mon). |
| Closed | January. |
| Directions | From Exeter A30 west to Whiddon Down, A382 south to Moretonhampstead, B3212 west to Postbridge. In village, left at pub. House signed straight ahead. |

Stephen & Karen Horn
Lydgate House Hotel
Postbridge,
Yelverton, PL20 6TJ

| | |
|---|---|
| Tel | +44 (0)1822 880209 |
| Email | info@lydgatehouse.co.uk |
| Web | www.lydgatehouse.co.uk |

## Prince Hall Hotel

A small country house lost to the world on beautiful Dartmoor. You spin down an avenue of beech trees, note the majestic view, then decant into this warm, friendly bolthole. It's one of those places that cleverly blends informality with good service – Fi, Chris and their lovely staff look after you in style. Potter about and find a sitting-room bar where you can sink into sofas in front of a wood-burner; binoculars in the drawing room, where views are framed by shuttered windows; then a smart restaurant for local food on a menu that changes daily, perhaps pigeon with prune purée, slow-roasted pork, chocolate torte with butterscotch sauce; the wine list is mostly organic. Bedrooms are all different, but it's worth splashing out on the big ones at the back – they have the view. Expect smart beds, warm colours, good bathrooms, perhaps a sofa. Those at the side, some beamed, are smaller, though none are small. Outside, lawns run down to fields, the river passes beyond, then moor, then sky; there's a shepherd's hut if you want to glamp. Guided walks can be arranged. Dogs are very welcome. *Minimum stay: 2 nights at weekends.*

| | |
|---|---|
| Rooms | 4 doubles, 4 twin/doubles: £160-£220. 1 shepherd's hut for 2: £115-£140. Dinner, B&B £95-£130 per person (3 big rooms dinner, B&B only May–September). |
| Meals | Lunch from £6.50. Dinner £39.50-£47.50. Sunday lunch from £21.50. |
| Closed | Never. |
| Directions | A38 to Ashburton, then follow signs through Poundsgate & Dartmeet. Hotel signed on left 1 mile before Two Bridges. |

Fi & Chris Daly
Prince Hall Hotel
Two Bridges, Princetown,
Yelverton, PL20 6SA
Tel      +44 (0)1822 890403
Email   info@princehall.co.uk
Web     www.princehall.co.uk

## Mill End

Mill End sits on the Two Moors Way, flanked on one side by the river Teign, as good a spot as any on Dartmoor. It's a firm favourite with walkers, foodies and dogs – your pooch is extremely welcome here. Outside, birds sing, rabbits hop, and mere mortals sit in the pretty garden digging into afternoon tea. Inside, warm interiors have timber frames, nooks and crannies, pretty art and games galore. You'll find a small bar for pre-dinner drinks, comfy sofas in front of an open fire, then an airy restaurant for some lovely food. Well-priced bedrooms have good beds, white linen, pretty colours, the odd antique. Most look the right way, a couple have padded window seats, one has a large balcony, others open onto a terrace. After long walks on the moors, return for a good meal, perhaps twice-baked Portland crab soufflé, haunch of Exmoor venison, warm treacle tart with chilli syrup. There's high tea for children, porridge with cream and brown sugar for breakfast, picnic hampers can be arranged. Castle Drogo, Fernworthy Resevoir and Buckland Abbey – home to Sir Francis Drake – all wait.

| Rooms | 9 doubles, 2 twins: £90–£160. |
| | 2 suites for 2: £145–£210. |
| | Singles from £75. Extra beds from £25. |
| Meals | Lunch from £6. |
| | Dinner, 3 courses, about £30. |
| | Sunday lunch £22–£26. |
| Closed | Rarely. |
| Directions | M5, then A30 to Whiddon Down. South on A382, through Sandy Park, over small bridge and on right. |

Tara & Nick Culverhouse
Mill End
Chagford,
Dartmoor, TQ13 8JN
Tel      +44 (0)1647 432282
Email    info@millend.com
Web      www.millendhotel.com

Inn

## The Lamb Inn

This 16th-century inn is adored by locals and visitors alike. It's a proper inn in the old tradition with gorgeous rooms and the odd touch of scruffiness to add authenticity to its earthy bones. It stands on a cobbled walkway in a village lost down tiny lanes, and those lucky enough to chance upon it leave reluctantly. Inside there are beams, but they are not sandblasted, red carpets with a little swirl, sofas in front of an open fire. Boarded menus trumpet irresistible food — carrot and orange soup, haunch of venison with a port jus, an excellent rhubarb crumble. You can eat wherever you want: in the bar, in the fancy restaurant, or out in the walled garden in good weather. There's a cobbled terrace, a skittle alley, maps for walkers and well-kept ales. Upstairs, seven rooms have a chic country style. Two have baths in the room, those in the barn have painted stone walls, the suite has a wood-burner and a private terrace. All are lovely with comfy beds, white linen, good power showers and flat-screen TVs. Kind staff chat with ease. Dartmoor waits, but you may well linger. Brilliant.

| | |
|---|---|
| Rooms | 5 doubles, 1 twin/double: £69–£130. 1 suite for 3: £150. |
| Meals | Lunch from £9. Dinner, 3 courses, £20–£30. Sunday lunch from £8.90. |
| Closed | Never. |
| Directions | A377 north from Exeter. 1st right in Crediton, left, signed Sandford. 1 mile up & in village. |

**Mark Hildyard & Katharine Lightfoot**
The Lamb Inn
Sandford,
Crediton, EX17 4LW

| | |
|---|---|
| Tel | +44 (0)1363 773676 |
| Email | thelambinn@gmail.com |
| Web | www.lambinnsandford.co.uk |

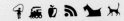

## The Lazy Toad Inn

Welcome to the rural idyll – a pretty village lost in fine country with a lovely inn that stands in the shadow of the church tower. Outside, you find a colourful courtyard for lunch in the sun. Inside, you get a beautiful fusion of old world and new. This isn't one of those places that sold its soul to an interior designer. On the contrary, its smart, homespun feel hits the spot perfectly: low ceilings, cool colours, painted settles and Elvis Presley framed on a wall. A fire smoulders in the bar, where you can grab a pint of Otter or try the local cider. Tables and chairs are scattered about, so grab one and order some seriously good food, perhaps caramelised onion soup, grilled sea bass with basil pesto, dark chocolate mousse with honeycomb and raspberry sorbet. Bedrooms have a warm country feel: pretty fabrics, comfy beds, crisp linen, iPod docks. Outside, there's a tiny back garden, then a polytunnel in a field beyond that serves the kitchen. A river passes beyond the church – perfect for wild swimming. You're only five miles from Exeter, but you'll think you're in the middle of nowhere. A gem. *All ages welcome to dine. Over 12s welcome to stay.*

| | |
|---|---|
| Rooms | 5 doubles: £85–£105. Singles from £75. Dinner, B&B £73–£88 per person. Extra bed/sofabed available £15–£25 per person per night. |
| Meals | Bar snacks from £3. Lunch from £5.35. Dinner from £12.50. Sunday lunch, 3 courses, £25. |
| Closed | Sun nights & Mon. |
| Directions | North from Exeter on A377 for Crediton. At roundabout at Cowley, take A377 for Brampford Speke. Right again after 1 mile & in village. |

Harriet & Mike Daly
The Lazy Toad Inn
Brampford Speke,
Exeter, EX5 5DP

| | |
|---|---|
| Tel | +44 (0)1392 841591 |
| Email | thelazytoad@outlook.com |
| Web | www.thelazytoadinn.co.uk |

## Magdalen Chapter

Where do we start? It might be simpler to confine ourselves to a bald statement of facts to describe this contemporary wonderland. An open fire, terrazzo floors, big warm colours and the odd sofa greet you in the entrance hall. Contemporary art hangs on every wall. There's a curated library, where you can sit and flick through glossy pages; a stunning sitting room bar with a Zen fireplace and a Hugo Dalton mural; an interior courtyard with walls of glass that looks onto an attractive garden. The brasserie is magnificent, open to the rafters with white pods of light hanging from on high and an open kitchen on display. In summer, glass doors fly open and you eat on the terrace, perhaps roast monkfish with wild garlic or a good steak. There are deckchairs on the lawn, a small kitchen garden, treatment rooms for stressed-out folk; there's even a small swimming pool that comes with a wood-burner. Bedrooms have an uncluttered, contemporary feel: iPads, flat-screen TVs, black-and-white photography, handmade furniture. Bathrooms are excellent; expect power showers, REN lotions and white bathrobes.

| | |
|---|---|
| Rooms | 52 doubles, 2 twin/doubles: £120–£250. 5 singles: £105. |
| Meals | Lunch from £8. Dinner from £12.95; à la carte about £30. |
| Closed | Never. |
| Directions | Sent on booking. |

Fiona Moores
Magdalen Chapter
Magdalen Street,
Exeter, EX2 4HY

| | |
|---|---|
| Tel | +44 (0)1392 281000 |
| Email | magdalen_ge@chapterhotels.com |
| Web | www.themagdalenchapter.com/ |

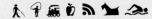

## Southernhay House

A beautiful small hotel on the loveliest square in town, a short stroll from the cathedral. The house dates to 1805 and was built for a major returning from the Raj. These days, it mixes quirky design with all the comforts you'd expect of a small, city hotel. It's central, welcoming, the rooms are lovely, the dining room serves great bistro food and there's a chic bar for cocktails or a pint of local ale. Downstairs, French windows at the back of the house draw you onto a small terrace, where you can eat in good weather, perhaps mussels in a white wine sauce, bangers and mash with a rich gravy, chocolate fondant with vanilla ice cream. Potter about and find electric blue sofas, 50s starlets framed on the wall, old style radiators and beautiful art. Stylish bedrooms wait upstairs – some are bigger, all are lovely. Expect bold colours, sumptuous fabrics, Indian art, hi-tech gadgetry. Cool bathrooms come as standard, bigger rooms have free-standing baths. Exeter has lots to offer: Roman walls, a 12th-century cathedral, the imperious Royal Albert Memorial Museum & Art Gallery. Topsham is close for river walks.

| Rooms | 10 doubles: £150–£240. |
|---|---|
| Meals | Lunch from £6.50. |
| | Afternoon tea from £19.50. |
| | Dinner, 3 courses, about £30. |
| Closed | Never. |
| Directions | Sent on booking. |

Deborah Clark & Tony Orchard
Southernhay House
36 Southernhay East,
Exeter, EX1 1NX
Tel        +44 (0)1392 435324
Email      home@southernhayhouse.com
Web        www.southernhayhouse.com

## Alexandra Hotel & Restaurant

Everything here is lovely, but the view is hard to beat, a clean sweep up the Jurassic coast towards Portland Bill. The hotel overlooks Lyme Bay; the only thing between you and it is the lawn. Below, the Cobb curls into the sea, the very spot where Meryl Streep withstood the crashing waves in *The French Lieutenant's Woman*. In summer, steamer chairs pepper the garden and guests fall asleep, books in hand, under an English sun. As for the hotel, it's just as good. Kathryn, ex-Firmdale, bought it from her mother and has refurbished brilliantly. You get stripped wood floors, windows everywhere, an airy bar for pre-dinner drinks, an attractive sitting room with plenty of books. The dining room could double as a ballroom, the conservatory brasserie opens onto a terrace; both provide excellent sustenance, perhaps Lyme Bay scallops, roast rump of Devon lamb, gingerbread pudding with vanilla ice-cream. Beautiful rooms hit the spot, most have the view. Expect super beds, padded headboards, robes in lovely bathrooms. Lyme, the beach and the fossil-ridden coast all wait. *Minimum stay: 2 nights at weekends.*

| | | |
|---|---|---|
| Rooms | 19 twin/doubles: £180–£245.<br>3 family rooms for 4: £293–£313.<br>2 singles: £90.<br>1 apartment for 6: £310–£360.<br>Dinner, B&B £125–£158 per person. |  |
| Meals | Lunch from £9.90.<br>Afternoon tea from £6.50.<br>Dinner, 3 courses, about £35.<br>Sunday lunch from £19.50. | |
| Closed | Rarely. | |
| Directions | In Lyme Regis up hill on high street;<br>keep left at bend; on left after 200m. | |

Kathryn Haskins
Alexandra Hotel & Restaurant
Pound Street,
Lyme Regis, DT7 3HZ
Tel       +44 (0)1297 442010
Email     enquiries@hotelalexandra.co.uk
Web       www.hotelalexandra.co.uk

## The Bull Hotel

The Bull – Dorset's first boutique hotel – sits on Bridport high street, a couple miles back from the coast. It's all things to all men, grand enough for a masked ball on New Year's Eve, informal enough for ladies who lunch to pop in unannounced. It's a big hit with the locals and lively most days, while the cool back bar rocks at weekends. All of which makes it a lot of fun for guests passing through. Downstairs, there's an open fire in reception, big art on the walls, then a cute bar for a slice of cake or a pint of London Pride. Outside, a flower-filled courtyard draws a crowd in summer; inside, there's a wood-burner in the restaurant, where good food waits, perhaps Lyme Bay scallops, ox cheek bourguignon, a caramelised lemon tart; moules frites is served every Wednesday night. Bedrooms – all different – have lots of style: beautiful beds, pashmina throws, chic wallpapers, perhaps a bath at the foot of your bed. Some have sofas, family rooms have bunk beds for kids. You get digital radios, flat-screen TVs and cool bathrooms. West Bay for Chesil Beach is close. *Minimum stay: 2 nights at weekends.*

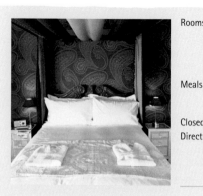

| | |
|---|---|
| Rooms | 10 doubles, 1 twin, 3 four-posters: £100–£200. 1 suite for 2: £235–£265. 3 family rooms for 4: £180–£200. 1 single: £90–£115. |
| Meals | Lunch, 2 courses, from £12. Dinner, 3 courses, around £35. Sunday lunch £19. |
| Closed | Never. |
| Directions | On main street in town. Car park at rear. |

Ali Pember
The Bull Hotel
34 East Street,
Bridport, DT6 3LF

| | |
|---|---|
| Tel | +44 (0)1308 422878 |
| Email | info@thebullhotel.co.uk |
| Web | www.thebullhotel.co.uk |

## BridgeHouse Hotel

Beaminster — or Emminster in Thomas Hardy's *Tess* — sits in a lush Dorset valley. From the hills above, you drop through glorious country, rolling down to this old market town, where the church tower soars towards heaven. As for this lovely hotel, it's a 13th-century priest's house and comes with original trimmings: stone flags, mullioned windows, old beams and huge inglenooks. It's intimate, friendly and deeply comfortable, with something beautiful at every turn. There are rugs on parquet flooring, a beamed bar with an open fire, a splendid dining room with Georgian panelling and a Robert Adam's fireplace. Beautiful lighting sets the mood for excellent food, perhaps Witchampton snails, an imperious steak and kidney pie, pear and rosemary tarte tatin. Rooms in the main house are bigger and smarter, those in the coach house are simpler and less expensive; all are pretty with chic fabrics, crisp linen, flat-screen TVs and stylish bathrooms. Breakfast is served in the conservatory, so watch the gardener potter about as you scoff your bacon and eggs. Chesil Beach at West Bay is close. *Minimum stay: 2 nights at weekends.*

| | |
|---|---|
| Rooms | 6 doubles, 3 twin/doubles, 2 four-posters: £95–£200. 2 family rooms for 4: £95–£200. Dinner, B&B from £82.50–£145 p.p. (obligatory on Fri & Sat, April–September). Extra beds: children under 17 £25; adults £35–£50. |
| Meals | Lunch from £8.50. Dinner, 3 courses, £25–£35. |
| Closed | Never. |
| Directions | From Yeovil A30 west; A3066 for Bridport to Beaminster. Hotel at far end of town as road bends to right. |

Mark & Jo Donovan
BridgeHouse Hotel
3 Prout Bridge,
Beaminster, DT8 3AY

Tel     +44 (0)1308 862200
Email   enquiries@bridge-house.co.uk
Web     www.bridge-house.co.uk

Fabulous food

## The Greyhound

It's hard to fault this little inn. It sits in one of Dorset's loveliest villages, lost in a lush valley with country views that shoot uphill. Outside, there's a colourful terrace that draws a crowd in summer. Inside, cool, rustic interiors mix old and new to great effect. You find stone walls, old flagstones, gilt mirrors and a wood-burner to keep things cosy. There's a lively locals' bar where you can grab a pint of Butcombe, then a chic little restaurant, where you dig into delicious food. The feel throughout is informal and you can eat wherever you want, so spin onto the terrace in good weather and try seared scallops, boeuf bourguignon, sticky toffee pudding. Six lovely rooms wait in an old skittle alley. They're not huge, but nor is their price, and what they lack in space, they make up for in comfort and style, with crisp linen, airy colours and pretty furniture. There's a DVD library, too, and Wellington boots if you want to walk. The Cerne Abbas giant is close, while the coast is on your doorstep: Lyme Regis for fossil hunters, West Bay for fine walking and fabulous Chesil Beach. *Minimum stay: 2 nights on Bank holidays.*

| | |
|---|---|
| Rooms | 6 doubles: £89–£99. Singles from £69. |
| Meals | Lunch from £5.50. Dinner, 3 courses, about £30 (not Sun evening). |
| Closed | Never. |
| Directions | South from Sherborne on A352. Right after 12 miles, signed Sydling St Nicholas. In village. |

Matthew Martinez
The Greyhound
26 High Street, Sydling St Nicholas,
Dorchester, DT2 9PD

| | |
|---|---|
| Tel | +44 (0)1300 341303 |
| Email | info@dorsetgreyhound.co.uk |
| Web | www.dorsetgreyhound.co.uk |

## Plumber Manor

A grand old country house that sits in a couple of acres of green and pleasant land with the river Divelish running through. It dates from 1650, with mullioned windows, huge stone flags and a fine terrace for afternoon tea. An avenue of horse chestnuts takes you to the front door. Inside, a pair of labradors rules the roost. Expect no designer trends – Plumber is old-school, defiantly so. Take the first-floor landing with its enormous sofa, gallery of family oils and grand piano thrown in for good measure. Bedrooms are split between the main house and converted barns. The latter tend to be bigger and are good for those with dogs. Décor is dated – 1980s florals – as are most bathrooms, though a couple now sparkle in travertine splendour. The family triumvirate of Brian (in the kitchen), Richard (behind the bar) and Alison (simply everywhere) excel in the art of old-fashioned hospitality. Delicious country food waits in the restaurant, try seared scallops with pea purée, rack of lamb with rosemary and garlic, lemon meringue pie. Bulbarrow Hill is close.

| | |
|---|---|
| Rooms | 2 doubles, 14 twin/doubles; 1 twin/double with separate bath: £150–£230. Singles £120–£140. Dinner, B&B £80–£120 per person. Extra bed/sofabed available £20 per person per night. |
| Meals | Sunday lunch £29.50. Dinner, 2-3 courses, £29–£36. |
| Closed | February. |
| Directions | West from Sturminster Newton on A357. Across traffic lights, up hill & left for Hazelbury Bryan. Follow brown tourism signs. Hotel signed left after 2 miles. |

Richard, Alison & Brian Prideaux-Brune
Plumber Manor
Plumber,
Sturminster Newton, DT10 2AF

| | |
|---|---|
| Tel | +44 (0)1258 472507 |
| Email | book@plumbermanor.com |
| Web | www.plumbermanor.com |

## Stapleton Arms

A perfect village inn: loads of style, lovely staff, super food, excellent prices. The Stapleton started life as a Georgian home, becoming an inn after the war. These days, warm, hip interiors carry a streak of country glamour. Downstairs, you'll find sofas in front of the fire, a piano for live music, a restaurant with shuttered windows and candles in the fireplace. You can eat whatever you want, wherever you want; delicious pork pies wait at the bar, but it's hard to resist a three-course feast, perhaps woodland mushrooms on toast, pan-fried sea bass with chilli and fennel, chocolate and Baileys soufflé with spiced orange ice cream. You'll find a beer menu to beat all others (ale matters here) and there's always a separate menu for kids – this is a very child-friendly place. Super rooms are soundproofed to ensure a good night's sleep. All have beautiful linen, fresh flowers, happy colours, excellent showers. You'll find maps and wellies if you want to walk and a playground for kids in the garden. Wincanton is close for the races if you want to lose your shirt. One of the best.

| | |
|---|---|
| Rooms | 4 doubles: £90–£120. Singles from £72. |
| Meals | Lunch & bar meals from £7. Dinner, 3 courses, about £30. |
| Closed | Rarely. |
| Directions | A303 to Wincanton. Into town right after fire station, signed Buckhorn Weston. Left at T-junction after 3 miles. In village, pub on right. |

Richard Smith
Stapleton Arms
Church Hill, Buckhorn Weston,
Gillingham, SP8 5HS

| | |
|---|---|
| Tel | +44 (0)1963 370396 |
| Email | relax@thestapletonarms.com |
| Web | www.thestapletonarms.com |

## Castleman Hotel & Restaurant

It's a little like stepping into the pages of a Hardy novel: an untouched corner of rural Dorset, a 400-year-old bailiff's house, sheep grazing in lush fields, a rich cast of characters pottering about. The Castleman — part country house, part restaurant with rooms — is a true one-off: quirky, intimate, defiantly English (you'll think you've landed in Ambridge). It pays no heed to prevailing fashions, not least because the locals would revolt if it did. Barbara runs the place in great style. Touches of grandeur are hard to miss: a panelled hall, art from Chettle House, a magnificent Jacobean ceiling in one of the sitting rooms. Follow your nose and find a cosy bar, fresh flowers everywhere and books galore. The restaurant has garden views, though your eyes are more likely to be fixed on Barbara's delicious old-school food, perhaps potted shrimp terrine, haunch of local venison, meringues with chocolate mousse and toasted almonds. Homely bedrooms fit the bill: comfortable, delightfully priced, a couple with claw-foot baths. Magical Dorset will fill your days with splendour. Don't miss it.

| | |
|---|---|
| Rooms | 4 doubles, 1 twin/double, 1 twin, 1 four-poster, 1 family room for 4: £95–£110. Singles from £70. |
| Meals | Sunday lunch £25. Dinner, 3 courses, about £27. |
| Closed | February. |
| Directions | A354 north from Blandford Forum. 3rd left (about 4 miles up) and on left in village. |

Barbara Garnsworthy
Castleman Hotel & Restaurant
Chettle,
Blandford Forum, DT11 8DB
Tel        +44 (0)1258 830096
Email     enquiry@castlemanhotel.co.uk
Web      www.castlemanhotel.co.uk

## La Fosse at Cranborne

This is a lovely restaurant with rooms in a pretty Dorset village – small and friendly, nicely homespun, owner-run and owner-cooked. Emmanuelle and Mark love their world, it's a way of life and they share it with guests happily and generously. Downstairs, there's a smart sitting room with stripped floors and maps for walkers. Upstairs, a clutch of pretty bedrooms wait with warm colours, attractive fabrics, comfy beds and spotless bathrooms. They're very well priced, so splash out on the bigger rooms and find a sofa or a separate sitting room. Not that you'll linger long. Mark's food is the big draw, much of it sourced within 20 miles. You eat in a pretty dining room with an open fire roaring beyond a couple of sofas. It's delicious stuff, perhaps game terrine with ale chutney, slow-cooked lamb with village vegetables, then pears poached in sloe gin with chocolate ice cream. Best of all is the cheese board, a tasting menu of ten local cheeses – utterly irresistible. You can walk it all off a few miles west at Hambledon Hill (a prehistoric hill fort) with big country views. Brilliant. *Minimum stay: 2 nights at weekends.*

| Rooms | 3 doubles, 2 twin/doubles: £89–£115. 1 suite for 2: £130–£150. |
|---|---|
| Meals | Dinner, 3 courses, £27.50. Not Sun. |
| Closed | Never. |
| Directions | A338 to Fordingbridge, then B3078 into Cranborne. Right at village shop and on right. |

Emmanuelle & Mark Hartstone
La Fosse at Cranborne
The Square, Cranborne,
Wimborne, BH21 5PR

| | |
|---|---|
| Tel | +44 (0)1725 517604 |
| Email | lafossemail@gmail.com |
| Web | www.la-fosse.com |

## The Priory Hotel

The lawns of this 16th-century priory run down to the river Frome. Boats float past, an old church rises behind, a gorgeous garden filled with colour wraps around you. As for this lovely country house, you'll find a grand piano in the drawing room, a first-floor sitting room with garden views, and a stone-vaulted dining room in the old cellar. Best of all is the terrace, where you can sit in the sun and watch the river pass – a perfect spot for lunch in summer. Bedrooms in the main house come in different sizes, some cosy in the eaves, others grandly adorned in reds and golds. You get Zoffany fabrics, padded window seats, bowls of fruit, the odd sofa. Eight have river views, others look onto the garden or church. Chic bathrooms – some dazzlingly contemporary – all come with white robes. Rooms in the boathouse, a 16th-century clay barn, are lavish, with oak panelling, stone walls and sublime views. Outside, climbing roses, a duck pond, and banks of daffs and snowdrops in Spring. Corfe Castle and Studland Bay are close. A slice of old England with delicious food to boot. *Minimum stay: 2 nights at weekends. Over 14s welcome.*

| | |
|---|---|
| Rooms | 12 twin/doubles: £220–£320. |
| | 5 suites for 2: £350–£380. |
| Meals | Lunch from £14.95. |
| | Dinner, 3 courses, £47.50. |
| Closed | Never. |
| Directions | West from Poole on A35, then A351 for Wareham and B3075 into town. Through lights, 1st left, right out of square, then keep left. Entrance on left beyond church. |

Jeremy Merchant
The Priory Hotel
Church Green,
Wareham, BH20 4ND

| | |
|---|---|
| Tel | +44 (0)1929 551666 |
| Email | reservations@theprioryhotel.co.uk |
| Web | www.theprioryhotel.co.uk |

## Urban Beach Hotel

A quirky little place close to the beach with cool interiors and a happy buzz in the bar. Mark and Fiona have a great way of doing things: they employ a Head of Happy and go out of their way to help their lovely staff flourish. It works brilliantly, if you stay it's hard not to notice a difference. Inside, the bar/restaurant is the hub of the house. Surf movies play silently, a couple of surf boards hang on the walls, you get big circular leather booths, then driftwood lamps and a house guitar. There's a table of cakes, a bar for cocktails, candle lanterns scattered about, the daily papers and a few cool tunes. Bedrooms upstairs are nicely priced, some bigger than others, but even the smaller rooms are lovely with warm colours, crisp linen and excellent bathrooms. A decked terrace outside is popular for summer barbecues, but the beach waits at the end of the road, seven miles of sand with a surf shop on the way down. Urban Reef, Mark and Fiona's cool sister restaurant, has a balcony and terrace overlooking the sea; they'll book you in for dinner, you can even have your breakfast there. *Minimum stay: 2 nights at weekends, 3 nights bank holidays.*

| | |
|---|---|
| Rooms | 9 doubles, 1 twin/double: £97–£180. 2 singles: £72. |
| Meals | Lunch & dinner £5–£25. |
| Closed | Never. |
| Directions | South from Ringwood on A338; left for Boscombe (east of centre). Over railway, right onto Centenary Way. Keep with the flow (left, then right) to join Christchurch Rd; 2nd left (St John's Rd); 2nd left. |

**Mark & Fiona Cribb**
Urban Beach Hotel
23 Argyll Road,
Bournemouth, BH5 1EB

| | |
|---|---|
| Tel | +44 (0)1202 301509 |
| Email | reception@urbanbeach.co.uk |
| Web | www.urbanbeach.co.uk |

## The Kings

This is one of those lovely places that delivers what many of us want: lots of style, delicious food, happy staff, attractive prices. The setting is just as good, a slice of Georgian England, with the river Stour to the left, the ruined castle to the right and the old bowling green in between. A riverside path leads down to Christchurch Quay, and another to the gardens at the priory – blissful stuff. As for the hotel, you'll find a cool new bar with big orange armchairs, green leather bar stools and candles everywhere at night – not a bad spot for champagne cocktails. Comfy bedrooms have lots of style: smart colours, fine beds, good bathrooms, perhaps a sofa if there's room. Three overlook the front, those in the eaves have a cute, cosy feel. Back downstairs you find the big draw – excellent food in the candlelit restaurant. Try Dorset cheddar soufflé, turbot with garlic and thyme, lemon meringues with limoncello. It's all local with menus from an amazing £15. Lobster nights bring in the locals, the Christchurch Food Festival comes in May with stalls on the bowling green. Perfect. *Minimum stay: 2 nights at weekends.*

| | |
|---|---|
| Rooms | 14 doubles, 6 twins: £99–£199. |
| Meals | Lunch from £6.50. Sunday lunch from £15. Dinner, 3 courses: table d'hôte £18.50; à la carte about £30. |
| Closed | Never. |
| Directions | West into Christchurch on A35. 2nd left onto High Street, then left at roundabout into Castle Street. On left after 200m. Parking on right in lay-by. |

Lukasz Dwornik
The Kings
18 Castle Street,
Christchurch, BH23 1DT

Tel     +44 (0)1202 588933
Email   kings@harbourhotels.co.uk
Web     www.thekings-christchurch.co.uk

## Captain's Club Hotel and Spa

The Captain's Club stands on the banks on the Stour, where a tiny ferry potters along the river dodging swans and ducks. In summer, you decant onto its lovely terrace and watch river life pass by. Inside, walls of glass weatherproof the view. The sprawling bar fills with light and comes with deep sofas, the daily papers and a grand piano. It's smart, stylish and very informal, with live music at weekends. The hotel also has its own boat, so you can take to the high seas and spin over to the Isle of Wight or Brownsea Island. Back on dry land uncluttered bedrooms have river views, low-slung beds, crisp white linen, neutral colours and excellent bathrooms. None are small, some are huge with separate sitting rooms, apartments have more than one bedroom, so perfect for families and friends. There's a spa, too, with a hydrotherapy pool, a sauna and four treatment rooms. Lovely food is on tap all day in the bar, while the mirrored restaurant ensures everyone has the view. Lobster, Dorset crab, sea bass and a good steak all wait. Christchurch is a short walk upstream. Brilliant. *Minimum stay: 2 nights at weekends.*

| | |
|---|---|
| Rooms | 17 doubles: £199–£259. |
| | 12 apartments for 2-6: £289–£649. |
| Meals | Bar meals all day from £6. |
| | Lunch from £15. Dinner £30–£35. |
| Closed | Never. |
| Directions | M27/A31 west, then A338/B3073 south into Christchurch. At A35 (lights at big r'bout) follow one-way system left. Double back after 100m. Cross r'bout heading west and 1st left into Sopers Lane. Signed left. |

Timothy Lloyd & Robert Wilson
Captain's Club Hotel and Spa
Wick Ferry, Wick Lane,
Christchurch, BH23 1HU

| | |
|---|---|
| Tel | +44 (0)1202 475111 |
| Email | reservations@captainsclubhotel.com |
| Web | www.captainsclubhotel.com |

## Rose & Crown

An idyllic village of mellow stone where little has changed in 200 years. The Rose and Crown dates from 1733 and stands on the green, next to the Saxon church. Roses ramble above the door in summer, so pick up a pint and search out the sun on the gravelled forecourt. Inside is just as good. You can sit at settles in the bar and roast away in front of the fire as you rifle through the *Teesdale Mercury*, or seek out sofas in the peaceful sitting room and tuck into afternoon tea. Bedrooms are lovely. Those in the converted barn are all cool grey and muted blue hues; those in the main house come with stylish furnishings and vibrant colours; all have Bose sound systems, quietly fancy bathrooms and lots of other extras. Delicious food can be eaten informally in the bar or restaurant. Try braised ox cheek with sautéed greens and triple cooked chips, followed by peanut butter mousse with caramel popcorn and maple glazed bacon. High Force waterfall and Barnard Castle are close – and you can take your wet togs to the drying room.

| | |
|---|---|
| Rooms | 8 doubles, 3 twins: £115-£160. 3 suites for 2: £180-£200. Singles from £95. Dinner, B&B from £79 per person. |
| Meals | Lunch from £10.50. Dinner, 3 courses, from £27. Sunday lunch £19.50. |
| Closed | 23-27 December & 1 week in January. |
| Directions | From Barnard Castle B6277 north for 6 miles. Right in village towards green. Inn on left. |

Thomas & Cheryl Robinson
Rose & Crown
Romaldkirk,
Barnard Castle, DL12 9EB

| | |
|---|---|
| Tel | +44 (0)1833 650213 |
| Email | hotel@rose-and-crown.co.uk |
| Web | www.rose-and-crown.co.uk |

## Houndgate Townhouse

Houndgate is a handsome townhouse hotel, the sort of place the term 'boutique' was coined to define. It has a chic contemporary style – airy interiors, cool colours, smart fabrics, the full works. But there's more to it than that. It's subtle, cleverly conceived, a design hotel with a level of craftsmanship you don't expect. At its heart, it's a cool little café/bar, where you can order a coffee, a bowl of soup, afternoon tea or cocktails before dinner. It sits on a smart Georgian street – Darlington itself is a beautiful surprise. Inside you find a mirrored ceiling in the elegant bar, a stylish restaurant with green leather booths, a terraced courtyard for lunch in the sun. Rooms are just as good: beautiful linen, excellent beds, robes in sparkling bathrooms. Two have a free-standing bath in the room, another a panel of original wallpaper that was discovered when refurbishing. Bistro-style food waits downstairs, perhaps moules with white wine, boeuf bourguignon, peanut butter parfait. Don't miss the Bowes Museum in Barnard Castle, a jewel of the North. Durham is close.

| | |
|---|---|
| Rooms | 4 doubles, 2 twin/doubles, 2 four-posters: £90–£145. Singles from £85. Dinner, B&B £65–£98 per person. |
| Meals | Lunch from £5. Afternoon tea £16. Dinner, 3 courses, £25–£30. |
| Closed | Never. |
| Directions | A1(M), then A167 into Darlington. Take the ring road to its southeastern roundabout and exit into Beaumont Street for its car park. Houndgate runs above, a 2-minute walk. |

Natalie Cooper
Houndgate Townhouse
11 Houndgate,
Darlington, DL1 5RF

| | |
|---|---|
| Tel | +44 (0)1325 486011 |
| Email | info@houndgatetownhouse.co.uk |
| Web | www.houndgatetownhouse.co.uk |

## The Sun Inn

This perennial favourite sits in an idyllic village made rich by mills in the 16th century. You're also in Constable country – the artist attended school in the village and often returned to paint the church. Best of all is the river – you can hire boats, grab a picnic from the inn, float down the sleepy Stour, then tie up on the bank for lunch al fresco. As for The Sun, you couldn't hope to wash up in a better spot. Inside, you find open fires, boarded floors, timber frames and an easy elegance. A panelled lounge comes with sofas and armchairs, the bar is made from a slab of local elm and the airy, beamed dining room offers fabulous food inspired by Italy, perhaps crab ravioli, squid with chilli and garlic, monkfish with truffle mash, chocolate mousse with Morello cherries. Rooms are gorgeous: creaking floorboards, timber-framed walls, a panelled four-poster. Those at the back are bigger and come in grand style, but all are lovely with crisp linen, local art and power showers in excellent bathrooms. There's afternoon tea on arrival if you book in advance and a garden for a pint in summer.

| | |
|---|---|
| Rooms | 5 doubles, 1 twin/double, 1 four-poster: £135. Singles £85. Dinner, B&B £95 per person. Extra bed/sofabed available £15 per person per night. |
| Meals | Lunch from £10.95. Dinner from £16.95. Not Monday lunch. |
| Closed | Christmas. |
| Directions | A12 north past Colchester. 2nd exit, signed Dedham. In village opposite church. |

Piers Baker
The Sun Inn
High Street, Dedham,
Colchester, CO7 6DF

| | |
|---|---|
| Tel | +44 (0)1206 323351 |
| Email | office@thesuninndedham.com |
| Web | www.thesuninndedham.com |

## Maison Talbooth

An outdoor swimming pool that's heated to 29°C every day, a chauffeur on hand to whisk you down to the hotel's riverside restaurant, a grand piano in the golden sitting room where those in the know gather for a legendary afternoon tea. They don't do things by halves at Maison Talbooth, a small-scale pleasure dome with long views across Constable country. The house, an old rectory, stands in three acres of manicured grounds, the fabulous pool house a huge draw with its open fire, honesty bar, beautiful art and treatment rooms. Interiors are equally alluring. There are no rooms, only suites, each divine. Some on the ground floor have doors onto terraces where hot tubs wait, but all pamper you rotten with flawless bathrooms, fabulous beds, vintage wallpapers, hi-tech excess. At dinner you're chauffeured to the family's restaurants (both within half a mile): Milsoms for bistro food served informally, Le Talbooth for more serious fare, perhaps roasted scallops with a Sauternes velouté, fillet of halibut with walnuts and apple, banoffee soufflé with caramelised banana crumble. A great escape.

| | |
|---|---|
| Rooms | 12 suites for 4: £210–£420. Singles from £170. |
| Meals | Dinner at Milsoms £25; at Le Talbooth £35–£50. |
| Closed | Never. |
| Directions | North on A12 past Colchester. Left to Dedham, right after S bend. Maison Talbooth is on right; follow brown signs. |

Paul & Geraldine Milsom
Maison Talbooth
Stratford Road, Dedham,
Colchester, CO7 6HN

| | |
|---|---|
| Tel | +44 (0)1206 322367 |
| Email | maison@milsomhotels.com |
| Web | www.milsomhotels.com |

## The Pier at Harwich

This attractive hotel was built in 1862 in the style of a Venetian palazzo and has remained in continuous service ever since. It sits above the historic Ha'Penny Pier with big skies above and watery views that shoot across the Stour estuary to Felixstowe. Inside you find a contemporary feel: boarded floors, a granite bar, deco travel posters framed on the wall, big arched windows to bring in the view. You can eat informally in the bistro downstairs (fish soup, rib-eye steak, warm treacle tart), or head upstairs to the beautiful first-floor restaurant, where you can watch the ferries glide past while tucking into Mersea rock oysters, rack of lamb, bitter chocolate pudding. Bedrooms are scattered about, some in the main house, others next door in a former inn. All are pretty, with padded bedheads, seaside colours, crisp white linen, and super bathrooms; if you want the best view in town, splash out on the Mayflower suite. Don't miss the coastal walks, the blue flag beach at Dovercourt, the ferry over to Felixstowe or the Electric Palace, the second oldest cinema in Britain.

| Rooms | 10 doubles, 3 twins: £120–£170. 1 suite for 2: £200–£230. Singles from £95. Dinner, B&B from £100 per person. |
| Meals | Lunch from £6.50. Sunday lunch from £19.50. Dinner à la carte £25–£40. |
| Closed | Never. |
| Directions | M25 junc. 28, A12 to Colchester bypass, then A120 to Harwich. Head for quay. Hotel opposite pier. |

Paul & Geraldine Milsom
The Pier at Harwich
The Quay,
Harwich, CO12 3HH

Tel    +44 (0)1255 241212
Email  pier@milsomhotels.com
Web    www.milsomhotels.com

## The Mistley Thorn

This welcoming inn fits the Sawday bill perfectly – lovely owners with fingers dipped into delicious local pies. Their kitchen shop and cooking school stand four doors down the street; Lucca, their popular wood-fired pizzeria, waits in Manningtree. As for their inn, it stands on the high street and dates to 1746. Interiors have an airy feel, the mood is laid-back with a great little bar, the food is local and utterly delicious. Expect tongue-and-groove panelling, a roaring wood-burner, padded benches and a happy vibe. Nicely-priced rooms (two above the kitchen shop) have a similar feel: pretty fabrics, warm colours, crisp linen on comfy beds, REN lotions for power showers and double-ended baths. There's good art, homemade shortbread and fresh fruit, too, while those at the front have views of the Stour estuary. As for the food, it's delicious stuff, perhaps smoked haddock chowder, mussels with garlic and herbs, sticky toffee pudding. The Witchfinder General lived here, you can walk along the river to Dedham, the Beth Chatto Gardens are close. Sunday nights are a steal: £100 for two with dinner.

| | |
|---|---|
| Rooms | 5 doubles, 3 twin/doubles: £110–£125. Singles from £90. Dinner, B&B from £75 per person. |
| Meals | Lunch from £4.95. Set lunch, 2 courses 12.50, 3 courses £15. Dinner, 3 courses, about £30. |
| Closed | Rarely. |
| Directions | From A12 Hadleigh/East Bergholt exit north of Colchester. Thro' East Bergholt to A137; signed Manningtree; continue to Mistley High St. 50 yds from station. |

David McKay & Sherri Singleton
The Mistley Thorn
High Street, Mistley,
Manningtree, CO11 1HE

| | |
|---|---|
| Tel | +44 (0)1206 392821 |
| Email | info@mistleythorn.co.uk |
| Web | www.mistleythorn.co.uk |

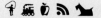

## Tudor Farmhouse Hotel

A gorgeous small hotel, one of the best. It sits on the edge of the Forest of Dean, a magical world of woodland walks, medieval castles, meandering rivers and bleating sheep. You're in the middle of a tiny village with country views all around. Step inside to find sparkling interiors — Colin and Hari have spent a small fortune turning their realm into something very special indeed. An airy elegance mixes with golden stone walls and original timber frames, the house bearing testament to its Tudor roots. Big or small, bedrooms are divine — stylishly uncluttered with smart fabrics, robes in fine bathrooms and super-comfy beds. Those in the main house have ancient beamed ceilings, those in the old barns have original stone walls. The bigger rooms are faultless: the best beds, claw-foot baths, enormous showers, the lap of luxury. Lovely local food waits downstairs, perhaps cider-cured salmon, haunch of venison, rhubarb Bakewell tart; there are home-laid eggs for breakfast, too. You can kayak on the Wye, forage in the forest, take to cycle tracks. Don't miss Puzzlewood or Clearwell Caves. *Minimum stay: 2 night stay on weekends.*

|  |  |
|---|---|
| Rooms | 10 doubles, 3 twins, 2 four-posters: £100–£200. 5 suites for 2: £180–£230. Singles from £90. Extra bed/sofabed available £25 per person per night. |
| Meals | Lunch from £6.95. Sunday lunch from £14.50. Dinner, 3 courses, £30–£40. |
| Closed | Never. |
| Directions | South from Monmouth on A466. Clearwell signed left after 3 miles. |

**Colin & Hari Fell**
Tudor Farmhouse Hotel
High Street,
Clearwell, GL16 8JS

Tel      +44 (0)1594 833046
Email    info@tudorfarmhousehotel.co.uk
Web     www.tudorfarmhousehotel.co.uk

AWARD WINNER

Hotel of the Year
England

## Three Choirs Vineyards

England's answer to the Napa Valley. After 15 years of tilling the soil (very sandy, good drainage), Thomas's 75 acres of Gloucestershire hillside now produce 300,000 bottles a year. There are regular tastings, a shop in which to buy a bottle or two, and paths that weave through the vines – a perfect stroll after a good meal. What's more, three fabulous lodges wait down by the lake, all with decks and walls of glass. You'll find claw-foot baths and comfy beds, so camp out in grand savannah style and listen to the woodpeckers. Rooms up at the restaurant are smart and spacious with terraces that overlook the vineyard. They come with padded bedheads, walls of colour, leather armchairs, flat-screen TVs and good bathrooms. Finally, the restaurant: claret walls, lovely views, sofas in front of an open fire. Excellent food waits, perhaps twice-baked Gloucester soufflé, fillet of bream with rocket and watercress, rhubarb crème brûlée with lemon shortbread. World wines are on the list, but you'll want something from the vines that surround you; there's a microbrewery, too. Brilliant. *Minimum stay: 2 nights at weekends.*

| | |
|---|---|
| Rooms | 6 doubles, 3 vineyard lodges, 2 twins: £140-£195. Singles from £135. |
| Meals | Lunch from £7.50. Dinner à la carte about £35. |
| Closed | Christmas & New Year. |
| Directions | From Newent north on B4215 for about 1.5 miles. Follow brown signs to vineyard. |

**Thomas Shaw**
Three Choirs Vineyards
Castle Tump,
Newent, GL18 1LS

| | |
|---|---|
| Tel | +44 (0)1531 890223 |
| Email | info@threechoirs.com |
| Web | www.three-choirs-vineyards.co.uk |

## No. 131

This funky new addition to Cheltenham's buzzing scene is a bone fide jaw-dropper — impeccable Georgian architecture outside, 21st-century chic within. Interiors mix all the lovely old stuff: stripped floors, chandeliers, ceiling friezes, period colours, with lots of lovely new stuff: enormous sofas, hanging lampshades, a cool collection of contemporary art. You'll find roaring fires, blue leather bar stools, vintage tiles, old wooden fridges piled high with hams and cheese. Downstairs, the bar has a retractable roof, turning itself into a terrace in summer, with a DJ station for the odd weekend. Upstairs, bedrooms have huge style: piles of art books, big beds, the best linen, perhaps a fancy bath in your room; all have robes and walk-in showers in flawless bathrooms. Downstairs, you mingle with happy locals in the bars and restaurants, where great food waits, perhaps grilled sardines with chilli and garlic, half a lobster or a juicy steak, treacle tart with clotted cream. In summer life spills onto the front terrace, overlooking Imperial Gardens. Don't miss the jazz festival in May.

| | |
|---|---|
| Rooms | 11 doubles: £150–£220. |
| Meals | Lunch from £7. |
| | Sunday lunch from £21. |
| | Dinner, 3 courses, about £40. |
| Closed | Never. |
| Directions | Pick up one-way system in the middle of town and follow it to its southwestern corner at Imperial Square; left onto the Promenade, signed 'M5, Gloucester, Oxford'. Hotel on right after 400m, before lights. |

**Stephen Wadcock**
No. 131
131 The Promenade,
Cheltenham, GL50 1NW

Tel     +44 (0)1242 822939
Email   reservations@no131.com
Web     www.no131.com

## No. 38

Not content with having one super-cool hotel in town, owners Sam and Georgina have opened another. The idea here is that you get the same chic style, but in the peace and privacy of a design B&B. Downstairs, there's an elegant sitting room with deep sofas, fresh flowers and contemporary art, then a stylish breakfast room, where you can sit on bar stools and watch the chef cook your bacon and eggs. In summer you can eat on the terrace, in winter there's a fire to keep things toasty. Drinks at the honesty bar are chilled in a wall of antique wooden refrigerators – nothing here is done by halves. Bedrooms are flawless. Smaller rooms have beautiful beds, mohair throws, fantastic art and walk-in showers. Bigger rooms have all that and more – perhaps a TV that rises at the end of your bed, a zinc bath in the room, then enormous wet rooms with showers for two. Pittville Park is opposite, the racecourse is up the road, taxis are provided to whisk you up to the other hotel, No. 131, for cocktails and a slap-up dinner. Take the whole place for a house party and a chef will come to cook. Dogs are welcome.

| | |
|---|---|
| Rooms | 13 doubles: £120–£180. |
| Meals | Breakfast £5–£12. Restaurants within 500m. Free taxis provided to their sister restaurant. |
| Closed | Never. |
| Directions | Head north from centre on A435, following signs to racecourse and Pittville Pump Room. On left, at crossroads/traffic lights, after 0.5 mile. |

Stephen Wadcock
No. 38
38 Evesham Road,
Cheltenham, GL52 2AH

| | |
|---|---|
| Tel | +44 (0)1242 822929 |
| Email | reservations@no38thepark.com |
| Web | www.no38thepark.com |

## Beaumont House

Fan and Alan have lived all over the world and came back to England to open the sort of hotel they like to stay in themselves. It's a very friendly place, nothing is too much trouble. Throw a few luxuries into the mix – stylish bedrooms, excellent breakfasts, an honesty bar in the airy sitting room – and you have a great base for all things Cheltenham. Spotless bedrooms spread over three floors. Some are simpler, others more extravagant, but all have lovely bathrooms and every budget will be happy. Compact, airy doubles on the lower ground floor are perfect for short stays. Rooms above are bigger, some with striking design. One has an African theme, another has far-eastern wood carvings, there are vast headboards, smart furniture and flat-screen TVs. You breakfast in an elegant dining room, perhaps freshly made porridge, American pancakes, smoked haddock, the full cooked works. Good restaurants wait in town (and there's live jazz at Daffodil's on Monday nights). As for Cheltenham, it has festivals coming out of its ears: folk, jazz, food, science, music, literature and horses. Brilliant.

| | |
|---|---|
| Rooms | 9 doubles, 2 twin/doubles: £90–£249. 2 suites for 4: £235–£300. 1 family room for 4: £235–£270. 2 singles: £75–£85. Extra bed/sofabed available £30 per person per night. |
| Meals | Restaurants within walking distance. |
| Closed | Rarely. |
| Directions | Leave one-way system in centre of town for Stroud (south) on A46. Straight ahead, through lights and right at 1st mini-roundabout. On left after 500m. |

Alan & Fan Bishop
Beaumont House
56 Shurdington Road,
Cheltenham, GL53 OJE

| | |
|---|---|
| Tel | +44 (0)1242 223311 |
| Email | reservations@bhhotel.co.uk |
| Web | www.bhhotel.co.uk |

## The Wheatsheaf

The Wheatsheaf stands at the vanguard of a cool new movement: the village local reborn in country-house style. It's a winning formula with locals and travellers flocking in for a heady mix of laid-back informality and chic English style. The inn stands between pretty hills in this ancient wool village on the Fosse Way. Inside, happy young staff flit about, throwing logs on the fire, ferrying food to diners, or simply stopping for a chat. Downstairs, you find armchairs in front of smouldering fires, noble portraits on panelled walls, cool tunes playing in the background. Outside, a smart courtyard garden draws a crowd in summer, so much so it has its own bar; English ales, jugs of Pimm's and lovely wines all wait. Back inside, beautiful bedrooms come as standard, some bigger than others, all fully loaded with comfort and style. Expect period colours, Hypnos beds, Bang & Olufsen TVs, then spectacular bathrooms with beautiful baths and/or power showers. As for the food, you feast on lovely local fare, perhaps devilled kidneys, coq au vin, pear and almond tart. Don't miss it.

| | |
|---|---|
| Rooms | 14 doubles: £120–£180. Extra bed £25 child, £50 adult. |
| Meals | Continental breakfast included, cooked extras £5–£12. Lunch from £9. Dinner, 3 courses, about £30. |
| Closed | Never. |
| Directions | North from Cirencester on A429 for 10 miles, then right for Northleach just before the A40. |

James Parn
The Wheatsheaf
West End, Northleach,
Cheltenham, GL54 3EZ

| | |
|---|---|
| Tel | +44 (0)1451 860244 |
| Web | www.cotswoldswheatsheaf.com |

## The Old Stocks Inn

Stow, a pretty market town, is nicely positioned for exploring the Cotswolds, with Stratford to the North, Cheltenham to the west, Oxford and Blenheim Palace to the east and the early stretches of the Thames to the south. As for this 17th-century inn, it's just been refurbished from top to toe. It sits on the market square with golden stone walls inside and out. Interiors mix original beams and timber frames with a big dollop of contemporary style – leather banquettes and hanging lamps in the stylish restaurant; panelled walls and an open fire in the cool little bar; a pretty coffee shop that overlooks the square. In summer, you spin onto a beautiful terrace for wood-fired pizzas in the sun. Super-comfy beds in beautiful rooms are wrapped in the crispest linen. You get coffee machines, iPod docks, Bakelite telephones, old Penguin books. All have chic bathrooms, some with claw-foot baths (a couple in the room). Three are dog-friendly, the family suite has bunk beds and an Xbox. Good food waits downstairs, perhaps cured salmon, a chargrilled steak, then lemon and lime mousse. *Minimum stay: 2 nights at weekends in high season.*

| | |
|---|---|
| Rooms | 10 doubles, 6 twin/doubles: £119–£229. |
| Meals | Lunch & dinner, £5–£35. |
| Closed | Never. |
| Directions | A429 to Stow-on-the-Wold. Inn on northeast corner of square in town. |

**Charlotte Knowles**
The Old Stocks Inn
The Square,
Stow-on-the-Wold, GL54 1AF
Tel       +44 (0)1451 830666
Email   info@oldstockshotel.co.uk
Web     www.oldstocksinn.com

## Wesley House Restaurant

Welcome to Winchcombe, the 6th-century capital of Mercia. Wesley House is a mere pup by comparison, a 15th-century timber-framed house that stands on the town's ancient High Street – John Wesley stayed in 1755, hence the name. Inside, you find two restaurants. The elder statesman comes in traditional style with sofas in front of a roaring fire, candles flickering on smartly dressed tables and a popular conservatory for delicious breakfasts with views of town and country. Next door, the young upstart is unashamedly contemporary with a smoked-glass bar, faux zebra-skin stools and hidden alcoves. Both buildings have original timber frames, beamed ceilings, stone flags and stripped boards. Bedrooms up in the eaves are small, but fine for a night or two. One has a balcony with views over rooftops to field and hill. All come in traditional style with good beds, floral fabrics, ultra-compact showers and wonky floors. Back downstairs, dig into good food, perhaps pan-fried scallops, roast duck with parsnips, plum and apple crumble. The Cotswold Way skirts the town, so bring your walking boots. *Minimum stay: 2 nights at weekends.*

| | |
|---|---|
| Rooms | 4 doubles, 1 twin: £75–£100. Singles from £65. Dinner, B&B (obligatory for 1-night stays on Sat) £185 per room. |
| Meals | Bar & grill: lunch & dinner from £9.50 (not Sun or Mon). Restaurant: lunch from £14.50, dinner £20–£25 or £39.50 on Sat. Not Sun nights (except B&B). |
| Closed | Boxing Day. |
| Directions | From Cheltenham B4632 to Winchcombe. Restaurant on right. Drop off luggage, parking nearby. |

Matthew Brown
Wesley House Restaurant
High Street, Winchcombe,
Cheltenham, GL54 5LJ
Tel    +44 (0)1242 602366
Email  enquiries@wesleyhouse.co.uk
Web    www.wesleyhouse.co.uk

## Horse & Groom

A happy pub informally run with lovely food, stylish interiors and wines and beers for all. It stands at the top of the hill with views on one side that pour over the Cotswolds. Inside, stripped floors, open fires and the odd stone wall give a smart rustic feel. Outside you can sit under the shade of damson trees and watch chefs gather eggs from the coop or carrots from the kitchen garden. Uncluttered bedrooms are nicely plush and come in contemporary country-house style with beautiful linen, pretty art, a padded window seat or two. One room is huge, the garden room opens onto the terrace, and those at the front are soundproofed to minimise noise from the road. This is a hive of youthful endeavour with two brothers at the helm. Will cooks, Tom pours the ales (or Cotswold Vodka), and a cheery conviviality flows. Delicious food waits. Most is sourced within 30 miles and it's much prized by canny locals, so come for fish soup, pork and chorizo meatballs, Granny G's unmissable toffee meringue. Breakfast is a feast with homemade croissants, local milk in bottles and blocks of patted butter. *Minimum stay: 2 nights at weekends.*

| | |
|---|---|
| Rooms | 5 doubles: £120–£170. Singles from £80. |
| Meals | Lunch from £4.75. Dinner, 3 courses, £25–£30. Not Sun night. |
| Closed | Christmas Day & New Year's Eve. |
| Directions | West from Moreton-in-Marsh on A44. Climb hill in Bourton-on-the-Hill; pub at top on left. Moreton-in-Marsh railway station 2 miles away. |

Tom & Will Greenstock
Horse & Groom
Bourton-on-the-Hill,
Moreton-in-Marsh, GL56 9AQ

| | |
|---|---|
| Tel | +44 (0)1386 700413 |
| Email | greenstocks@horseandgroom.info |
| Web | www.horseandgroom.info |

## The Churchill Arms

This lovely inn is back where it belongs – in good hands. It sits in a tiny village with views across open country at the front and you can follow footpaths across the fields to Chipping Campden. Outside, stone walls drip with wisteria. Inside, a beautiful refurbishment has delivered cool colours and an airy feel. You'll find a smart bar for local ales, low beamed ceilings, painted panelling and a roaring fire. It's exactly the sort of place lots of us love these days: stylish and informal with fantastic food. Nick, a Gordon Ramsay scholar who cooked at Soho House, hung up his London apron to come home and do his own thing. Good food lies at the heart of it all – nothing overly complicated, just great produce cooked to perfection, perhaps smoked haddock soufflé, pork T-bone with apple and crackling, chocolate and salted caramel tart; the rare roast beef on Sundays is worth a detour. There's a small garden for summer days, then a couple of cute rooms with wonky floors, old style radiators, padded bedheads and good bathrooms; more are on the way. Stratford and Oxford are close. Don't miss it.

| | |
|---|---|
| Rooms | 2 doubles: £120. Singles £60-£75. |
| Meals | Lunch from £5.95. Dinner, 3 courses, £25-£35. Sunday lunch from £14.50. |
| Closed | Sun nights & Mon. |
| Directions | North from Moreton-in-Marsh for 4 miles on A429, then left onto B4035, signed Paxford. Left again onto B4479. On left in village opposite church. |

Nick Deverell-Smith
The Churchill Arms
Paxford,
Chipping Campden, GL55 6XH
Tel        +44 (0)1386 593159
Email    enquiries@churchillarms.co
Web      www.churchillarms.co

## Chewton Glen

Chewton Glen is one of England's loveliest country-house hotels. It opened in 1964 with eight bedrooms and even though it now has 70, it remains delightfully intimate. Fifty years of evolution have brought a pillared swimming pool, a hydrotherapy spa, a golf course and a tennis centre. It recently added 12 treehouse suites, which sit peacefully in their own valley with hot tubs on balconies and wood-burners waiting inside. As for the hotel, beauty waits at every turn: stately sitting rooms, roaring fires, busts and oils, a bar that opens onto a sun-trapping terrace. Bedrooms are the best. Some come in country-house style, but most have a contemporary feel. Expect marble bathrooms, private balconies, designer fabrics, faultless housekeeping. Outside, four gardeners tend 130 acres of lawns and woodland, with a kitchen garden that helps the restaurant, so you'll eat well; perhaps Dorset crab, Devon duck, Charantais melon soup. You can atone in style: a walk on the beach, mountain biking in the New Forest, croquet on the lawn in summer. *Minimum stay: 2 nights at weekends.*

| | |
|---|---|
| Rooms | 5 doubles, 30 twin/doubles: £325–£685. 23 suites for 2: £610–£1,580. 12 treehouses for 2: £700–£1,450. Prices per night. |
| Meals | Breakfast: £21–£26. Lunch, 3 courses, £25. Sunday lunch £39.50. Dinner, 3 courses, £55–£65. Tasting menu £70. Light meals available throughout day. |
| Closed | Never. |
| Directions | A337 west from Lymington. Through New Milton for Christchurch. Right at r'bout, for Walkford. Right again; on right. |

Andrew Stembridge
Chewton Glen
Christchurch Road,
New Milton, BH25 7QT

| | |
|---|---|
| Tel | +44 (0)1425 275341 |
| Email | reservations@chewtonglen.com |
| Web | www.chewtonglen.com |

## The Mill at Gordleton

Another wormhole back to old England, a 400-year-old mill on Avon Water with mallards, lampreys and Indian runners to watch from the terrace in summer. The house stands in three acres of gardens that are filled with art and beautiful things. Inside, cosy interiors mix old and new delightfully: low ceilings, wonky walls, busts and mirrors, smouldering fires. Colour tumbles from pretty fabrics, there's a panelled bar for pre-dinner drinks, then bedrooms which are full of character. The suite above the wheelhouse has a fabulous bathroom, you'll find lots of colour, sheets and blankets, bowls of fruit. Three rooms have watery views (you can fall asleep to the sound of the river), most have fancy new bathrooms. The main suite has robes, all have White Company oils; and while a lane passes outside, you are more likely to be woken by birdsong. Downstairs, the beautifully refurbished restaurant continues to draw a happy crowd for its delicious local food, perhaps wild mushroom ravioli, Creedy Carver free-range duck, blackberry soufflé with apple crumble ice cream. The forest and coast are both on your doorstep. *Min stay: 2 nights at weekends April-October.*

| | |
|---|---|
| Rooms | 3 doubles, 3 twin/doubles: £150–£195. 2 suites for 2: £150–£275. Singles from £115. |
| Meals | Lunch from £6.95. Sunday lunch from £21.50. Dinner £22.50–£27.50; à la carte about £40. |
| Closed | Christmas Day. |
| Directions | South from Brockenhurst on A337 for 4 miles. After 2nd roundabout 1st right, signed Hordle. On right after 2 miles. |

Liz Cottingham
The Mill at Gordleton
Silver Street, Sway,
Lymington, SO41 6DJ
Tel       +44 (0)1590 682219
Email    info@themillatgordleton.co.uk
Web      www.themillatgordleton.co.uk

Entry 107   Map 3

## The Manor at Sway

A big house in a small village in the middle of the New Forest — lovely gardens run down to woodland, the odd deer comes in to nibble the roses. Inside, country-house interiors have a distinctly contemporary feel — airy and nicely stylish with wood floors, pretty wallpapers and a relaxed feel. You'll find smart sofas in the sitting room, then a chic bar with a wall of glass that opens onto the terrace, perfect for afternoon tea in the sun. Bedrooms are lovely. They come in different shapes and sizes, but all have the same comforts: excellent beds, crisp linen, warm colours, sparkling bathrooms. Three are dog-friendly, those in the eaves are warmly cosy, larger rooms have armchairs, most have garden views. The big surprise is the delicious food, so work up an appetite in the forest by day, then come home for a feast, perhaps scallops with curried cauliflower, local venison in a port sauce, Bakewell tart with blackberry jam. There are simpler dishes, too: posh fish and chips, pork belly with buttered greens, beetroot tarte tatin. Fabulous walking, mountain bike trails and sun loungers in the garden wait. *Minimum stay: 2 nights at weekends.*

| Rooms | 12 doubles, 3 twin/doubles: £90–£210. |
|---|---|
| Meals | Lunch from £6. |
| | Dinner, 3 courses, £30–£40. |
| | Sunday lunch £19.50–£24.50. |
| Closed | Rarely. |
| Directions | From Brockenhurst, B3055 west for Sway. Right in village for railway station. On right opposite garage. |

Tim Holloway
The Manor at Sway
Station Road, Sway,
Lymington, SO41 6BA

| Tel | +44 (0)1590 682754 |
| Email | info@swaymanor.com |
| Web | www.themanoratsway.com |

## Daisybank Cottage Boutique B&B

This cute B&B in the New Forest mixes a warm contemporary style with some fine, old-fashioned hospitality – Ciaran and Cheryl go out of their way to make your stay special. As for their Arts & Crafts house, it sits on the southern fringes of Brockenhurst with a pretty garden at the back, where free-range hens strut their stuff. Inside, spoiling bedrooms come with airy colours, plantation shutters, then Vi-Spring mattresses for beautiful beds and robes in striking bathrooms. One has a small courtyard, another a claw-foot bath, the room at the back opens onto the garden. All have coffee machines, silent fridges in which to chill drinks, iPod docks and flat-screen TVs. Breakfast is a local feast – eggs from the garden, artisan jams and honey, home-baked soda bread and granola, bacon and sausages from a New Forest farm. After which you can walk by the sea, hire bikes and explore the forest or spin across to the Isle of Wight. A shepherd's hut in the garden may soon be available for B&B. Good restaurants wait in town (a ten-minute stroll); posher ones are further afield. *Children over 10 welcome.*

| | |
|---|---|
| Rooms | 5 doubles: £100–£140. |
| | Singles from £90. |
| | Extra beds £40. |
| Meals | Local restaurants within half a mile. |
| Closed | One week over Christmas. |
| Directions | M27, junc. 1, then A337 south for Lymington. Right onto B3055 as you approach Brockenhurst. Over x-roads and signed left after half a mile. |

Cheryl & Ciaran Maher
Daisybank Cottage Boutique B&B
Sway Road,
Brockenhurst, SO42 7SG

| | |
|---|---|
| Tel | +44 (0)1590 622086 |
| Email | info@bedandbreakfast-newforest.co.uk |
| Web | www.bedandbreakfast-newforest.co.uk |

## The Master Builder's House Hotel

A beautiful spot on the water: lawns roll down to the river, curlews race about gracefully, a vast sky hangs above. The house, built in 1729, was home to the shipwrights who built Nelson's fleet, with Agamemnon, Euryalus and Swiftsure all going on to fight at Trafalgar. Flags commemorating his victories hang in the hall, bedrooms are named after his ships. As for the hotel, there's a pretty sitting room that opens onto a smart terrace, a yachtsman's bar for a pint of ale, then open fires, warm colours, and good food in the chic restaurant, perhaps smoked salmon and mackerel cannelloni, Gressingham duck with spicy red cabbage, ginger beer jelly with poached rhubarb. There's a barbecue in the garden at weekends that's popular with walkers, then a giant chess board for visiting grand masters. Bedrooms in the main house have lots of colour, bags of character, big views and Indian furniture. Those in the annexe are small, standard hotel rooms, though bathrooms are good. Walk by the river, take a ferry up to the estuary or bring your bike and explore the forest.

| | |
|---|---|
| Rooms | 7 doubles, 1 suite for 2: £110–£205. Annexe: 18 twin/doubles: £110–£155. 2 cottages for 4: £205. Singles £100. Dinner, B&B from £85 per person. |
| Meals | Lunch from £7.50. Dinner, 3 courses, £22–£30. |
| Closed | Never. |
| Directions | From Lyndhurst B3056 south past Beaulieu turn-off. 1st left, signed Buckler's Hard. Hotel signed left after 1 mile. |

Clive Watts
The Master Builder's House Hotel
Buckler's Hard, Beaulieu,
Brockenhurst, SO42 7XB

| | |
|---|---|
| Tel | +44 (0)1590 616253 |
| Email | enquiries@themasterbuilders.co.uk |
| Web | www.themasterbuilders.co.uk |

## The Montagu Arms Hotel

Beaulieu, an ancient royal hunting ground, was gifted to Cistercian monks by King John in 1204. Their abbey took 40 years to build and you can see its ruins in the nearby grounds of Palace House, seat of the Montagu family since 1538. As for the village, its tiny high street is a hotchpotch of 17th-century timber-framed houses that totter by the tidal estuary drinking in the view. The hotel dates to 1742, but was re-modelled in 1925 and interiors have an Edwardian country-house feel. You'll find roaring fires, parquet flooring, a library bar and a courtyard garden, where you can eat in summer. Traditional bedrooms vary in size, but all come with pretty fabrics, period furniture, good bathrooms, a sofa if there's room. Downstairs, a Michelin star in the dining room brings with it some fabulous food, so try Dover sole with brown shrimps, saddle of roe deer with parsnip purée, praline soufflé with dark chocolate ice-cream. There's a gastro pub if you want something lighter: local fish pie, great steaks, ham and chips with poached eggs from resident hens. Beautiful walks start from the front door. *Minimum stay: 2 nights at weekends.*

| | |
|---|---|
| Rooms | 7 doubles, 3 twin/doubles, 4 four-posters: £157–£317. 5 suites for 2: £257–£377. Singles from £129. Dinner, B&B from £277 per person. |
| Meals | Lunch £6.50–£25. Sunday lunch £29.50. Dinner, 3 courses, £70 (not Mon nights in main restaurant). |
| Closed | Never. |
| Directions | South from M27, junc. 1 to Lyndhurst on A337, then B3056 for Beaulieu. Left into village and hotel on right. |

Sunil Kanjanghat
The Montagu Arms Hotel
Palace Lane, Beaulieu,
Brockenhurst, SO42 7ZL

| | |
|---|---|
| Tel | +44 (0)1590 612324 |
| Email | reservations@montaguarmshotel.co.uk |
| Web | www.montaguarmshotel.co.uk |

## Castle House

Hereford's loveliest hotel stands 200 paces from the city's magnificent 11th-century cathedral, home to the Mappa Mundi. It's English to its core with a beautiful garden that overlooks what remains of the castle moat – in summer you can eat here watching ducks glide by. Inside, the lap of luxury: a fine staircase, painted panelling, a delicious restaurant for the best food in town. Big bedrooms are lavish. Those in the main house are more traditional (the top-floor suite runs all the way along the front of the house); those in the townhouse (a 30-second stroll) are distinctly 21st century. All have a smart country-house feel with beautiful fabrics, super-comfy beds, crisp white linen, excellent bathrooms. Seriously good food, much from the owner's nearby farm, waits in the restaurant, perhaps beetroot panna cotta, roast bream with saffron mash, banana mousse with chocolate brownies. You can walk it off along the river Wye, which runs through the park behind. Hereford has lots to offer: pop-up opera, guided walks, Evensong in the cathedral, the Three Choirs Festival in July.

| | |
|---|---|
| Rooms | 11 suites for 2: £195–£230. |
| | 4 singles: £130. |
| | Townhouse – 4 doubles: £150–£190. |
| | Townhouse – 5 suites for 2: £195–£230. |
| Meals | Lunch from £5. |
| | Sunday lunch from £18.50. |
| | Dinner, 3 courses, about £35. |
| Closed | Never. |
| Directions | Follow signs to Hereford city centre, then City Centre east. Right off Bath St into Union St, through St Peters Sq to Owen's St, right into St Ethelbert St. Hotel on left as road veers right. |

Michelle Marriott-Lodge
Castle House
Castle Street,
Hereford, HR1 2NW

| | |
|---|---|
| Tel | +44 (0)1432 356321 |
| Email | info@castlehse.co.uk |
| Web | www.castlehse.co.uk |

## The Verzon

The Verzon, once a Georgian farmhouse, sits on the road between Hereford and Ledbury with long views across fields to the Malvern Hills. It's owned by William and Kate Chase, farmers who turn potatoes and apples into Chase vodka and gin; tours of their distillery up the road are easily arranged. Not that this is the limit of their endeavours, far from it. They also rear cattle and pigs and have a vineyard in the Lubéron. The Verzon is where it all comes together – a gin and tonic before dinner, then delicious local food washed down by good French wines. Most of the food is sourced within 30 miles, the producers listed on the menu, perhaps Hereford rarebit, a Chase steak, Evesham rhubarb crumble. Inside, contemporary touches mix with original features. Timber frames and Union-Jack sofas wait in the bar, so grab a pint of Ledbury Gold (brewed next door) and roast away in front of the fire. Bedrooms upstairs have warm colours, crisp linen and robes in good bathrooms. Two have baths in the room, one of the suites is huge, those at the back have the view. Don't miss Hereford cathedral for the Mappa Mundi.

| | |
|---|---|
| Rooms | 5 twin/doubles: £100-£120. |
| | 2 suites for 2: £150. |
| | 1 single: £80-£90. |
| Meals | Lunch, 2 courses, from £16 |
| | (sandwiches from £5). |
| | Sunday lunch, 2 courses, from £20. |
| | Dinner, 3 courses à la carte, £25-£35. |
| Closed | Never. |
| Directions | A438 west from Ledbury for 4 miles. |
| | On right, signed. |

|  | Will & Kate Chase |
|---|---|
| | The Verzon |
| | Hereford Road, Trumpet, |
| | Ledbury, HR8 2PZ |
| Tel | +44 (0)1531 670381 |
| Email | info@verzonhouse.com |
| Web | www.verzonhouse.com |

## Wilton Court Restaurant with Rooms

This Grade-II listed house dates to 1510 and looks across the lane to the river Wye: herons dive, otters swim, kingfishers nest. Roses ramble outside, happy guests potter within. This is a small hotel with pretty rooms, good food and owners that care. Bedrooms upstairs come in different shapes and sizes, but all have style. Those at the front have watery views, William Morris wallpaper, lots of space, perhaps a four-poster. A couple of rooms are small (as is their price), but, along with several others, have recently been refurbished. Expect lots of colour, a wall of paper, white bathrooms and sofas in the bigger rooms. Back downstairs there's a bar for pre-dinner drinks, a wood-burner in the panelled sitting room, then a conservatory restaurant for tasty food, perhaps Shropshire blue cheese soufflé, Herefordshire beef with savoy cabbage, caramel panna cotta with vanilla ice cream. Berries from a Grade-I listed mulberry tree in the garden are turned into sorbets and pies. You can cross the lane to a second garden for drinks by the river in summer. Ross is a five-minute stroll. *Minimum stay: 2 nights at weekends.*

| | |
|---|---|
| Rooms | 4 doubles, 5 twin/doubles, 1 four-poster: £135–£185. 1 family room for 4: £165–£205. Singles from £100. |
| Meals | Lunch snacks from £6.95. Lunch, 2-3 courses, £16.95–£19.95. Dinner, 2-3 courses, £27.50–£32.50. 3 courses à la carte £35–£40. |
| Closed | Rarely. |
| Directions | South into Ross at A40/A49 Wilton roundabout. 1st right into Wilton Lane. Hotel on right. |

Roger & Helen Wynn
Wilton Court Restaurant with Rooms
Wilton Lane, Wilton,
Ross-on-Wye, HR9 6AQ

| | |
|---|---|
| Tel | +44 (0)1989 562569 |
| Email | info@wiltoncourthotel.com |
| Web | www.wiltoncourthotel.com |

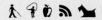

## The George Hotel

You get the best of two worlds here – the loveliest hotel on the island and the prettiest town, too. Yarmouth has the feel of a cute seaside village from the 1960s. As for the George, it's been around for over 400 years and has never looked better. Dianne bought the place recently and has poured in love and money, restoring former glories; Charles II stayed in 1671, but he didn't have it this good. Step off the street, pass wellington boots in the porch, then find yourself in a grand hall, where flowers scent the air. Outside, a beautiful garden and terrace overlook the water, flanked on one side by the east wall of Yarmouth Castle, a fine spot for lunch in the sun. Inside, you find panelled walls in an elegant sitting room, then a roaring fire in the beautiful bar. Two restaurants await: a brasserie that opens onto the terrace, then Isla's, a chic dining room, for delicious food, perhaps hand-dived scallops, roasted brill, caramelised banana bavarois. Bedrooms are gorgeous. Four have been refurbished, others will follow soon. Expect smart beds, fabulous bathrooms, perhaps a balcony for sea views. *Minimum stay: 2 nights at weekends.*

| | |
|---|---|
| Rooms | 17 twin/doubles: £135–£375. Singles from £110. Extra beds £20. Cots £15. |
| Meals | Lunch from £6. Dinner: in the brasserie from £14.50; 3 courses in the restaurant £65. |
| Closed | Rarely. |
| Directions | Lymington ferry to Yarmouth, then follow signs to town centre. |

Dianne Thompson
The George Hotel
Quay Street,
Yarmouth, PO41 0PE
Tel       +44 (0)1983 760331
Email    res@thegeorge.co.uk
Web      www.thegeorge.co.uk

## Hillside

A lovely small hotel with a cool Scandinavian feel that stands at the foot of forested hills with fine views over Ventnor and out to sea. Outside, five and a half acres of lawn, field and woodland with beehives, Hebridean sheep, red squirrels and white doves; there's an extensive kitchen garden, too, that provides much for the table. Inside, a pristine wonderland in white. There's a cosy bar with books, newspapers and a wood-burner, a sitting room/gallery with Danish leather sofas, a conservatory that opens onto a manicured terrace, and an airy restaurant with great art on the walls. Spotless bedrooms upstairs have a smart, uncluttered feel with comfy beds, vintage throws, more good art and lovely bathrooms. Those at the front look out to sea. Back downstairs, tasty food flies from the kitchen. The hotel has a share in a local fishing boat and lands its own fish, rears its own cattle in nearby fields and harvests fresh vegetables from the kitchen garden. It also has a bistro with an open-kitchen in town, so you can make the most of two culinary worlds. Beaches, gardens and the coastal path wait. *Minimum stay: 2 nights at weekends.*

| | |
|---|---|
| Rooms | 6 doubles, 2 twin/doubles, 1 twin: £146–£196. 3 singles: £68–£133. 2 apartments for 4: £196–£262. Singles £68–£133. Dinner, B&B £99 per person. |
| Meals | Lunch and dinner from £5. |
| Closed | Never. |
| Directions | South to Ventnor on A3055, then right (on approach to town) onto B3277. Past tennis courts, up hill, on right. |

Gert Bach
Hillside
151 Mitchell Avenue,
Ventnor, PO38 1DR

| | |
|---|---|
| Tel | +44 (0)1983 852271 |
| Email | mail@hillsideventnor.co.uk |
| Web | www.hillsideventnor.co.uk |

## Priory Bay Hotel

This lovely old house stands one field up from the sea with woodland paths leading down to the hotel's sandy beach. Medieval monks, Tudor farmers and Georgian gentry have all lived here. The house dates from the 14th century and stands in 60 acres of sprawling grounds. Inside, high ceilings, huge windows and a baby grand wait in the drawing room, but it's all very relaxed with a sitting-room bar and a playroom for children. The odd bag of golf clubs waits for the six-hole course, sunloungers flank the pool in summer, croquet hoops stand on the lawn. Bedrooms have an uncluttered feel: warm colours, tongue-and-groove bathrooms, a sofa if there's room. Some are enormous with timber frames, while luxurious yurts on the estate have claw-foot baths and terraces that look out to sea. As for the food, it's serious stuff, mostly local, some foraged, the fish from the waters around you, the meat from the hills behind. You eat in a stylish brasserie with walls of glass to bring in the view; try Bembridge crab, a tasty steak, Eton Mess with Isle of Wight strawberries and cream. *Minimum stay: 2 nights at weekends.*

| | |
|---|---|
| Rooms | 16 twin/doubles: £160–£300. |
| | 2 family rooms for 4: £240–£330. |
| | 2 barns for 6: £300–£455. |
| | 2 yurts: £200. |
| | Singles from £90. |
| Meals | Lunch from £8. Afternoon tea £20. |
| | Dinner, 3 courses £25–£35. |
| Closed | Never. |
| Directions | South from Ryde on B3330. Through Nettlestone and hotel signed left and left again. |

Andrew Palmer
Priory Bay Hotel
Priory Road,
Seaview, PO34 5BU

| | |
|---|---|
| Tel | +44 (0)1983 613146 |
| Email | enquiries@priorybay.co.uk |
| Web | www.priorybay.co.uk |

## Hever Castle Luxury Bed & Breakfast

Hever is out of this world, a 13th-century moated castle that was home to Anne Boleyn, second wife to Henry VIII, mother of Elizabeth I. It is one of those places that thrills at every turn. It has all the regal trimmings: 625 acres of green and pleasant land with formal gardens and a 38-acre lake. You either stay in the Astor Wing or the Anne Boleyn wing, both built in Tudor style in 1903. Bedrooms are fit for a queen. Expect period colours, panelled walls, perhaps a golden chaise longue or a glimpse of the castle through leaded windows. Lots have pretty wallpaper, one has a vaulted ceiling, several have four-poster beds, while bigger rooms have sofas. Bathrooms are faultless, some with claw-foot baths, others with walk-in power showers; a few have both. There's a panelled sitting room, a timber-framed billiard room, and a small courtyard for summer sun, but don't linger too long – entrance to the castle and gardens is included in your room price. You can boat on the lake, have picnic dinners, they even host the odd spot of jousting. The village pub for a good dinner is a short stroll. Unbeatable.

| | |
|---|---|
| Rooms | 22 doubles, 3 twins: £155–£205.<br>2 singles: £105–£120.<br>Extra bed/sofabed available £50 per person per night. |
| Meals | Picnic lunches by arrangement.<br>Restaurants within 0.25 miles. |
| Closed | Rarely. |
| Directions | Castle signed west out of Edenbridge. |

Roland Smith
Hever Castle Luxury Bed & Breakfast
Hever,
Edenbridge, TN8 7NG

| | |
|---|---|
| Tel | +44 (0)1732 861800 |
| Email | stay@hevercastle.co.uk |
| Web | www.hevercastle.co.uk |

## Leicester Arms

Rescued from closure and refurbished with style and panache in late 2013 by Julian Leefe-Griffiths, the creeper-clad 16th-century inn stands in picture-postcard Penshurst, opposite the gates to Penshurst Place and Gardens. Expect heavy oak doors and wooden floors, wall timbers and leaded windows, glowing woodburning stoves and candles on darkwood tables – perfect for supping a pint of local Larkins Traditional. At polished tables in the purple panelled dining room, quite grand with gilt-framed family portraits and chandeliers, enjoy some classic British food – lunchtime steak sandwich with horseradish cream and chips, or ham hock with fennel pickle and mustard mayo, followed by Old Spot toad-in-the-hole with mash and kale, and sticky toffee pudding with cobnut ice cream. Bedrooms ramble across two floors, all sport heritage hues, Hypnos mattresses and the best linen on antique beds, eclectic furnishings, posh tiled Aston Matthews bathrooms, and gorgeous views to Penshurst church or across rolling countryside. Hever Castle is close; stunning estate walks start from the front door.

| | |
|---|---|
| Rooms | 6 doubles, 3 four-posters: £119–£159. 2 family rooms for 4 (extra people over 14 £25 per night): £159. 2 singles: £99–£119. |
| Meals | Continental breakfast included, full cooked £8. Lunch from £4.50. Sunday lunch from £12.95. Dinner, 3 courses, £25–£30. |
| Closed | Never. |
| Directions | South from Tonbridge on A26, then right onto B2176. In village, after 3 miles, on left, opposite church. |

Melissa Porter
Leicester Arms
High Street, Penshurst,
Tonbridge, TN11 8BT

| | |
|---|---|
| Tel | +44 (0)1892 871617 |
| Email | info@theleicesterarmshotel.com |
| Web | www.theleicesterarmshotel.com |

## The Tunbridge Wells Hotel

Charles I put Tunbridge Wells on the map when he came to take the waters in 1630. By the end of the century the town had flourished and the great and good gathered to stroll along the Pantiles, the colonnaded terraces in the middle of town. They remain every bit as lovely today, with pavement cafés, antique shops, the odd concert and a weekly farmers' market. Hogging the limelight is this newly-refurbished hotel, which spills onto the terrace outside, a lovely spot to eat in summer. Inside, you find a buzzing brasserie that will make you think you've crossed the channel: clumps of lampshades hang from the ceilings, French art is crammed on the walls, a happy vibe runs throughout. The food is excellent, French to its core, perhaps lobster bisque, coq au vin, then tarte tatin, all of which you wash down with impeccable French wines. Bedrooms above have a simple elegance: warm colours, smart beds, pretty furniture, lovely prices. Good bathrooms have power showers, some a roll-top bath, one of which is in the room. The Downs wait across the road to work off any excess so come to make merry.

| | |
|---|---|
| Rooms | 11 doubles, 4 twins: £109-£139. 2 suites for 2, 2 family rooms for 4: £139-£195. 1 single: £75-£85. |
| Meals | Continental breakfast included, cooked dishes from £3.50. Lunch & dinner £5-£30. |
| Closed | Never. |
| Directions | Sent on booking. |

Julian Leefe-Griffiths
The Tunbridge Wells Hotel
58 The Pantiles,
Tunbridge Wells, TN2 5TD

| | |
|---|---|
| Tel | +44 (0)1892 530501 |
| Email | info@thetunbridgewellshotel.com |
| Web | www.thetunbridgewellshotel.com |

## Leeds Castle

This iconic English castle has a just smidgeon of history to it! Six queens of England lived here, it was a favourite haunt of Edward I and a pleasure palace to Henry VIII, who stayed here with Catherine of Aragon before setting off to meet Francis I at the Field of the Cloth of Gold in 1520. It dates back to 1119 and is every bit as spectacular as you'd expect, its 500 acres home to lakes and rivers and beautiful gardens, then a Tudor tithe barn that doubles as a restaurant. In the 18th century the castle was remodelled in country-house style and from the 1930s the great and the good gathered here at weekends for riotous house parties. These days you can stay in the pretty courtyard rooms, on the island in Maiden's Tower with sublime views, or in the castle itself, spilling with history, with spectacular interiors, stately bedrooms and butlers to serve dinner. The castle is mostly for parties taking eight rooms or more, but rooms are available for one-off events: concerts in the park, special weekends. You can punt on the moat, picnic in the grounds, try your hand at falconry. Unbeatable. *Castle bookings on enquiry.*

| | |
|---|---|
| Rooms | Courtyard rooms – 17 twin/doubles: £120–£150. Maiden's – 5 doubles: £220–£280. Dinner, B&B from £90 per person. |
| Meals | Dinner, 3 courses, about £25 in the Courtyard Restaurant. |
| Closed | Christmas Eve & Christmas Day. |
| Directions | M20, junc. 8, then A20 south. Ignore brown signs to castle, pass Park Gate Inn, then 1st right and right again into castle. |

**Mark Flavell**
Leeds Castle
Maidstone, ME17 1PL
Tel        +44 (0)1622 767823
Email    accommodation@leeds-castle.co.uk
Web      www.leeds-castle.com

## The Milk House

The gardens at Sissinghurst Castle, designed by Vita Sackville-West, are some of the loveliest in the land and if you stay at this cute village pub, you can stroll over after breakfast, via apple orchards and bluebell woods. As for The Milk House, it's a great base from which to explore this deeply rural area – stylish, welcoming, nicely priced. It's also a place for a very good meal, seasonal and mostly sourced within 20 miles. In summer, you decant onto a smart terrace with an outside bar and wood-fired pizza oven, not a bad spot for a jug of Pimm's and a crispy margherita. There's a duck pond, too, lawns for a pint in the sun, then views over open country. Airy interiors have an easy style: woven willow lampshades hanging above the bar, a timber-framed dining room, where you dig into fabulous food, perhaps home-cured smoked salmon, free-range Park Farm beef, chocolate tart with kirsch-soaked cherries; there are matchless local cheeses, too. Beautiful bedrooms are crisply uncluttered. Expect chic fabrics, relaxing colours, excellent bathrooms and a sofa if there's room. *Minimum stay: 2 nights at weekends.*

|  |  |
|---|---|
| Rooms | 3 doubles, 1 twin: £100–£120. |
| Meals | Lunch from £4. |
|  | Dinner, 3 courses, about £30. |
|  | Sunday roast from £12.95. |
| Closed | Rarely. |
| Directions | East into Sissinghurst on A262. In village, on left. |

Dane & Sarah Allchorne
The Milk House
The Street, Sissinghurst,
Cranbrook, TN17 2JG
Tel       +44 (0)1580 720200
Email    fresh@themilkhouse.co.uk
Web      www.themilkhouse.co.uk

## Cloth Hall Oast

This attractive Kentish oast house dates to 1780 and sits in peace a mile across the fields from Cranbrook. Mrs Morgan, the star of the show, lived in the 15th-century manor next door for 40 years; now she's turned her perfectionist's eye upon these five acres. The garden is beautiful – well-groomed lawns, a carp-filled pond, pergola, summer house, heated swimming pool, flower beds full of colour. You breakfast grandly at a mahogany table with the hall open to the rafters above, a sparkling chandelier hanging gracefully, a grand piano on the minstrels' gallery; in good weather you nip outside and eat on the deck overlooking the pond. Three bedrooms wait: a circular four-poster in the roundel on the ground floor, then a family room and a small double above. Colours are soft, fabrics are frilled, but nothing is busy or overdone. You'll find spotless bathrooms, fine mattresses, crisp linen, flowered chintz. In summer, the pool is yours, with sun loungers to take the strain. There are good local pubs for dinner and a Michelin starred restaurant in the village. Sissinghurst Gardens are close. *No credit cards.*

| | |
|---|---|
| Rooms | 1 double, 1 four-poster: £90–£135. 1 family room for 3: £125–£135. |
| Meals | Dinner from £25, by arrangement. Pub & restaurant 1 mile. |
| Closed | Christmas. |
| Directions | Leave village with windmill on left, taking Golford Road east for Tenterden. After a mile right, before cemetery. Signed right. |

Katherine Morgan
Cloth Hall Oast
Course Horn Lane,
Cranbrook, TN17 3NR

| | |
|---|---|
| Tel | +44 (0)1580 712220 |
| Email | clothhalloast@aol.com |
| Web | www.clothhalloast.co.uk |

## Elvey Farm

This old farmhouse stands in six acres of blissful peace, half a mile up a private drive. It's a deeply rural position, a nostalgic sweep back to old England. White roses run riot on red-brick walls, a thick vine shades the veranda, trim lawns run up to colourful borders. Inside you find timber frames at every turn, but the feel is airy with contemporary furniture sitting amid stripped boards and old beams. Bedrooms come in similar vein. Two homely rooms in the main house are family-friendly, those in the stable block have chunky beds, small sitting rooms and good wet rooms; two have slipper baths. Best of all are the two fancy rooms in the granary. Expect timber-framed walls in chic bathrooms and massive beds under original rafters; one room comes with a hot tub in a secret garden. Italian food waits in the restaurant, perhaps gnocchi with mozzarella and fresh basil, lamb with rosemary and anchovies, limoncello mousse. The Greensand Way runs through the grounds, so come to walk through Kent's soft landscapes. Leeds Castle is close, *The Darling Buds of May* was filmed in the village.

| | |
|---|---|
| Rooms | 1 double, 1 four-poster: £105–£245. Oast – 2 doubles: £105–£245. Granary – 2 suites for 2: £105–£245. Stables – 3 suites for 2, 2 suites for 4: £105–£245. Singles from £85. Dinner, B&B from £74.50 per person. |
| Meals | Dinner £26–£37. Not Mondays. Sunday lunch from £26. |
| Closed | Never. |
| Directions | M20 junc. 8; A20 to Lenham. At Charing r'bout 3rd exit for A20 Ashford. Right at lights to Pluckley. Bypass village, down hill, right at pub, right & right again. |

Simon Peek
Elvey Farm
Pluckley,
Ashford, TN27 0SU

| | |
|---|---|
| Tel | +44 (0)1233 840442 |
| Email | bookings@elveyfarm.co.uk |
| Web | www.elveyfarm.co.uk |

## The Relish

It's not just the super-comfy interiors that make The Relish such a tempting port of call. There's a sense of generosity here: a drink on the house each night in the sitting room; tea and cakes on tap all day; free internet throughout. This is a grand 1850s merchant's house on the posh side of town – lovely old bricks and mortar, softly contemporary interiors. Laura and Rakesh took over recently and have already pulled out the paintbrushes, so wind up the cast-iron staircase to find bedrooms that make you smile. You get Hypnos beds with padded headboards, crisp white linen and pretty throws. There's a sense of space, a sofa if there's room, big mirrors and lovely bathrooms. All are great value for money. Downstairs candles flicker on the mantelpieces above an open fire, the high-ceilinged dining room comes with stripped floors and padded benches and in summer you can decamp onto the terrace for breakfast, a communal garden stretching out beyond. You're one street back from Folkestone's cliff-top front for big sea views. Steps lead down to smart gardens, the promenade and waterside restaurants. *Minimum stay: 2 nights at weekends in summer.*

| | |
|---|---|
| Rooms | 9 doubles: £98–£150. |
| | 1 single: £75. |
| Meals | Restaurants nearby. |
| Closed | 22 December to 2 January. |
| Directions | In centre of town, from Langholm Gardens, head west on Sandgate Road. 1st right into Augusta Gardens/Trinity Gardens. Hotel on right. |

Laura & Rakesh Sharma
The Relish
4 Augusta Gardens,
Folkestone, CT20 2RR

| | |
|---|---|
| Tel | +44 (0)1303 850952 |
| Email | reservations@hotelrelish.co.uk |
| Web | www.hotelrelish.co.uk |

## Albion House

This is quite some house, a Regency pile that dates to 1790, with huge rooms, high ceilings and grandeur at every turn. It stands at the top of a hill in the middle of town with fine views over the Royal Harbour. Incredibly, it was left to decay by its last inhabitants, Ramsgate Town Council, whose headquarters this was until 2008. Now, after a long renovation, interiors shine, mixing contemporary design with the feel of a colonial gentleman's club. There's a fire in reception, watery views through big windows in the restaurant, then a fabulous bar with a grand piano, exotic pot plants, a roaring fire, and sofas everywhere. Classical prints are jammed on the wall, the bar itself came from the town hall. The whole place is a work of art, nothing is here by accident. Downstairs, there's a treatment room, a steam room, a meeting room that doubles as a cinema, then a vaulted cavern for wine tastings. Big bedrooms get smaller as you climb the house, but the best views are at the top. Expect good beds, crisp linen, neutral colours, robes in white marble bathrooms. Don't miss afternoon tea. Brilliant.

| Rooms | 12 twin/doubles, |
| --- | --- |
| | 1 four-poster: £125–£220. |
| | 1 suite for 2: £220–£375. |
| Meals | Continental breakfast included, |
| | full English £10. Lunch from £14. |
| | Dinner, 3 courses, £25–£35. |
| | Sunday lunch from £16. |
| Closed | Rarely. |
| Directions | M2, A299, then B2054 into Ramsgate. |
| | Follow signs for town centre, pick up |
| | coast on right, down hill, up the other |
| | side, on left at top. |

|  | Ben & Emma Irvine |
| --- | --- |
| | Albion House |
| | Albion Place, |
| | Ramsgate, CT11 8HQ |
| Tel | +44 (0)1843 606630 |
| Email | enquiries@albionhouseramsgate.co.uk |
| Web | www.albionhouseramsgate.co.uk |

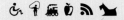

## Read's Restaurant with Rooms

A gorgeous country-house restaurant with rooms, Read's stands in five acres of lawned grounds with a half-acre kitchen garden that supplies much for the table. Inside, you find warm elegance at every turn. There's a sitting room bar for pre-dinner drinks, then a couple of beautiful dining rooms where you eat at smartly clothed tables surrounded by ornamental fireplaces and lots of good art. As for the food, it's some of the best in Kent. David and Rona came here 33 years ago, and locals and travellers come for their delicious delights: a hot soufflé of Montgomery's Cheddar on a bed of smoked haddock, local venison with pickled pears and walnut croquettes, a chestnut and whisky parfait with toasted hazelnuts and Seville orange curd meringues. The bedrooms are just as good — country-house splendour in spades. Expect decanters of sherry, Roberts radios, huge beds dressed in crisp white linen, wonderful bathrooms with robes to pad about in. Canterbury, Whitstable and Leeds Castle are close, as is Rochester for all things Dickens.

| Rooms | 5 doubles, 1 twin/double: £165–£195. Singles from £125. Dinner, B&B from £135 per person. |
|---|---|
| Meals | Lunch £26. Dinner £60. |
| Closed | Sun & Mon. 1st week in January, 1st 2 weeks in September. |
| Directions | M2, junc. 7, then A2 west into Faversham. Past petrol station and signed left after 400m. |

David & Rona Pitchford
Read's Restaurant with Rooms
Macknade Manor, Canterbury Road,
Faversham, ME13 8XE

| Tel | +44 (0)1795 535344 |
|---|---|
| Email | enquiries@reads.com |
| Web | www.reads.com |

AWARD WINNER
Fabulous food

## The Cartford Inn

Patrick and Julie know how to run a great little inn: whisk up some fabulous food, throw in a pinch of quirky style, then add lovely bedrooms and serve informally. The inn stands on the banks of the river Wyre – views from the restaurant drift upstream with the Trough of Bowland looming beyond. The front bar, with its cool art, roaring fire and friendly locals is a great place to stop for a pint of local ale, though a courtyard garden will draw you out in good weather. In typically relaxed style you can eat whatever you want wherever you want, perhaps a smoked black pudding doughnut, oxtail and beef pudding with green beans and mash, a crème caramel with banana crisp. Bedrooms are just as good – gilded sleigh beds, signature wallpapers, crisp white linen and river views. All have lovely bathrooms with REN lotions, two have roll-top baths in the room, the penthouse suite has a shower for two and a rooftop terrace. You can walk by the river – a two-mile circular walk will spin you round – head east into the Yorkshire Dales, or spin off to Blackpool and jump on a rollercoaster.

| | |
|---|---|
| Rooms | 10 doubles, 1 twin: £120–£130. 1 suite for 2: £200. 2 family rooms for 3-4: £140. Singles from £65. |
| Meals | Lunch from £8.50. Not Mon lunch. Dinner, 3 courses, £25–£35. |
| Closed | Christmas Day. |
| Directions | M6 junc. 32, M55 junc. 3, then A585 north. Right at T-junction onto A586 for Garstang. Little Eccleston signed left. |

Patrick & Julie Beaume
The Cartford Inn
Cartford Lane, Little Eccleston,
Preston, PR3 0YP

| | |
|---|---|
| Tel | +44 (0)1995 670166 |
| Email | info@thecartfordinn.co.uk |
| Web | www.thecartfordinn.co.uk |

## The Inn at Whitewell

It is almost impossible to imagine a day when a better inn will grace the English landscape. Everything here is perfect. The inn sits just above the river Hodder, and doors in the bar lead onto a terrace where guests can enjoy five-mile views across parkland to rising fells. Inside, fires roar, newspapers wait, there are beams, sofas, maps and copies of *Wisden*. Bedrooms, some in the Coach House, are exemplary and come with real luxury, perhaps a peat fire, a lavish four-poster, a fabulous Victorian power shower. All have beautiful fabrics, top linen and gadgets galore; many have the marvellous view – you can fall asleep at night to the sound of the river. There are bar meals for those who want to watch their weight (the Whitewell fish pie is rightly famous) or a restaurant for splendid food, so dig into seared scallops, Bowland lamb, a plate of local cheese (the Queen once popped in for lunch). Elsewhere, a wine shop in reception, seven miles of private fishing and countryside as good as any in the land. Dogs and children are very welcome. Magnificent.

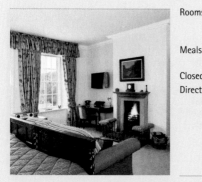

| | |
|---|---|
| Rooms | 17 doubles, 5 twin/doubles: £120–£215. 1 suite for 2: £210–£240. Singles £92–£204. |
| Meals | Bar meals from £8. Dinner £25–£35. |
| Closed | Never. |
| Directions | M6 junc. 31A, B6243 east through Longridge, then follow signs to Whitewell for 9 miles. |

Charles Bowman
The Inn at Whitewell
Dunsop Road, Whitewell,
Clitheroe, BB7 3AT

| | |
|---|---|
| Tel | +44 (0)1200 448222 |
| Email | reception@innatwhitewell.com |
| Web | www.innatwhitewell.com |

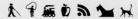

## Washingborough Hall

In its day Lincoln was one of the most important cities in England. Its castle holds a copy of the Magna Carta and was built by William the Conqueror in 1068; its cathedral dates to 1090 and remains one of the finest in Europe. All of which makes it a great city to visit, and if you want to beat a peaceful retreat into the country at the end of the day, this is the place to stay. It sits two miles east of town in a small village on the river Witham – footpaths by the water lead back into town. As for this Georgian rectory, you'll find smart lawns to the front, then a big welcome within – Edward and Lucy go out of their way to make your stay special. There's a wood-burner in the hall, a breakfast room with garden views, a sitting-room bar for afternoon tea, then a light-filled orangery restaurant. Stylish bedrooms offer unstinting comforts. Rooms at the front are bigger and have the view, all have good beds, bold wallpapers, excellent bathrooms, a sofa if there's room. As for the food, there's posh fish and chips in the bar or sea bass with spring greens in the orangery.

| | |
|---|---|
| Rooms | 6 doubles, 3 twin/doubles, 2 four-posters: £85-£175. Singles from £75. |
| Meals | Lunch from £5.50. Dinnner, 3 courses, £25-£35. Sunday lunch from £18.50. |
| Closed | Never. |
| Directions | East out of Lincoln on B1190. In village, right at mini r'bout onto Church Hill. On left after 500m. |

Lucy & Edward Herring
Washingborough Hall
Church Hill,
Washingborough, LN4 1BE

| | |
|---|---|
| Tel | +44 (0)1522 790340 |
| Email | enquiries@washingboroughhall.com |
| Web | www.washingboroughhall.com |

## The Castle Hotel

Lincoln, a medieval powerhouse, has been at the centre of British life for 2,000 years. Romans, Vikings and Normans ruled here, the cathedral is one of the finest in Europe, an original copy of the Magna Carta sits in its castle. As for the hotel, it's a splendid spot from which to explore the city. It stands in the old town with views to the front of the castle's enormous walls and the cathedral's towers soaring two streets east. Paul and Saera renovated from top to toe, rescuing it from neglect. Now there's an airy bar in reception, an attractive restaurant for fancy food and a clutch of bedrooms waiting above. Expect contemporary colours, smart fabrics, padded bedheads, excellent bathrooms. Lincoln's wonders wait: the castle and its dungeon, the jaw-dropping cathedral, then Steep Hill (old-world charm with lots of tearooms) which leads down to Brayford Pool, where you can sit on café terraces and watch the world go by. The Christmas market in early December is one of the best in Britain. Come by train, it's only two hours from London.

| | |
|---|---|
| Rooms | 16 twin/doubles: £110–£130. |
| | 1 suite for 2: £140. |
| | 1 single: £90. |
| | Dinner, B&B from £90 per person. |
| Meals | Lunch & bar meals from £10. |
| | Dinner £30–£35. |
| Closed | Rarely. |
| Directions | Sent on booking. |

Paul Catlow & Saera Ahmad
The Castle Hotel
Westgate,
Lincoln, LN1 3AS

Tel     +44 (0)1522 538801
Email   info@castlehotel.net
Web     www.castlehotel.net

## The William Cecil

This attractive townhouse hotel stands yards from the gates of the Burghley estate. Inside, interiors offer a pleasing mix of English quirkiness and splendour. Downstairs, informality reigns. There are armchairs in front of the fire in the bar, smart wicker tables in the conservatory, doors onto a lovely terrace in summer, then hanging lamps and half-panelling in the colourful restaurant. The food is fresh and local with seasonal delights that include game from the estate. You might find lobster mousse with avocado ice-cream, slow-cooked Burghley venison casserole, lemon curd pie with lime sorbet. You can walk it all off with a stroll through historic Stamford or spin over to Burghley for one of the finest Elizabethan houses in the realm. Come back to country-house bedrooms that mix eclectic Rajasthan furniture with a little English decorum. You'll find beautiful art, a wall of paper, perhaps a day bed or a ceiling rose. Some have views onto the estate, all have good bathrooms, the best with roll top tubs and vast walk-in showers. Dogs don't fare badly either with Union Jack beds.

| | |
|---|---|
| Rooms | 20 doubles, 7 twin/doubles: £125. |
| Meals | Lunch from £6.50. |
| | Dinner from £12. |
| | Sunday lunch, 3 courses, £24.50. |
| Closed | Never. |
| Directions | A1 north past Easton-on-the-Hill, then B1081 for Stamford. On right as you enter town. |

Paul Brown
The William Cecil
St Martins,
Stamford, PE9 2LJ

| | |
|---|---|
| Tel | +44 (0)1780 750070 |
| Email | enquiries@thewilliamcecil.co.uk |
| Web | www.thewilliamcecil.co.uk |

## SACO Holborn – Lamb's Conduit Street

Lamb's Conduit Street is cool, quirky and pedestrianised with a sprinkling of cafés and restaurants and the legendary bookshop Persephone. A recent refurbishment has made these serviced apartments a great central base. You get the equivalent of a hotel suite, then excellent kitchens thrown in for free. Sparkling top-floor apartments open onto vast decked terraces while those below have walls of glass overlooking the street. It's all a big surprise given the utilitarian 60s exterior: there's space and style, with open-plan living rooms, excellent bathrooms, comfy bedrooms and lots of appealing extras such as washing machines, dishwashers and flat-screen TVs; the reception staff are great, too. The building stands directly opposite Great Ormond Street Hospital – quiet at night and devoid of the crowds. It's also extremely central: you can walk to St Paul's, Covent Garden, Oxford Street and the British Museum. Waitrose for shopping and Russell Square for the tube are both a step away, as is the Renoir, a small London cinema for great independent films. Off-street parking available by arrangement.

| Rooms | 2 apartments for 6, 10 apartments for 4, 24 apartments for 2: £201-£462. |
|---|---|
| Meals | Self-catered. Restaurants nearby. |
| Closed | Never. |
| Directions | Train: Liverpool Street. Tube: Russell Square. Bus: 19, 38, 55, 243. Private parking from £15 a day. |

**Tim Ripman**
SACO Holborn – Lamb's Conduit Street
Spens House, 72-84 Lamb's Conduit
Street, Holborn, London, WC1N 3LT

| Tel | +44 (0)20 7269 9930 |
| Email | london@sacoapartments.com |
| Web | www.sacoapartments.com |

## 22 York Street

A Regency townhouse in W1, a family home for over 60 years. Definitely not your average place to stay in London – in fact it defies all attempts to pigeonhole it. There may be 10 bedrooms, but you should still expect the feel of home: Liz and Michael, friendly and easy-going, are determined to keep things as informal and unfussy as possible. This might explain the convivial breakfasts taken communally around a curved wooden table in the big and bright kitchen/dining room, where visitors meet to chat and don't feel under any pressure to hurry. There's always something to catch your eye, be it the red-lipped oil painting outside the dining room or the old boots on the landing. Wooden floors run throughout, and the house has a huge sitting room, with sofas, books, backgammon, and a baby grand piano, which, of course, you are welcome to play. Expect good beds with pretty quilts and lots of space in the bedrooms: all are spotless and very comfy with antiques and rugs. This is Sherlock Holmes country and Madame Tussauds, Regent's Park and Lord's are all close by, as are hundreds of restaurants. A very friendly place.

| Rooms | 5 doubles, 2 twins: £150. |
|---|---|
| | 3 singles: £95–£120. |
| Meals | Continental breakfast included. |
| | Pubs/restaurants nearby. |
| Closed | Never. |
| Directions | Train: Paddington (to Heathrow). |
| | Tube: Baker Street (2-minute walk). |
| | Bus: 2, 13, 30, 74, 82, 113, 139, 274. |
| | Parking: £25 a day, off-street. |

Michael & Liz Callis
22 York Street
Marylebone, London, W1U 6PX

Tel        +44 (0)20 7224 2990
Email      mc@22yorkstreet.co.uk
Web        www.22yorkstreet.co.uk

## The Portobello Hotel

In 1969, in the days of Bowie and the Rolling Stones, this small hotel opened its doors, making it London's first boutique hotel. It was a new idea, a hip little place, not dull and formal like other hotels, but relaxed and friendly with lots of colour and a bohemian feel. These days, not much has changed, and it remains a popular base for artists and movie stars, designers and musicians, a star-studded list of regulars who come for its seductive combination of privacy, informality and style. It stands in the middle of Notting Hill, peacefully hidden away on a side street yet close to the tube, with Portobello Road and the shops and cafés of Westbourne Grove a short stroll. Inside, a beautiful sitting room has pine bay windows and carved ceiling roses, then fresh flowers, big art and views onto communal gardens. Bedrooms vary in size, not style. Lots have claw-foot baths in the room, one has a small terrace, another a high four-poster with library steps to help you up. Bigger rooms have sofas, all have cool colours, antique furniture, coffee machines and robes for the bathroom.

| | |
|---|---|
| Rooms | 19 doubles: £195–£395.<br>2 singles: £155–£175. |
| Meals | Continental breakfast included, cooked dishes from £5. Light bites from £6.<br>Good restaurants within 500m. |
| Closed | Never. |
| Directions | Tube: Notting Hill Gate.<br>Bus: 12, 27, 28, 52, 70, 94.<br>Parking: £25 per 24 hrs. |

**David Smith**
The Portobello Hotel
22 Stanley Gardens,
Notting Hill Gate, London, W11 2NG

Tel      +44 (0)20 7727 2777
Email    stay@portobellohotel.com
Web      www.portobellohotel.com

## Temple Lodge Club

Temple Lodge, once home to the painter Sir Frank Brangwyn, is sandwiched between a courtyard and a lushly landscaped garden. The peace is remarkable making it a very restful place – simple yet human and warmly comfortable, a nourishing experience. Michael and his devoted team run it with quiet energy. You breakfast overlooking the garden, there are newspapers to browse, a library instead of TVs. Bedrooms are surprisingly stylish: pretty art, crisp linen, no clutter, a hint of country chic. They're exceptional value for money, too, so book well in advance. Some rooms have garden views, only two have their own bathrooms and loo; if you don't mind that, you'll be happy. The Thames passes by at the end of the road, the Riverside Studios is round the corner for theatre and film, and the Gate Vegetarian Restaurant is across the courtyard, a well-known eatery, its food so good even committed carnivores can't resist. It was also Brangwyn's studio, hence the artist's window. The house is a non-denominational Christian centre with two services a week, which you may take or leave as you choose.

| | |
|---|---|
| Rooms | 1 double, 1 double with separate wc; 1 double with separate bathroom; 1 double sharing bath & shower, 2 twins sharing baths & shower with singles: £76–£120. 5 singles sharing baths & shower: £58–£72. Extra bed/sofabed available from £12–£14 per person per night. |
| Meals | Continental breakfast included. Vegetarian restaurant across courtyard. |
| Closed | Never. |
| Directions | Tube: Hammersmith (5-minute walk). Bus: 9, 10, 27, 295. |

**Michael Beaumont**
Temple Lodge Club
51 Queen Caroline Street,
Hammersmith, London, W6 9QL

| | |
|---|---|
| Tel | +44 (0)20 8748 8388 |
| Email | templelodgeclub@btconnect.com |
| Web | www.templelodgeclub.com |

## The Georgian House

Serena's great-great grandfather was commissioned by Thomas Cubitt to build this row of houses and liked the results so much he kept one for himself. They were built to rival Belgravia and have the same august credentials: pillars at the door, porticos and friezes, then high-ceilinged interiors as befits elegant Georgian architecture. Fast forward 160 years and the house, still in the same family, is now a B&B hotel, with a friendly brigade of international staff and a lovely sitting room in reception, where you can make a coffee and read the papers. As for the bedrooms, they come in two styles: rooms that haven't been recently refurbished and those that have. The former are due to be upgraded soon, but are simpler altogether: compact with blond wood. The latter are lovely: bigger, with white walls, a roll of paper, pretty fabrics, perhaps a sofa. Breakfast hits the spot with free-range eggs and Musk's sausages (also popular with Her Majesty). You're close to Victoria (and the train to Gatwick) and Buckingham Palace. A couple of Harry Potter themed rooms are popular with younger guests.

| | |
|---|---|
| Rooms | 35 doubles, 12 triples: £99–£219. 4 family rooms for 4: £159–£239. 8 singles: £99–£125. Bower House – 7 doubles: £145–£195. Bower House – 3 singles: £125–£155. 2 apartments for 5, 2 apartments for 6: £259–£349. |
| Meals | Pubs/restaurants within walking distance. |
| Closed | Never. |
| Directions | Tube: Victoria, Pimlico, Sloane Square. Train: Victoria (for Gatwick). Bus: 6, 11, 16, 24, 38, 52, 73, 82, 185, 211, 239, C10 |

Serena von der Heyde
The Georgian House
35-37 St. Georges Drive,
Pimlico, London, SW1V 4DG

Tel +44 (0)20 7834 1438
Email reception@georgianhousehotel.co.uk
Web www.georgianhousehotel.co.uk

## Artist Residence London

In the future, if a book is written about London hotels, they will divide it into two periods – before and after Artist Residence London. Because this gorgeous small hotel is a game changer, a new template of British cool, a space designed wholly to exercise your pleasure receptors. It proves resoundingly that small is more beautiful than big ever can be and while large hotels will try to copy it, they'll fail miserably, unable to match its intimacy, or the fantastic staff who look after you all the way. So what do you get? A small slice of heaven between Pimlico and the King's Road. It's a phoenix from the ashes, a Thomas Cubitt pub recently rescued from neglect. The cellar bar, with pop art and exposed brick walls, must qualify as one of London's coolest; the sitting room has fat sofas in front of a roaring fire; the Cambridge Street Café offers lovely food in a stylish, relaxed setting. Bedrooms are flawless: cool art, chic fabrics, the best beds, power-showered bathrooms. Smaller rooms are divine, bigger rooms have sofas, the suites have free-standing baths. Battersea Park is close.

| | |
|---|---|
| Rooms | 8 doubles: £180-£295. |
| | 2 suites for 2: £295-£410. |
| Meals | Lunch from £6. |
| | Dinner, 3 courses, about £30. |
| Closed | Never. |
| Directions | Tube: Victoria, Pimlico, Sloane Square. |
| | Train: Victoria (for Gatwick). |
| | Bus: 6, 11, 16, 24, 38, 52, 73, 82, 185, |
| | 211, 239, C10. |

Charlie Newey & Justin Salisbury
Artist Residence London
52 Cambridge Street,
Pimlico, London, SW1V 4QQ

Tel      +44 (0)20 7828 6684
Email    london@artistresidence.co.uk
Web      www.artistresidencelondon.co.uk

## Lime Tree Hotel

You'll be hard pressed to find better value in the centre of town. The Lime Tree — two elegant Georgian townhouses — stands less than a mile from Buckingham Palace, with Westminster, Sloane Square and Piccadilly easy strolls. Add warm interiors, kind owners and one of the capital's loveliest pubs waiting round the corner and you've unearthed a London gem. There's Cole & Son wallpaper in the airy dining room, so dig into an excellent breakfast (included in the price), then drop into the tiny sitting room next door for guide books and a computer for guests to use. Rooms — one on the ground floor with doors onto the garden and the quietest at the back — are just the ticket: smart without being lavish. Expect warm colours, crisp linen, pretty wallpaper and excellent bathrooms (most have super showers). Those at the front on the first floor have high ceilings and fine windows, those at the top (a few stairs!) are cosy in the eaves. Charlotte and Matt are hands-on and will point you in the right direction. Don't miss the Thomas Cubitt pub (50 paces from the front door) for seriously good food. *Minimum stay: 2 nights at weekends.*

| | |
|---|---|
| Rooms | 12 doubles, 4 twins: £175–£205. |
| | 1 family room for 4: £235. |
| | 6 singles: £115–£150. |
| | 2 triples: £220. |
| Meals | Restaurants nearby. |
| Closed | Never. |
| Directions | Train: Victoria (to Gatwick). |
| | Tube: Victoria or Sloane Square. |
| | Bus: 11, 24, 38, 52, 73, C1. |
| | Parking: £34 a day off-street. |

**Charlotte & Matt Goodsall**
Lime Tree Hotel
135 Ebury Street, Victoria,
London, SW1W 9QU

| | |
|---|---|
| Tel | +44 (0)20 7730 8191 |
| Email | info@limetreehotel.co.uk |
| Web | www.limetreehotel.co.uk |

## The Levin Hotel

A great London base for shopaholics — Harrods waits at one end of the street, Harvey Nicks at the other. As for the hotel, it sits quietly on Basil Street, a peaceful retreat in the middle of Knightsbridge. There's no sitting room, but a lively café/bar/restaurant, which acts as the social hub. Bedrooms spread over four floors with a lift to carry you up, though you may prefer to walk — a contemporary chandelier with an 18-metre drop fills the stairwell. As for the rooms, some are bigger, others smaller, but all have the same chic style: bold colours, Art Nouveau furnishings, hand-stitched beds, white marble bathrooms. Bigger rooms have sofas, all have Bose radios, flat-screen TVs, white robes and beautiful linen. You can breakfast on croissants from the owner's bakery, nip back early for afternoon tea, or dine on lovely comfort food, perhaps salmon fishcakes, shepherd's pie, Eton Mess with mixed berries. If that's not enough, there's a Michelin star next door at the Capital (their sister hotel). All rooms are air conditioned, there's a full concierge service and iPads are available at reception. *Pets by arrangement.*

| | |
|---|---|
| Rooms | 3 doubles, 8 twin/doubles: £240–£479. 1 suite for 2: £375–£619. Extra beds for under 12s £30. |
| Meals | Lunch from £5.50. Dinner, 3 courses, about £30. Afternoon tea from £22.99. |
| Closed | Never. |
| Directions | Tube: Knightsbridge (for Heathrow). Station: Victoria (for Gatwick). Bus: 09, 10, 19, 22, 52, 137, C1. Car parks £45 a day. |

|  |  |
|---|---|
| | Harald Duttine The Levin Hotel 28 Basil Street, Knightsbridge, London, SW3 1AS |
| Tel | +44 (0)20 7589 6286 |
| Email | reservations@thelevinhotel.co.uk |
| Web | www.thelevinhotel.co.uk |

## The Troubadour

The Troubadour is a one-off, a quirky coffee house and bar that has kept true to its 60s roots. It's a famous old music venue, too – Dylan, Joni Mitchell and the Stones all played here, as did Jimi Hendrix, whose pictures, shot here, adorn the walls; bands still play most nights. Outside, pavement tables make the best of the weather. Inside, rows of teapots sit in the windows, as they have for 60 years. The ceiling drips with musical instruments – the largest collection of long-neck banjos outside the British Museum hangs above your head. It's all informally run, the kitchen is open all day, and if you wear a hat on Tuesday nights, pudding is free. Next door, above their wine shop, two apartments wait on high with views over London rooftops. You get bold colours, comfy beds, books and vintage luggage, then a sofabed in the sitting room, making this a great base for families. You also get a kitchen, yours to use whenever you want, though the food below is tempting, perhaps steak and eggs for breakfast or coq au vin for dinner. "Character pours from every cupboard," as one guest said. Brilliant.

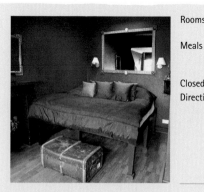

| | |
|---|---|
| Rooms | 2 suites for 2-4 with sofabed: £175-£225. Singles from £160. |
| Meals | Continental breakfast included, cooked extras from £4.50. Lunch & dinner £5-£25. |
| Closed | 25 & 26 December; 1 January. |
| Directions | Tube: Earl's Court or West Brompton (both 5-minute walk). Bus: 74, 328, 430, C1, C3. Car parks £35 a day. |

Simon & Susie Thornhill
The Troubadour
263-267 Old Brompton Road,
Earls Court, London, SW5 9JA

| | |
|---|---|
| Tel | +44 (0)20 7370 1434 |
| Email | susie@troubadour.co.uk |
| Web | www.troubadour.co.uk |

## The Royal Foundation of St Katharine

London is full of surprises and this is one of them. St Katharine's was founded by Queen Matilda in 1147, a hospital for the poor and infirm that originally stood next to the Tower of London. In 1273, after a dispute over its control, it passed into the hands of English queens, in whose patronage it has remained ever since (the Queen Mother was a frequent visitor). It moved East and grew into a village on the banks of the Thames, giving its name to St Katharine's Docks (a short walk). In 1825 it moved to Regent's Park, returning to the East End in 1948; it now sits between Tower Bridge and Canary Wharf. Inside, you find a world at odds with the roar of the city: a courtyard garden for quiet reflection; a beautiful chapel that fills with light; a fine old house with muralled meeting rooms. You get comfy sofas in the sitting room, a dining room for simple breakfasts, then bedrooms that give a sense of retreat, some with garden views, all with good beds, power showers and no TVs. Limehouse station (DLR) is a two-minute walk, the London marathon passes outside. There's free parking, too.

| | |
|---|---|
| Rooms | 22 doubles, 1 twin/double, 2 twins: £90–£175. 3 family rooms for 4: £140–£200. 11 singles: £75–£110. |
| Meals | Continental breakfast included. Restaurants nearby. |
| Closed | Christmas. |
| Directions | Docklands Light Railway: Limehouse. Tube: Stepney Green (0.75 mile). Bus: 15, 100, 115, D3. Free parking. |

Mark Aitken
The Royal Foundation of St Katharine
2 Butcher Row, Limehouse,
London, E14 8DS

| | |
|---|---|
| Tel | +44 (0)300 111 1147 |
| Email | reservations@rfsk.org.uk |
| Web | www.rfsk.org.uk |

## The Tommyfield

The Tommyfield is a cool little find – a lively pub for a good pint, a restaurant serving tasty food, a small hotel with well-priced rooms that deliver in spades. It sits between Vauxhall and Kennington, with two tube lines to whizz you into town and three buses passing outside. Inside, you find wooden floors, high ceilings and the odd ionic pillar. Lamps hang above the bar, where you can order a pint of Wandle, then dig into posh fish and chips. Leather banquettes run along big windows, an open kitchen is on display, a couple of booths are nicely private. Rooms are the big surprise, some with painted panelling, others with planked walls. You get pop art, good beds, coffee machines and flat-screen TVs. Excellent bathrooms have walk-in power showers, two have claw-foot baths. On weekdays a continental breakfast is left in your fridge, on weekends the full English is on tap below. As for the food – half-price for residents – pies, steaks and burgers sit alongside pumpkin ravioli, Chateaubriand and banoffee pie. Tuesday is quiz night, Oval is close for the cricket. *Cots available.*

| | |
|---|---|
| Rooms | 4 doubles, 2 twin/doubles: £99–£139. |
| Meals | Continental breakfast included, cooked breakfast on weekends £6–£9. Lunch and dinner from £12.50. Sunday lunch from £13.50. |
| Closed | Never. |
| Directions | Tube: Vauxhall, Kennington, Oval (all a 5-minute walk). Bus: 3, 59, 159. Train: Vauxhall (for Gatwick/Victoria). |

|  | Daniel Glackin |
|---|---|
| | The Tommyfield |
| | 185 Kennington Lane, |
| | Kennington, London, SE11 4EZ |
| Tel | +44 (0)20 7735 1061 |
| Email | info@thetommyfield.co.uk |
| Web | www.thetommyfield.com |

## Strattons

Strattons isn't a hotel, it's a place that tickles your senses. First there's the house, a beautiful Queen Anne villa that wouldn't look out of place in the French countryside. Then you step inside and you're immediately surrounded by art, not one or two interesting pieces, but a treasure trove of wonderful stuff that spills from every corner, sits on every wall or dangles from the odd ceiling. You'll find august busts, contemporary chandeliers, murals by the dozen. Bedrooms are just as good: a carved four-poster in priestly red, Botticelli's angels hovering on a wall, bedside lights that hang from the ceiling. Some have double-ended baths in the room, others a roof terrace with sun loungers. As for the food, there's a deli across the courtyard for homemade treats: naughty cakes, sweet smelling bacon rolls, local cheeses and oils to take home. The restaurant (turn right at the chaise longue), is another art-filled room where local food follows the seasons, perhaps game pie with honey and fennel, slow-cooked beef with roasted roots, hazelnut tart with crème fraîche. Don't miss the Brecks for magical walking.

| | |
|---|---|
| Rooms | 6 doubles, 1 twin/double: £109–£185. |
| | 5 suites for 2: £155–£275. |
| | 2 apartments for 2: £172–£275. |
| | Singles from £92. |
| Meals | Lunch (deli), Mon–Sat, from £6. |
| | Sunday lunch (hotel), from £12. |
| | Dinner, 3 courses, about £30. |
| Closed | Never. |
| Directions | Ash Close runs off north end of market place between W H Brown estate agents & fish & chip restaurant. |

Vanessa & Les Scott
Strattons
4 Ash Close,
Swaffham, PE37 7NH

| | |
|---|---|
| Tel | +44 (0)1760 723845 |
| Email | enquiries@strattonshotel.com |
| Web | www.strattonshotel.com |

## Chalk & Cheese

Andrew and Bridget's quirky Victorian schoolhouse stands on the village green. If its exterior gives the impression of rural decorum, then its interiors do the opposite – this is a whimsical world of antiques and vintage collectibles. It's all refreshingly original, a poke in the eye to the minimalist movement. The big room takes centre stage, its high ceiling and stained glass windows giving an ecclesiastic feel. Mismatching sofas wait below, there's a rocking chair in front of the fire, a bust of Aristotle draped in a feather boa and a lovely bar with lampshades descending from on high. Homely bedrooms are warmly simple and nicely priced. One has a four-poster, another a slipper bath, two next door in a cute cottage can be taken together to self-cater. As for the food, lunch menus are written by hand, a wood-fired pizza oven works overtime at weekends, and you can sup on pea and ham soup, homemade cottage pie and sticky toffee pudding for under £20. There's a conservatory breakfast room, a terrace for summer, even a farm shop and art gallery. Lovely local walking waits as does the coast. *Self-catering option.*

| | |
|---|---|
| Rooms | 3 doubles, 1 twin, 1 four-poster: £70-£95. Singles from £60. Extra beds from £10. |
| Meals | Lunch from £4.50. Dinner, 3 courses, £20-£25 (not Monday or Tuesday). |
| Closed | Never. |
| Directions | North of A1122 between Swaffham and Downham Market. In village, on green. |

Andrew & Bridget Archibald
Chalk & Cheese
1 Eastgate Street, Shouldham,
King's Lynn, PE33 0DD

| | |
|---|---|
| Tel | +44 (0)1366 348039 |
| Email | info@chalkandcheesenorfolk.co.uk |
| Web | www.bed-and-breakfast-west-norfolk.co.uk |

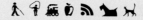

## Congham Hall

This is a lovely old Georgian merchant's house set in 30 acres of parkland, but it's also a cool little spa hotel with an indoor pool and treatment rooms, a perfect blend of old and new. Outside, three gardeners grow flowers for the house, vegetables for the kitchen and keep the gardens looking utterly lovely. Inside, a recent refurbishment has brought contemporary elegance into this smart country house. There's an open fire and beautiful art in the sitting room, a cool little bar with low-hanging lampshades, then an airy dining room for tasty food, perhaps Norfolk asparagus with a soft poached egg, Breckland duck with carrots and parsnips, lemon panna cotta with raspberry sorbet. After which you'll need to atone, so grab a robe from your room and roast away in the sauna before jumping in the pool for a few lengths; some might prefer the hot tub on the terrace. Bedrooms are lovely. Those in the house are more traditional, those in the courtyard have doors onto private terraces. Sandringham is close, as is the North Norfolk coast. Children are very welcome and have their own menu.

| | |
|---|---|
| Rooms | 25 twin/doubles: £125-£245. |
| | 1 suite for 2: £250-£270. |
| Meals | Lunch from £6.50. |
| | Dinner £12.95-£40. |
| | Afternoon tea from £8.75. |
| Closed | Rarely. |
| Directions | A10 to King's Lynn, then A149 north. At second roundabout, take A148 east for 500m, then right for Grimston. Hotel signed. |

Julie Woodhouse
Congham Hall
Grimston,
King's Lynn, PE32 1AH
Tel        +44 (0)1485 600250
Email     info@conghamhallhotel.co.uk
Web      www.conghamhallhotel.co.uk

## The Kings Head

This Edwardian inn was once part of the Sandringham estate. A hundred years on and you can't help noticing it's cut its ties with the old world – this is a small contemporary hotel that serves some of the best food in North Norfolk. It sits in peace on the edge of a small village four miles back from the coast, with the Wash to the west and the beach at Holkham to the north. Airy interiors have a big city feel: a grand piano in the sitting room; sleek sofas in front of an open fire; an attractive bar, where French wines, American cocktails and English ales share the same menu. There's big art on the walls, doors onto a pretty side terrace, a play area for children and a garden for summer. A glass staircase sweeps you up to good rooms. Some are big, some smaller, all have the same comforts: warm colours, smart fabrics, good beds, perhaps a sofa. Bathrooms hit the spot, too. Back downstairs, delicious food waits in the restaurant, perhaps Cromer crab, local game, Armagnac brûlée with Agen prunes. Sandringham and Houghton Hall are both close. Hanseatic King's Lynn is a big surprise.

| | |
|---|---|
| Rooms | 1 double, 11 twin/doubles: £95-£175. Singles from £85. Extra beds £25. Dinner, B&B from £80 per person. |
| Meals | Lunch from £6. Dinner, 3 courses, £25-£35. |
| Closed | Never. |
| Directions | A148 east from King's Lynn, then B1153 north after Hillington. On left after 4 miles. In village. |

Craig Jackson
The Kings Head
Lynn Road, Great Bircham,
King's Lynn, PE31 6RJ

Tel     +44 (0)1485 578265
Email   info@thekingsheadhotel.co.uk
Web    www.the-kings-head-bircham.co.uk

## Magazine Wood

If you want big views, deep peace and a thick slice of luxury up on the North Norfolk coast, then Magazine Wood may well be for you. Jonathan and Pip's boutique B&B sits deep in the country on the family farm, but only a couple of miles back from the coast. It's a bit like those places in Southeast Asia, a self-contained suite away from the main house with a super-smart bathroom, a big stylish bedroom, then doors onto a terrace, where you sit for hours gazing out over fields; sunsets are amazing, starry skies on clear nights astound. Inside, you find the lap of luxury: contemporary design, chic fabrics, calming colours, the best linen on terrific beds. You get binoculars, a small sofa and a dining table, then tablets for movies on demand, the daily papers and a guide to local restaurants. A continental breakfast is left in your room – croissants, juice, cereals, fruit salad – but you can order cooked dishes, too. You're on the Peddars Way, walks start from the front door. A clutch of local pubs wait for a good dinner; taxis can be arranged to whisk you there and back. *Minimum stay: 2 nights June – September.*

| | |
|---|---|
| Rooms | 3 doubles: £105–£139. |
| Meals | Continental breakfast included, full English £6. Pubs and restaurants nearby. |
| Closed | One week at Christmas. |
| Directions | West from Docking on B1454. Enter village at 40mph sign and right after 1st house. On left. |

**Pip & Jonathan Barber**
Magazine Wood
Peddars Way, Sedgeford,
Hunstanton, PE36 5LW

| | |
|---|---|
| Tel | +44 (0)1485 570422 |
| Email | relax@magazinewood.co.uk |
| Web | www.magazinewood.co.uk |

## The White Horse

A smart little inn on the North Norfolk coast with beautiful views that shoot across tidal marshes to Scolt Head Island. At high tide boats bob, birds swoop and the water laps at the garden edge; at low tide, the marshes appear and fishermen come to harvest the mussels and oysters. In summer you can eat on the terrace and drink it all in, then drop down to the coastal path at the bottom of the garden and follow your nose. But the view here is weather-proofed – a big conservatory restaurant looks out on it all. It's a popular haunt for locals and visitors alike, who come for consistently good food, perhaps oysters from the bay, sea bass with squid risotto, lemon tart with a chocolate macaroon. There's a sunken garden that catches the sun, then an open fire in the locals' bar, where you'll find well-kept ales, the daily papers, bar billiards and sofas for a game of scrabble. Chic, uncluttered bedrooms have seaside colours, robes for spotless bathrooms, good beds and fine linen. Some in the main house have the view, dog-friendly garden rooms have terraces. Sandringham is close. *Minimum stay: 2 nights at weekends.*

| Rooms | 11 doubles, 4 twins: £100–£230. Extra beds £30. Cots £5. Dogs £10. |
|---|---|
| Meals | Lunch & bar meals from £9.95. Dinner from £13.95. |
| Closed | Never. |
| Directions | Midway between Hunstanton & Wells-next-the-Sea on A149. |

Cliff & James Nye
The White Horse
Brancaster Staithe, PE31 8BY
Tel     +44 (0)1485 210262
Email   reception@whitehorsebrancaster.co.uk
Web     www.whitehorsebrancaster.co.uk

## The Hoste

Nelson was a local, now it's farmers and film stars who jostle at the bar. In its 300-year history the Hoste has been a court house, a livestock market and a brothel. These days it's a Norfolk institution, a default destination for those in search of a little luxury. It's all things to all men: a fabulous restaurant, a conservatory café, a beautiful country pub. Inside, stylish interiors come as standard with warm colours, panelled walls and beautiful art everywhere. Best of all, it never stands still. The airy new garden room hums with happy guests, a fine spot for breakfast with a wall of glass that opens onto a lawned terrace. Elsewhere, four new bedrooms are predictably lovely, like all rooms at the Hoste, each refurbished every five years. You get sofas, four-posters, sleigh beds and fabulous bathrooms, you can even sleep in a railway carriage over at Railway House. As for the food, it's as local as possible, perhaps Brancaster oysters, Norfolk rib-eye, treacle tart with blood orange ice-cream. There's a beauty spa, live jazz and a magical coastline for windswept walks.

| | |
|---|---|
| Rooms | 45 twin/doubles: £170–£230. 9 self-catering cottages for 6: £160–£200. Railway House – 7 twin/doubles: £130–£190. Railway House – 1 train carriage for 2: £170–£230. Singles from £110. Dinner, B&B from £85 per person. |
| Meals | Lunch from £6. Dinner, 3 courses, from £25. Sunday lunch from £14. |
| Closed | Never. |
| Directions | On B1155 for Burnham Market. By green & church in village centre. |

Martin DeSousa
The Hoste
The Green, Burnham Market,
King's Lynn, PE31 8HD

| | |
|---|---|
| Tel | +44 (0)1328 738777 |
| Email | reservations@thehoste.com |
| Web | www.thehoste.com |

## The Globe Inn at Wells-next-the-Sea

Wells is one of the prettiest towns on the North Norfolk coast. Fisherman land their catch on the quay, a sandy beach runs for a mile or two, pine trees soar above local fields. As for the Globe, it sits on The Buttlands, a smart square of Georgian houses that rings the village green. There's a terrace at the front for a pint in the sun, a courtyard to the side for dinner in summer, then an airy bar that floods with light through big bay windows. Inside, you find wooden floors, the odd sofa, seaside colours and a wood-burner for chilly days. Bedrooms, all recently refurbished, have a wall of paper, padded heads, crisp white linen on excellent beds and waffled robes in pretty bathrooms. Three have views of the green, all have local art and flat-screen TVs. Back downstairs, there's good food in the restaurant, which opens onto the courtyard, perhaps pan-fried fillet of sea bass, a venison burger or Norfolk duck with ginger and rhubarb. Rooms connect for families, dogs are very welcome. Don't miss Titchwell for migrating birds or Blakeney for lounging seals. Boat trips can be arranged, too. *Minimum stay: 2 nights at weekends.*

| | |
|---|---|
| Rooms | 5 doubles, 2 twin/doubles: £110–£160. Extra bed/sofabed available £30 per person per night. |
| Meals | Lunch from £6. Dinner, 3 courses, £25–£30. |
| Closed | Rarely. |
| Directions | A149 east into Wells. In village, above quay, on green. |

|  |  |
|---|---|
|  | Antonia & Stephen Bournes |
|  | The Globe Inn at Wells-next-the-Sea |
|  | The Buttlands, |
|  | Wells-Next-The-Sea, NR23 1EU |
| Tel | +44 (0)1328 710206 |
| Email | hello@theglobeatwells.co.uk |
| Web | www.theglobeatwells.co.uk |

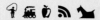

## The Blakeney Hotel

The view here is matchless, a clean sweep across the salt marshes up to Blakeney Point. The estuary passes five paces from the front door and guests are prone to fall into graceful inertia and watch the boats slide by. You can do this from a sun-trapping terrace, a convivial bar, a traditional restaurant and the stunning first-floor sitting room that comes with binoculars to follow the wildlife. Most bedrooms have been refurbished in a contemporary country-house style with lovely fabrics, cool colours, an armchair or sofa, then gorgeous bathrooms; those at the front have the view. Six traditional rooms remain – simpler, but still pretty, with yellow and red chintz, good beds and crisp linen. There's a bar for light lunches, a drawing room with an open fire, then a stylish indoor pool with steam room and sauna; a snooker room and children's games' room wait too. Outside, paths lead down to the marshes, there are seals to spot, birds to watch, links golf at Sheringham and Cromer. Lovely food awaits your return, perhaps potted brown shrimps, Gressingham duck, sticky toffee pudding.

| | |
|---|---|
| Rooms | 19 doubles, 36 twin/doubles: £182-£322. 8 singles: £91-£149. |
| Meals | Lunch from £9.50. Dinner, 3 courses, £29-£43.50. |
| Closed | Never. |
| Directions | A148 north from Fakenham, then B1156 north to Blakeney. In village on quay. |

Stannard Family
The Blakeney Hotel
The Quay, Blakeney,
Holt, NR25 7NE

| | |
|---|---|
| Tel | +44 (0)1263 740797 |
| Email | reception@blakeneyhotel.co.uk |
| Web | www.blakeneyhotel.co.uk |

## Cley Windmill

The setting here is magical: rushes flutter in the salt marsh, raised paths lead off to the sea, a vast sky hangs overhead. The windmill, now with new sails, dates to 1713. It became a house in the 1920s, the family home of James Blunt no less. Square rooms are bigger, a couple have sofas, while round rooms in the tower are impossibly romantic (one is for mountaineers only). Six rooms are in the mill and you really want to go for these, though the cottage is set up for self-catering and visiting dogs. Inside, you find the loveliest drawing room – low ceiling, open fire, stripped floorboards and a cute little window seat. Bedrooms have a chic feel with Farrow & Ball colours, beautiful fabrics, the odd claw-foot bath. Those in the tower (with compact shower rooms) get smaller as you rise, but the view improves with every step; there's a viewing platform halfway up for all. You eat in a pretty dining room, perhaps crab fishcakes, Norfolk Lamb, pear tarte tatin with cinnamon ice cream. But plans are afoot to build an orangery and when it's ready, you'll eat there surrounded by the walled garden. *Minimum stay: 2 nights.*

| | |
|---|---|
| Rooms | 6 doubles, 2 twin/doubles: £159-£219. 1 self-catering cottage for 4: £390 for 3 days; extra days £50-£130; 7 days £495-£625. Children under 12, £30. |
| Meals | Dinner, 3 courses, £27.50-£32.50. |
| Closed | Christmas. |
| Directions | Head east through Cley on A149. Mill signed on left in village. |

Simon Whatling
Cley Windmill
The Quay, Cley,
Holt, NR25 7RP

| | |
|---|---|
| Tel | +44 (0)1263 740209 |
| Email | info@cleywindmill.co.uk |
| Web | www.cleywindmill.co.uk |

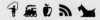

## Saracens Head

Lost in the lanes of deepest Norfolk, an English inn that's hard to match. Outside, Georgian red-brick walls stand to attention at the front, but nip round the back and find them at ease in a beautiful courtyard where you can knock back a pint of Wherry in the evening sun before slipping inside to eat. Tim and Janie upped sticks from the Alps, unable to resist the allure of this lovely old inn. A sympathetic refurbishment has worked its magic, but the spirit remains the same: this is a country-house pub with lovely staff who go the extra mile. Downstairs the bar hums with happy locals who come for Norfolk ales and good French wines, while the food in the restaurant is as good as ever: Norfolk pheasant and rabbit terrine, wild duck or Cromer crab, treacle tart and caramel ice-cream. Upstairs, there's a sitting room on the landing, then six pretty rooms. All have have smart carpets, wooden furniture, comfy beds and sparkling bathrooms. There's masses to do: ancient Norwich, the coast at Cromer, golf on the cliffs at Sheringham, Blickling Hall, a Jacobean pile. Don't miss Sunday lunch.

| | |
|---|---|
| Rooms | 5 twin/doubles: £100-£110. 1 family room for 4: £110-£140. Singles from £70. |
| Meals | Lunch from £6.50. Sunday lunch from £13.50 Dinner, 3 courses, £25-£35. Not Mon; or Tue lunch October-June. |
| Closed | Christmas. |
| Directions | From Norwich A140 past Aylsham, then 3rd left for Erpingham. Right into Calthorpe, through village, straight out the other side (not right). On right after about 0.5 miles. |

Tim & Janie Elwes
Saracens Head
Wolterton,
Norwich, NR11 7LZ

Tel +44 (0)1263 768909
Email info@saracenshead-norfolk.co.uk
Web www.saracenshead-norfolk.co.uk

## Beechwood Hotel

The Beechwood is charming, an old-school hotel in a sleepy corner of England with an impressive level of service. It sits between Norwich and Cromer in a small market town where Nelson spent his schooldays. Its hallmarks are generous prices, lovely staff, and Don and Lindsay, who look after their guests in style. Outside, you find an Virginia creeper-clad façade, inside, you get smartly tiled floors, a sitting-room bar, an attractive restaurant for local food and a pretty garden for afternoon tea in summer. There's a small library for the daily papers, then a collection of Agatha Christie novels – she was a frequent visitor in the 1920s and occasionally came to write. Bedrooms have a warm, traditional feel: pretty florals, oak furniture, crisp white linen for Vi-Spring mattresses. Two are small, most have sofas, garden rooms have slipper baths. You get robes and good showers, usually a bath, too. As for the food, most is sourced within ten miles, perhaps Morston mussels, fillet of beef, sticky toffee pudding. Cliff-top walks and sandy beaches wait, as does beautiful Norwich.
*Minimum stay: 2 nights dinner, B&B at weekends.*

| | |
|---|---|
| Rooms | 12 doubles, 2 twins, 3 four-posters: £100–£175. |
| Meals | Dinner, 3 courses, £40. |
| Closed | Rarely. |
| Directions | North from Norwich on B1150 and into North Walsham. Under railway bridge, left at traffic lights, right at next traffic lights, on left after 500m. |

| | |
|---|---|
| | **Don Birch & Lindsay Spalding** |
| | Beechwood Hotel |
| | 20 Cromer Road, |
| | North Walsham, NR28 0HD |
| Tel | +44 (0)1692 403231 |
| Email | info@beechwood-hotel.co.uk |
| Web | www.beechwood-hotel.co.uk |

## The Fritton Arms

This is a small, chic, country-house inn on the Somerleyton estate – well worth the detour to this far-flung realm. And stately it is, 5,000 acres of green and pleasant land, with parkland behind running down to Fritton Lake. Inside, airy interiors mix original features with contemporary design. You'll find period colours, rugs on stripped floors, 16th-century sand-blasted beams, then beautifully upholstered armchairs in front of a lovely old fireplace. There are sofas in the sitting room, fresh flowers on the piano, a roaring fire in the well-stocked bar. Food is served here and there: at green leather booths in the Fish Room; in the low-ceilinged restaurant with original brick walls; or out on the gravelled terrace in summer. Try wood-fired pizzas, sizzling steaks, perhaps ham hock terrine, sea bass with chorizo, a plate of local cheeses. Attractive bedrooms have warm colours, smart fabrics, comfy beds, white robes for good bathrooms. Some in the eaves are open to the rafters, bigger rooms may have a sofa. Don't miss Somerleyton Hall, one of the finest in the land. The Broads are close.

| | |
|---|---|
| Rooms | 6 doubles, 3 twin/doubles: £110–£140. Singles from £95. Extra beds £25. |
| Meals | Lunch from £5.50. Dinner, 3 courses, £25-30. Sunday lunch from £12.50. |
| Closed | Rarely. |
| Directions | From Beccles A143 north for Great Yarmouth. In Fritton, right, signed Fritton Lake. Hotel on right before lake. |

Ben Davenport
The Fritton Arms
Church Lane, Fritton,
Great Yarmouth, NR31 9HA

| | |
|---|---|
| Tel | +44 (0)1493 484008 |
| Email | info@frittonarms.co.uk |
| Web | www.frittonarms.co.uk |

## The Pheasant Inn

A super little inn lost in beautiful country, the kind you hope to chance upon. The Kershaws run it with great passion and an instinctive understanding of its traditions. The bars are wonderful. Brass beer taps glow, 100-year old photos of the local community hang on stone walls, the clock above the fire keeps perfect time. Fires burn, bowler hats and saddles pop up here and there, varnished ceilings shine. House ales are expertly kept, Timothy Taylor's and Wylam waiting for thirsty souls. Fruit and vegetables come from the garden, while Robin's lovely food hits the spot perfectly, perhaps twice-baked cheese soufflé, slow-roasted Northumberland lamb, brioche and marmalade bread and butter pudding; as for Sunday lunch, *The Observer* voted it 'Best in the North'. Bedrooms in the old hay barn are light and airy, cute and cosy, great value for money. You're in the Northumberland National Park – no traffic jams, not too much hurry. You can sail on the lake, cycle round it or take to the hills and walk. For £10 you can also gaze into the universe at the Kielder Observatory (best in winter). Brilliant. *Minimum stay: 2 nights at weekends.*

| | |
|---|---|
| Rooms | 4 doubles, 3 twins: £95–£100. |
| | 1 family room for 4: £95–£140. |
| | Singles from £65. |
| | Dinner, B&B from £70 per person. |
| | Extra bed/sofabed available £15 per person per night. |
| Meals | Bar meals from £9.95. |
| | Sunday lunch from £11.50. |
| | Dinner, 3 courses, £20–£30. |
| Closed | Christmas. |
| Directions | From Bellingham follow signs west to Kielder Water & Falstone for 9 miles. On left, 1 mile short of Kielder Water. |

Walter, Irene & Robin Kershaw
The Pheasant Inn
Stannersburn,
Hexham, NE48 1DD

| | |
|---|---|
| Tel | +44 (0)1434 240382 |
| Email | stay@thepheasantinn.com |
| Web | www.thepheasantinn.com |

## Eshott Hall

An utterly gorgeous Palladian mansion set in 35 acres of medieval woodlands and pasture. Wisteria fans out at the front, there's an ancient fernery, paths that weave past rare trees, an extremely productive kitchen garden. Inside is equally grand, and all the better for a recent refurbishment. You find Corinthian columns and a fine ornate ceiling in the drawing room, a roaring fire and leather sofas in the striking library, then a panelled dining room from which you may spot the odd deer tucking into the garden roses. Nip up the stairs, passing a stained-glass window designed by William Morris, and find a clutch of light-filled bedrooms. A couple come with free-standing baths in the room, others have high ceilings, garden views, perhaps a sofa or a four-poster bed. Chic bathrooms have natural stone, white robes and spoiling oils. There's tennis in the garden, peace at every turn, then white beaches, Hadrian's Wall, Holy Island and Alnwick Castle. Come back for a good dinner, perhaps potted Craster crab, Ingram Valley lamb, pear tarte tatin with mascarpone ice-cream. Fabulous.

| | |
|---|---|
| Rooms | 11 twin/doubles: £120–£250. |
| | Eshott Grange: 5 doubles: £120–£250. |
| | Singles from £90. |
| | Dinner, B&B from £95 p.p. |
| Meals | Lunch from £6. |
| | Dinner, 3 courses, about £35. |
| | Sunday lunch from £17.50. |
| Closed | Never. |
| Directions | East off A1 7 miles north of Morpeth, 9 miles south of Alnwick, at Eshott signpost. Hall gates approx. 1 mile down lane. |

Mark Rawlings–Lloyd
Eshott Hall
Eshott,
Morpeth, NE65 9EN

| | |
|---|---|
| Tel | +44 (0)1670 787454 |
| Email | info@eshotthall.co.uk |
| Web | www.eshotthall.co.uk |

## Hart's Nottingham

A small enclave of good things. You're on the smart side of town at the end of a cul-de-sac, thus remarkably quiet. You're also at the top of the hill and close to the castle with exceptional views that sweep south for ten miles; at night, a carpet of light sparkles. Inside, cool lines and travertine marble greet you in reception. Bedrooms are excellent, not huge, but perfectly adequate and extremely well designed. All come with wide-screen TVs, Bose sound systems, super little bathrooms and king-size beds wrapped in crisp white cotton. Those on the ground floor open onto a fine garden, each with a terrace where you can breakfast in good weather; rooms on higher floors have better views (six overlook the courtyard). A cool little bar, the hub of the hotel, is open for breakfast, lunch and dinner, and Hart's Restaurant across the courtyard offers fabulous food, perhaps pan-fried wood pigeon with blackberries, free-range chicken with wild garlic, tarte tatin with caramel ice cream. There's a private car park for hotel guests and a small gym for those who must.

| | |
|---|---|
| Rooms | 29 doubles: £129–£179. |
| | 2 suites for 2: £265. |
| | 1 family room for 4: £139–£197. |
| Meals | Continental breakfast £9, full English £14. |
| | Bar snacks from £3.50. |
| | Lunch from £14.95. |
| | Dinner, 3 courses, from £24. |
| Closed | Never. |
| Directions | M1 junc. 24, then follow signs for |
| | city centre and Nottingham Castle. |
| | Left into Park Row from Maid Marian |
| | Way. Hotel on left at top of hill. |
| | Parking £8.50/night. |

Adam Worthington
Hart's Nottingham
Standard Hill, Park Row,
Nottingham, NG1 6GN

Tel      +44 (0)115 988 1900
Email    reception@hartshotel.co.uk
Web      www.hartsnottingham.co.uk

## Langar Hall

Langar Hall is one of the loveliest places in this book – reason enough to come to Nottinghamshire – and Imogen's exquisite style and natural joie de vivre make this a mecca for those in search of an informal country house with a touch of bohemian flair. The house sits at the top of a hardly noticeable hill in glorious parkland, bang next door to the church. Imo's family came 150 years ago, building on the site of Admiral Lord Howe's burned-down home. Much of what fills the house arrived then and it's easy to feel intoxicated by beautiful things: statues and busts, a pillared dining room, ancient tomes in overflowing bookshelves, an eclectic collection of oil paintings. Bedrooms are wonderful, some resplendent with antiques, others with fabrics draped from beams or trompe l'œil panelling. Heavenly food is a big treat, too, perhaps wild garlic soup, local venison, pistachio soufflé with lemon sorbet. There's a pretty conservatory for afternoon tea that opens onto a terrace, then grounds all around for medieval fishponds, an adventure play area and, once a year, Shakespeare on the lawn. One of a kind.

| | |
|---|---|
| Rooms | 7 doubles, 2 twins, 1 four-poster: £100–£199. 1 suite for 2: £199. 1 chalet for 2: £100–£199. |
| Meals | Lunch from £18.50. Dinner, 3 courses, £25–£35. |
| Closed | Never. |
| Directions | From Nottingham A52 towards Grantham. Right, signed Cropwell Bishop, then straight on for 5 miles. House next to church on edge of village, signed. |

Imogen Skirving
Langar Hall
Church Lane, Langar,
Nottingham, NG13 9HG

| | |
|---|---|
| Tel | +44 (0)1949 860559 |
| Email | info@langarhall.co.uk |
| Web | www.langarhall.com |

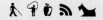

## The Trout at Tadpole Bridge

A 17th-century Cotswold inn on the banks of the Thames; pick up a pint, drift into the garden, watch the world float by. Inside you find all the trimmings of a lovely old pub: timber frames, exposed stone walls, a wood-burner to keep things toasty, local ales on tap at the bar. Logs are piled high in alcoves, good art hangs on the walls, pretty rugs cover old flagstones. Delicious food ranges from bar classics to posh nosh, perhaps fish and chips or steak and ale pie, then rack of lamb with a rosemary crust or Gressingham duck with ginger purée. Bedrooms at the back are away from the crowd; three open onto a small courtyard where wild roses ramble. You get smart fabrics, trim carpets, monsoon showers (one room has a claw-foot bath), DVD players, flat-screen TVs and a library of films. Sleigh beds, brass beds, smartly upholstered armchairs... one room even has a roof terrace. You can watch boats pass from the breakfast table, feast on local sausages, tuck into homemade marmalade courtesy of Helen's mum. Oxford is close, there are maps for walkers, you can even get married in the garden. *Minimum stay: 2 nights at weekends.*

| | |
|---|---|
| Rooms | 2 doubles, 3 twin/doubles: £130. 1 suite for 2: £160. Singles from £85. |
| Meals | Lunch from £5. Dinner, 3 courses, about £30. Sunday lunch from £14.95. |
| Closed | Christmas Day & Boxing Day. |
| Directions | A420 southwest from Oxford for Swindon. After 13 miles right for Tadpole Bridge. Pub on right by bridge. |

Gareth & Helen Pugh
The Trout at Tadpole Bridge
Buckland Marsh,
Faringdon, SN7 8RF

| | |
|---|---|
| Tel | +44 (0)1367 870382 |
| Email | info@trout-inn.co.uk |
| Web | www.trout-inn.co.uk |

## Old Bank Hotel

You're in the heart of old Oxford, with Merton College and Christ Church Meadow to the south, the Radcliffe Camera and the Bodleian Library to the north, and University College and the Botanic Gardens at Magdalen Bridge to the east. As for the Old Bank, its stylish interiors are home to an exceptional collection of modern art and photography. The hub is the old tiller's hall, now a cocktail bar and brasserie, with six arched windows overlooking the high street. Food is on tap all day long, anything from a pizza or a steak to afternoon tea, with meat from the owner's farm and fish from the Channel Islands. Bedrooms are gorgeous: fine beds, piles of cushions, original art, robes in chic bathrooms. Some have padded window seats, others have sofas, all have flat-screen TVs and good WiFi. Staff are lovely, beds are turned down, the daily papers delivered to your door. There's a decked courtyard for breakfast in summer, free off-street parking, then daily walking tours for guests. The University Church of St Mary stands opposite, so climb its tower for the best views of Oxford. *Minimum stay: 2 nights at weekends.*

| | |
|---|---|
| Rooms | 20 doubles, 21 twin/doubles: £170–£290. 1 suite for 5: £305–£500. |
| Meals | Breakfast £5–£15. Lunch & dinner £5–£30. Afternoon tea from £6.95. |
| Closed | Never. |
| Directions | Cross Magdalen Bridge for city centre. Straight through 1st set of lights, then left into Merton St. Follow road right; 1st right into Magpie Lane. Car park 2nd right. |

Ben Truesdale
Old Bank Hotel
92-94 High Street,
Oxford, OX1 4BJ

| | |
|---|---|
| Tel | +44 (0)1865 799599 |
| Email | info@oldbank-hotel.co.uk |
| Web | www.oldbank-hotel.co.uk |

## Old Parsonage Hotel

The Old Parsonage has been at the centre of Oxford life for over 350 years. It stands in the middle of town on land owned by University College and was once home to Oscar Wilde. It is one of the loveliest places to stay in town, not least due to a spectacular refurbishment that has touched every corner. Chief among its virtues are its shaded dining terrace, its exceptional art collection, and its first-floor library (curated by Philip Blackwell), which opens onto a small roof terrace. Inside, logs smoulder in an ancient fireplace, newspapers wait by mullioned windows, fresh flowers scent the air. The restaurant doubles as an art gallery, its charcoal walls crammed with portraits. It's a theatrical setting for a good meal, perhaps Jersey crab, duck with dandelion, rhubarb crumble with rhubarb ice cream. Bedrooms are delicious: pale greys, Oxford art, sublime white marble bathrooms with robes and pots of spoiling oils. Expect the best beds, the crispest linen, pretty throws and padded bedheads. As for Oxford, there are free guided walking tours for guests every day and picnics for lunch by the river. *Minimum stay: 2 nights at weekends.*

| | |
|---|---|
| Rooms | 24 doubles, 5 twins: £195-£405. 6 suites for 3: £315-£485. |
| Meals | Breakfast £5-£15. Lunch from £18.50. Afternoon tea from £9. Dinner, 3 courses, about £35. |
| Closed | Never. |
| Directions | From A40 ring road, south onto Banbury Road; thro' Summertown and hotel on right just before St Giles church. |

Rebecca Mofford
Old Parsonage Hotel
1 Banbury Road,
Oxford, OX2 6NN

| | |
|---|---|
| Tel | +44 (0)1865 310210 |
| Email | info@oldparsonage-hotel.co.uk |
| Web | www.oldparsonage-hotel.co.uk |

## The Feathers Hotel

Woodstock is a slice of old England, its golden cottages stitched together seamlessly. It's intrinsically linked to Blenheim Palace, one of Britain's finest houses, seat of the Dukes of Marlborough, birthplace of Winston Churchill. You can stroll up in five minutes, drop your jaw, then come back for afternoon tea. The hotel sits serenely on the high street with a carriage arch leading into a stone courtyard where you sit in summer sipping Pimm's; just heavenly. Inside, elegant, uncluttered interiors keep things simple: beautiful art, smouldering fires, a wall or two of original panelling, flowers everywhere. Ancient windows flood the place with light, there are colourful rugs on polished wooden floors, then more gin than you can shake a stick at in the sitting-room bar (181 different bottles). Bedrooms are dreamy with beautiful fabrics, lovely beds, mohair throws, delicious wallpapers. Some have sofas, all come with robes in fancy bathrooms. Back downstairs you'll find delicious food in the restaurant, perhaps crab risotto, grilled lemon sole, treacle tart with chocolate ice-cream. Oxford is close. *Minimum stay: 2 nights at weekends in summer.*

| | |
|---|---|
| Rooms | 13 doubles, 3 twin/doubles: £169–£229. 5 suites for 2: £259–£319. Singles from £129. |
| Meals | Lunch from £5. Dinner £39.95–£49.95 (not Sun eve). |
| Closed | Never. |
| Directions | North from Oxford on A44. In Woodstock left after traffic lights & hotel on left. |

Dominic Bishop
The Feathers Hotel
Market Street,
Woodstock, OX20 1SX

| | |
|---|---|
| Tel | +44 (0)1993 812291 |
| Email | enquiries@feathers.co.uk |
| Web | www.feathers.co.uk |

## The Kings Head Inn

The sort of inn that defines this country: a 16th-century cider house made of ancient stone that sits on the green in a Cotswold village with free-range hens strutting their stuff and a family of ducks bathing in the pond. Inside, locals gather to chew the cud, scoff great food and wash it down with a cleansing ale. The fire burns all year, you get low ceilings, painted stone walls, country rugs on flagstone floors. Bedrooms, all different, are scattered about; all are well priced. Those in the main house have more character, those in the courtyard are bigger (and quieter). You'll find painted wood, lots of colour, pretty fabrics, spotless bathrooms; most have great views, too. Breakfast and supper are taken in a pretty dining room (exposed stone walls, pale wood tables), while you can lunch by the fire in the bar on Cornish scallops, steak and ale pie, then a plate of British cheeses. There are lovely unpompous touches like jugs of cow parsley in the loo, and loads to do: antiques in Stow, golf at Burford, walking and riding through gorgeous terrain. The front terrace teems with life in summer. *Minimum stay: 2 nights at weekends.*

| | |
|---|---|
| Rooms | 9 doubles, 3 twin/doubles: £100–£135. Singles from £80. |
| Meals | Lunch from £7.50. Dinner, 3 courses, about £30. Sunday lunch £15. |
| Closed | 25 December to 27 December. |
| Directions | East out of Stow-on-the-Wold on A436, then right onto B4450 for Bledington. Pub in village on green. |

Archie & Nicola Orr-Ewing
The Kings Head Inn
The Green, Bledington,
Chipping Norton, OX7 6XQ

| | |
|---|---|
| Tel | +44 (0)1608 658365 |
| Email | info@kingsheadinn.net |
| Web | www.kingsheadinn.net |

## The Swan

Free-range bantams strut in the garden, a pint of Hooky waits at the bar. This lovely old pub sits in glorious country with the river Windrush passing ten paces from the front door and the village cricket pitch waiting beyond. It started life as a water mill and stands on the Devonshire estate, hence all the pictures of the Mitford sisters hanging on the walls. Outside, wisteria wanders along golden stone and creepers blush red in the autumn sun. Interiors are delicious: low ceilings, open fires, beautiful windows, stone walls. Over the years thirsty feet have worn grooves into 400-year-old flagstones, so follow in their footsteps and stop for a drink at the bar, then eat from a seasonal menu that brims with local produce: curried sweet potato soup, Foxbury Farm chargrilled steak, dark chocolate and ginger pot. Doors in the conservatory restaurant open onto the garden terrace in fine weather. Bedrooms in the old forge hit the spot: very pretty, nicely priced, super-comfy beds. Expect 15th-century walls, 21st-century interior design and a pink chaise longue in the suite. Burford is close.

| | |
|---|---|
| Rooms | 4 doubles, 1 twin: £125–£130. 1 suite for 2: £180–£195. Cottage Rooms: 5 twin/doubles: £125–£150. Singles from £70. |
| Meals | Lunch from £5. Dinner, 3 courses, about £30. Sunday lunch from £14.95. |
| Closed | Christmas Day & Boxing Day. |
| Directions | West from Oxford on A40 for Cheltenham/Burford. Past Witney & village signed right at 1st r'bout. |

Archie & Nicola Orr-Ewing
The Swan
Swinbrook, Burford, OX18 4DY

| | |
|---|---|
| Tel | +44 (0)1993 823339 |
| Email | info@theswanswinbrook.co.uk |
| Web | www.theswanswinbrook.co.uk |

## Burford House

This pretty town of golden stone slips down hill to the river Windrush, which flows past a Norman church on its way into the country. It's a lovely spot with footpaths you can follow into Cotswold heaven, but there's history, too. Cromwell held a band of Levellers here in 1649 and their murals survive in the church, which doubled as their prison. Halfway up the hill you find Burford House, a Grade II-listed draper's shop that came to life after the civil war. Interiors sweep you back to the soft elegance of old England: a smart sitting room with the daily papers, a smouldering wood-burner in the attractive bar, a pretty courtyard for lunch in the sun. You find timber frames, stone walls, mullioned windows, freshly-cut flowers. Bedrooms are lovely, two across the courtyard in the coach house. You get period colours, the odd beam, perhaps an old four-poster or a claw-foot bath. All come with super beds, woollen blankets and robes in good bathrooms. Breakfast is a treat, too, and you eat in a smart dining room with theatre posters on the wall. Good restaurants are on the doorstep. Brilliant. *Min. stay: 2 nights at weekends during summer.*

| | |
|---|---|
| Rooms | 4 twin/doubles, 2 four-posters: £125-£225. 1 family room for 4: £175-£250. |
| Meals | Lunch from £6.95. Restaurants on the high street. |
| Closed | Rarely. |
| Directions | In centre of Burford, halfway down hill. Free on-street parking, free public car park nearby. |

Ian Hawkins
Burford House
99 High Street,
Burford, OX18 4QA

| | |
|---|---|
| Tel | +44 (0)1993 823151 |
| Email | stay@burfordhouse.co.uk |
| Web | www.burford-house.co.uk |

## The Feathered Nest Country Inn

The village is tiny, the view is fantastic, the bar is lively, the rooms are a treat. This 300-year-old malthouse sits in 55 acres of green and pleasant land and is utterly gorgeous inside and out. The view from the garden is one of the best in the Cotswolds – a five-mile sweep across quilted fields to a distant ridge. Interiors are just as good. A warm rustic style mixes beautifully with original timbers and old stone walls. A fire smoulders in the lovely bar, doors in the restaurant open onto the terrace, the garden room has tartan walls and the white wine cellar on display. Bedrooms delight. One is enormous, two have the view, beds are dressed in crisp linen. Most have power showers, one has a claw-foot bath, all have robes. You get coffee machines and iPod docks, too. Delicious food waits downstairs, perhaps octopus with lemon and garlic, pollock with saffron and fennel, tarte tatin with vanilla ice cream. You eat on the terrace in summer looking out on the lake and distant farms. A couple of luxurious cabins are soon to be sprinkled across the grounds – Amanda and Tony do nothing by halves. Magical. *Minimum stay: 2 nights at weekends.*

| | |
|---|---|
| Rooms | 3 doubles: £190-£250. |
| | Singles from £160. |
| Meals | Lunch & dinner £6.50-£30. |
| | Not Sunday night. |
| Closed | Mondays (except Bank Holidays). |
| Directions | North from Burford on A424 for |
| | Stow-on-the-Wold. After 4 miles right |
| | for Nether Westcote. In village. |

|  | Tony & Amanda Timmer |
|---|---|
| | The Feathered Nest Country Inn |
| | Nether Westcote, |
| | Chipping Norton, OX7 6SD |
| Tel | +44 (0)1993 833030 |
| Email | reservations@thefeatherednestinn.co.uk |
| Web | www.thefeatherednestinn.co.uk |

## The Olive Branch

A lovely pub in a sleepy Rutland village, where bridle paths lead out across peaceful fields. It dates to the 17th century and is built of Clipsham stone, as is York Minster. Inside, a warm, informal, rustic chic hits the spot perfectly with open fires, old beams, stone walls and choir stalls in the bar. But there's more here than cool design. This is a place to come and eat great food, the lovely, local seasonal stuff that's cooked with passion by Sean and his brigade, perhaps potted pork and stilton with apple jelly, haunch of venison with a juniper fondant, then a boozy rhubarb trifle. Bedrooms in Beech House across the lane are gorgeous. Three have terraces, one has a free-standing bath, all come with crisp linen, pretty beds, Roberts radios and real coffee. Super breakfasts — smoothies, boiled eggs and soldiers, the full cooked works — are served in a stone-walled barn with flames leaping in the wood-burner. The front garden fills in summer, the sloe gin comes from local berries, and Newark is close for the biggest antiques market in Europe. Picnic hampers can be arranged. A total gem.

| | |
|---|---|
| Rooms | 5 doubles, 1 family room for 4: £115–£195. Singles from £97.50. Extra beds £30. |
| Meals | Lunch from £6.25. Dinner, 3 courses, £25–£35. Sunday lunch from £17.50. |
| Closed | Rarely. |
| Directions | A1 5 miles north of Stamford, then exit onto B668. Right & right again for Clipsham. In village (Beech House across the road from The Olive Branch). |

AWARD
WINNER

Fabulous food

Ben Jones & Sean Hope
The Olive Branch
Main Street, Clipsham,
Oakham, LE15 7SH
Tel       +44 (0)1780 410355
Email    info@theolivebranchpub.com
Web      www.theolivebranchpub.com

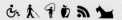

## Hambleton Hall Hotel & Restaurant

A sublime country house, one of the loveliest in England. The position here is matchless. The house stands on a tiny peninsular that juts into Rutland Water. You can sail on it or cycle around it, then come back to the undisputed wonders of Hambleton: sofas by the fire in the panelled hall, a pillared bar in red for cocktails, a Michelin star in the dining room. French windows in the sitting room (beautiful art, fresh flowers, the daily papers) open onto fine gardens. Expect clipped lawns and gravel paths, a formal parterre garden that bursts with summer colour and a walled swimming pool with views over grazing parkland to the water. Bedrooms are the very best. Hand-stitched Italian linen, mirrored armoires, Roberts radios, fabulous marble bathrooms; Stefa's eye for fabrics, some of which coat the walls, is faultless. The Pavilion, a supremely comfortable two-bedroom suite, has its own terrace. Polish the day off with incredible food, perhaps breast of wood pigeon, fallow venison with Asian pear, passion fruit soufflé with banana sorbet. Don't miss the hotel's bakery up the road. Irreproachable. *Minimum stay: 2 nights at weekends.*

| | |
|---|---|
| Rooms | 15 twin/doubles: £270–£540. 1 suite for 4: £440–£660. Singles from £195. Dinner, B&B from £195 per person. Extra bed/sofabed available £35 per person per night. |
| Meals | Lunch from £26.50. Sunday lunch £55. Dinner, 3 courses, £68. Tasting menu £80. |
| Closed | Never. |
| Directions | From A1, A606 west towards Oakham for about 8 miles, then left, signed Hambleton. In village bear left and hotel signed right. |

Tim & Stefa Hart
Hambleton Hall Hotel & Restaurant
Ketton Road, Hambleton,
Oakham , LE15 8TH

| | |
|---|---|
| Tel | +44 (0)1572 756991 |
| Email | hotel@hambletonhall.com |
| Web | www.hambletonhall.com |

## The Castle Hotel

This thriving medieval market town sits amid some of the loveliest country in the land, a launch pad for walkers and cyclists alike, with Offa's Dyke, Long Mynd and the Kerry Ridgeway all close. After a day in the hills, roll back to this quirky hotel for a night of gentle carousing. You'll find heaps of country comforts: hearty food, impeccable ales, super rooms with honest prices. Downstairs, there's a coal fire in the pretty snug, oak panelling in the breakfast room, and Millie the short-haired dachshund who patrols the corridors with aplomb. Stylish bedrooms upstairs have all been refurbished. Expect good beds, warm colours, flat-screen TVs, an armchair if there's room. Some are up in the eaves, several have views of the Shropshire hills, two have baths in the room. Back downstairs you find the sort of food you'd want after a day in the hills, perhaps hot garlic prawns, beef and ale pie, sticky toffee pudding. Don't miss the hugely popular real ale festival in July, the beer drinker's equivalent of Glastonbury. The garden terrace, with long country views, is a fine spot for a sundowner.

| | |
|---|---|
| Rooms | 9 doubles, 1 twin: £95–£150. |
| | 2 family rooms for 4: £130–£155. |
| | Singles from £75. |
| | Dinner, B&B from £82.50 per person. |
| | Extra beds for children £20. |
| Meals | Lunch from £4.50. |
| | Dinner, 3 courses, about £25. |
| Closed | Christmas Day & 10 days in January. |
| Directions | At top of hill in town, off A488. |

**Henry & Rebecca Hunter**
The Castle Hotel
Bishop's Castle, SY9 5BN

| | |
|---|---|
| Tel | +44 (0)1588 638403 |
| Email | stay@thecastlehotelbishopscastle.co.uk |
| Web | www.thecastlehotelbishopscastle.co.uk |

## Pen-y-Dyffryn Country Hotel

In a blissful valley lost to the world, a small country house that sparkles on the side of a peaceful hill. This is one of those lovely places where guests return again and again, mostly due to Audrey and Miles, who run a very happy ship. Outside, fields tumble down to a stream that marks the border with Wales. Daffodils erupt in spring, the lawns are scattered with deckchairs in summer, paths lead into the hills for fine walking. Lovely interiors are just the ticket: Laura Ashley wallpaper and an open fire in the quirky bar; colourful art and super food in the pretty restaurant; the daily papers and the odd chaise longue in the sitting room. Bedrooms hit the spot. Most have the view, one has a French sleigh bed, a couple have jacuzzi baths for two. Four lovely rooms outside are dog-friendly and have their own patios. You get warm colours, crisp linen, pretty fabrics and sparkling bathrooms. After a day in the hills come back for a good dinner, perhaps wild mushroom risotto, pan-fried wood pigeon, hot chocolate fondant with vanilla ice-cream. Offa's Dyke and Powis Castle are close. *Minimum stay: 2 nights at weekends.*

| | |
|---|---|
| Rooms | 8 doubles, 4 twins: £120–£190. Singles from £86. |
| Meals | Light lunch (for residents) by arrangement. Dinner £30–£37. |
| Closed | Rarely. |
| Directions | From A5 head to Oswestry. Leave town on B4580, signed Llansilin. Hotel 3 miles up. Approach Rhydycroesau, left at town sign, first right. |

Miles & Audrey Hunter
Pen-y-Dyffryn Country Hotel
Rhydycroesau,
Oswestry, SY10 7JD
Tel      +44 (0)1691 653700
Email   stay@peny.co.uk
Web     www.peny.co.uk

AWARD
WINNER

Old favourite

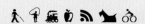

## Sebastian's

This cute little restaurant with rooms occupies an old merchant's house that dates from 1640. Michelle and Mark have been at the helm for some 25 years cooking up a fine reputation – not only for their delicious food, but for the quirky, old-world interiors in which they serve it. Inside you find huge beams, timber frames, half panelling and stripped floors. Big warm colours sit on the walls, smartly clothed tables are lit by candles, deco posters of the Orient Express hang in every room (Mark supplies the train with canapés and desserts). Back in the restaurant, sofas wait in front of a fire that smoulders from morning to night in winter. Here you drool over the menu before digging into delicious food, perhaps scallop ravioli with lemon grass and ginger, short rib of beef in a red wine sauce, dark chocolate mousse with honey ice cream. Six nicely-priced rooms wait, two in the main house (timber frames, lots of colour), four off the attractive courtyard (comfy sofas, lovely bathrooms). Plans are afoot for a couple of suites. Welsh hills wait to the west, so bring your walking boots.

| | |
|---|---|
| Rooms | 4 doubles, 2 twin/doubles: £75. Singles £65. |
| Meals | Breakfast £6.95–£11.95. Dinner, 3-course set menu, £22.50 (Tue–Thur); 5 courses £44.50 (Tue–Sat). Not Sun or Mon. |
| Closed | Rarely. |
| Directions | In middle of Oswestry on B4580. |

**Michelle & Mark Sebastian Fisher**
Sebastian's
45 Willow Street,
Oswestry, SY11 1AQ

| | |
|---|---|
| Tel | +44 (0)1691 655444 |
| Email | sebastians.rest@virgin.net |
| Web | www.sebastians-hotel.co.uk |

## Old Downton Lodge

The last time anything really happened here was in 1067 when Edric the Wild got a bit shirty with invading Normans. Fast forward five hundred years and Old Downton is taking shape. It's a fine old building, a little like walking onto the set of Wolf Hall, with original timbers, mighty crossbeams and beautiful stone walls. It sits in pristine country. Pheasants strut, hills roll, woodlands sprawl along distant ridges; a stunning walk across it all takes you over to Ludlow. Back at the house Pippa and Willem look after you in great style. There's a lovely sitting room in the old dairy with a roaring fire and an honesty bar, then a dining room in an 11th-century barn that resembles a medieval banqueting hall. In summer, life moves into the courtyard (once used for cattle auctions), where you can eat, drink and make merry in good weather. Big bedrooms mix timber frames, stone walls, flagged floors and oak furniture, while bathrooms have robes and lashings of hot water. Back outside, follow the river Teme up to Downton Gorge for ferns, otters, Roman baths and bluebells in spring. Blissful.

| Rooms | 5 doubles, 2 twins, 2 four-posters: £125-£165. Extra beds £30. |
| --- | --- |
| Meals | Dinner, 5-7 courses, £40-£50 (not Sun or Mon). |
| Closed | February. |
| Directions | North from Ludlow on A49, then west after 2 miles on A4113. 1st left (after 2 miles). Keep straight for four miles and on right. |

Willem & Pippa Vlok
Old Downton Lodge
Downton-on-the-Rock,
Ludlow, SY8 2HU

| Tel | +44 (0)1568 771826 |
| --- | --- |
| Email | bookings@olddowntonlodge.com |
| Web | www.olddowntonlodge.com |

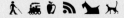

## The Swan

The Swan is gorgeous, a contemporary take on a village local. It's part of a new wave of pubs that open all day and do so much more than serve a good pint. The locals love it. They come for breakfast, pop in to buy a loaf of bread, then return for afternoon tea and raid the cake stands. It's right on the bustling street, with a sprinkling of tables and chairs on the pavement in French-café style. Interiors mix old and new brilliantly. You get Farrow & Ball colours and cool lamps hanging above the bar, then lovely old rugs on boarded floors and a wood-burner to keep things toasty. Push inland to find an airy restaurant open to the rafters that overlooks the garden. Here you dig into Tom Blake's fabulous food (he's ex-River Cottage), anything from a Cornish crab sandwich with lemon mayo to a three-course feast, maybe Wye Valley asparagus, Wedmore lamb chops, bitter chocolate mousse with chocolate cookies. Bedrooms are lovely. Two have fancy baths in the room, you get vintage French furniture, iPod docks, colourful throws and walk-in power showers. Glastonbury is close, as are the Mendips.

| | |
|---|---|
| Rooms | 4 doubles, 2 twin/doubles: £85–£120. Extra bed £20. Cots available. |
| Meals | Lunch from £5. Dinner, 3 courses, about £25. Sunday lunch from £14. Bar meals only Sun night. |
| Closed | Rarely. |
| Directions | M5, junc. 22, then B3139 to Wedmore. In village. |

Jen Edwards
The Swan
Cheddar Road,
Wedmore, BS28 4EQ

| | |
|---|---|
| Tel | +44 (0)1934 710337 |
| Email | info@theswanwedmore.com |
| Web | www.theswanwedmore.com |

## The Talbot Inn at Mells

A timeless village — ancient church, manor house, unspoilt stone cottages — with this 15th-century coaching inn hogging the limelight. It's an absolute stunner, with huge oak doors that lead into a cobbled courtyard, where life gathers in good weather. There's a tithe-barn sitting room with big sofas and a Sunday cinema, then the Coach House Grill, where you eat at weekends under hanging beams. As for the main house, it's a warren of ancient passageways, nooks and crannies and low doorways — the décor may be contemporary, but the past lives on. You'll find rugs on wood floors, crackling log fires, a lovely bar for a pint of Butcombe, then cosy rooms where you dig into tasty food, perhaps leek and potato soup, lemon sole with greens and beets, apple and rosemary tarte tatin. Bedrooms are the best, some small, others huge with claw-foot baths beside modern four-posters. Nothing is too much trouble for the spoiling staff. There's a colourful garden, then further afield some great local walking, so bring your boots. The First World War poet, Siegfried Sassoon, is buried in the churchyard.

| | |
|---|---|
| Rooms | 8 doubles: £95–£150. |
| Meals | Lunch & dinner £5–£30. |
| | Sunday lunch, 2 courses, £15. |
| Closed | Never. |
| Directions | From Frome A362 for Radstock; left turn for Mells. At mini-roundabout take right to Mells. After 1 mile turn right to Mells. |

Matt Greenlees
The Talbot Inn at Mells
Selwood Street, Mells,
Frome, BA11 3PN

| | |
|---|---|
| Tel | +44 (0)1373 812254 |
| Email | info@talbotinn.com |
| Web | www.talbotinn.com |

## At The Chapel

Every now and then, someone comes along and changes the game. Before Catherine and Ahmed opened At The Chapel, Bruton was a sleepy town only a few people had heard off. These days, visitors and locals come in their droves, drawn by the friendly staff, the cool design and the lovely food. At the front, you find an irresistible bakery – if you stay, they leave freshly baked croissants outside your room in the morning, a pre-breakfast snack. Back downstairs, one huge room draws you in. This is an old Baptist chapel that Catherine and Ahmed bought ten years ago; the chapel itself, now a restaurant/café/art gallery/theatre, was once their sitting room. You get white walls, vast windows, contemporary art and a rather cool bar. The food is perfect, nothing too posh, just seriously tasty stuff – fabulous pizza, fish from Lyme Bay, an ambrosial baked aubergine with parmesan and basil. Outside, a pretty terrace looks out over the town onto green hills. Above, flawless bedrooms come with white marble bathrooms; one has a terrace. We've run out of space, come to see for yourself. And expect the best.

| | |
|---|---|
| Rooms | 5 doubles, 2 twin/doubles: £100-£200. 1 suite for 2: £250. |
| Meals | Breakfast from £2.50. Lunch & dinner £5-£35. |
| Closed | Rarely. |
| Directions | Bruton is 5 miles north of the A303 at Wincanton. On High Street. |

Catherine Butler & Ahmed Sidki
At The Chapel
High Street,
Bruton, BA10 0AE

| | |
|---|---|
| Tel | +44 (0)1749 814070 |
| Email | mail@atthechapel.co.uk |
| Web | www.atthechapel.co.uk |

## The Pilgrims Restaurant with Rooms

Medieval pilgrims in search of King Arthur's tomb would stop here for sustenance before heading out across the marshes on their way to Glastonbury Abbey. These days, the food, the welcome and the rooms are all so lovely you're more likely to suffer a crisis of faith and stay put. Jools is to blame – his food is far too good to miss, good enough to alter the DNA of these walls – the Pilgrims is not an inn these days, but a restaurant with rooms. All the lovely old stuff survives – stone walls, timber frames, panelled walls and a couple of sofas in front of the fire. Tables in the restaurant are nicely spaced apart with subtle lighting and service that hits the spot. As for the food, expect local ingredients cooked to perfection, perhaps Lyme Bay scallops, rack of lamb, smooth dark chocolate pot with a hint of stem ginger. Five lovely bedrooms wait in the old skittle alley. Three have cathedral ceilings, all come with exposed stone walls, flat-screen TVs and crisp linen on good beds. As for the bathrooms, expect double-ended baths, separate power showers, fluffy robes. Wells and Glastonbury are close.

| | |
|---|---|
| Rooms | 4 doubles, 1 twin/double: £70–£110. Singles from £60. |
| Meals | Lunch from £8. Dinner, 3 courses, about £30. Sunday lunch £19. Not Mon. |
| Closed | Rarely. |
| Directions | On B3153 between Castle Cary & Somerton. In village by traffic lights. |

Julian & Sally Mitchison
The Pilgrims Restaurant with Rooms
Lovington,
Castle Cary, BA7 7PT

| | |
|---|---|
| Tel | +44 (0)1963 240597 |
| Email | jools@thepilgrimsatlovington.co.uk |
| Web | www.thepilgrimsatlovington.co.uk |

## The White Hart

Cool inns with lovely rooms in interesting parts of the land are a big hit with lots of us — we like the easy style, the local food, the good prices and the happy staff. The White Hart is a case in point, a beautifully refurbished inn. It sits on Somerton's ancient market square, 16th-century bricks and mortar, 21st-century lipstick and pearls. Inside, old and new mix beautifully: stone walls and parquet flooring, lovely sofas in front of the fire, funky lamps hanging above the bar. You'll find soft colours, padded window seats, country rugs, antler chandeliers. There's a cute booth in a stone turret, then cathedral ceilings in the airy restaurant, where lovely food waits, perhaps a chargrilled steak, smoked mackerel fishcakes, a pizza cooked in the wood-fired oven. In summer, you spill onto a smart courtyard or into the garden for views of open country. Upstairs, fabulous bedrooms await. You might find timber frames, a claw-foot bath, a wall of paper or stripped boards. All have super beds, flat-screen TVs, lovely bathrooms and a nice price. Beautiful Somerset is all around, don't miss it.

| | |
|---|---|
| Rooms | 8 doubles: £85–£130. |
| Meals | Lunch from £6. |
| | Dinner, 3 courses, £25–£30. |
| | Sunday lunch from £15. |
| Closed | Never. |
| Directions | South from Glastonbury on B3151. Right for Somerton, left into village and on left in square. |

Natalie Patrick
The White Hart
Market Place,
Somerton, TA11 7LX

| | |
|---|---|
| Tel | +44 (0)1458 272273 |
| Email | info@whitehartsomerton.com |
| Web | www.whitehartsomerton.com |

## The Devonshire Arms

What makes a great little inn these days? The Devonshire Arms has all the ingredients: lots of style, good prices, a community feel, some lovely rooms. It's in the right place, too, bang on the village green, with a terrace at the front, a garden at the back and a courtyard in between. Inside, is just as good. This isn't one of those places where every table is laid up for food; on the contrary, the best seats in the house are in the bar – a couple of armchairs in front of the fire. Step inside and find stylish interiors throughout. You get painted panelling in the restaurant – a sort of contemporary take on an 18th-century gentleman's club – then cool colours in the bar, where you can grab a pint of Butcombe, then spin outside to watch village life pass by. Lovely rooms have terrific prices. You'll find good beds, white linen, pretty furniture and excellent bathrooms; one has a free-standing bath. Elsewhere, red leather banquettes, fresh flowers, kind staff, the daily papers. As for the food, it's just the ticket: local partridge, fillet of bream, treacle tart with buttermilk ice cream.

| | |
|---|---|
| Rooms | 8 doubles, 1 twin/double: £95–£140. Singles from £85. Extra bed/sofabed £20 per person per night. |
| Meals | Lunch from £5.95. Dinner, 3 courses, about £30. Sunday lunch from £12.95. |
| Closed | 25th/26th December. |
| Directions | A303, then north on B3165, through Martock to Long Sutton. On village green. |

Philip & Sheila Mepham
The Devonshire Arms
Long Sutton,
Langport, TA10 9LP

| | |
|---|---|
| Tel | +44 (0)1458 241271 |
| Email | mail@thedevonshirearms.com |
| Web | www.thedevonshirearms.com |

## Little Barwick House

A beautiful restaurant with rooms lost in peaceful lanes south of Yeovil. Tim and Emma rolled west 14 years ago and now have a legion of fans who come to feast on their ambrosial food. Their small Georgian country house stands privately in three acres of peace. Horses graze in the paddock below, afternoon tea is served in the garden to the sound of birdsong in summer. Inside, chic interiors flood with light thanks to fine windows that run along the front. There's an open fire in the bar, eclectic reading in the sitting room, then contemporary art in the high-ceilinged dining room. Gorgeous bedrooms have a country-house feel and come with warm colours, pretty fabrics, Roberts radios, a sofa if there's room. You'll find fresh garden flowers, antique furniture, White Company oils in compact bathrooms. Dinner is the main event, heaven in three courses. Everything is homemade and cooked by Tim and Emma, an equal partnership in the kitchen – perhaps Lyme Bay scallops, saddle of wild venison, dark chocolate tort with armagnac ice-cream. Posh wines by the glass come courtesy of clever technology. *Children over 5 welcome.*

| | |
|---|---|
| Rooms | 4 doubles, 2 twins: £100–£170. Singles from £75. Dinner, B&B from £105 per person. Extra bed/sofabed available £25 per person per night. |
| Meals | Lunch, 2-3 courses, £25.95–£29.95. Dinner, 2-3 courses, £41.95–£47.95. Not Sun night, Mon or Tue lunch. |
| Closed | Mon & Sun nights. |
| Directions | From Yeovil A37 south for Dorchester; left at 1st r'bout. Down hill, past church, left in village and house on left after 200 yds. |

Emma & Tim Ford
Little Barwick House
Rexes Hollow Lane, Barwick,
Yeovil, BA22 9TD

| | |
|---|---|
| Tel | +44 (0)1935 423902 |
| Email | reservations@barwick7.fsnet.co.uk |
| Web | www.littlebarwickhouse.co.uk |

## Lord Poulett Arms

An idyllic inn that's hard to beat. It's like stepping onto the pages of a Jane Austen novel. A clipped country elegance runs throughout – old stone walls and period colours, then noble portraits on the walls and beautiful old settles to take the strain. There are drawbacks – sooner or later you will have to leave, probably with a touch of envy for the locals. Smart rusticity abounds. A fire burns on both sides in the dining room, where you eat under beams at antique tables. You'll find the daily papers, sofas in the locals' bar, a pile of logs at the back door, then an informal French garden with a piste for boules. Bedrooms upstairs have a lovely style with fancy flock wallpaper, pretty fabrics and fresh flowers, perhaps a small chandelier or a carved wooden bed. Two rooms have slipper baths in the room; two have claw-foot baths in bathrooms one step across the landing; the suite is enormous and has an open fire. The food is just as lovely, perhaps pea and ham soup, confit pork belly, praline fondant with coffee ice cream. Don't miss Sunday lunch or summer barbecues. An affordable treat.

| | |
|---|---|
| Rooms | 2 doubles; 2 doubles with separate bath: £85–£95. 1 suite for 3: £100–£150. Singles from £60. |
| Meals | Lunch from £5. Dinner, 3 courses, £20–£35. Sunday lunch £18–£21. |
| Closed | Never. |
| Directions | A303, then A356 south for Crewkerne. Right for West Chinnock. Through village, 1st left for Hinton St George. Pub on right in village. |

Steve & Michelle Hill
Lord Poulett Arms
High Street,
Hinton St George, TA17 8SE

| | |
|---|---|
| Tel | +44 (0)1460 73149 |
| Email | reservations@lordpoulettarms.com |
| Web | www.lordpoulettarms.com |

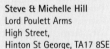

## Farmers Arms

A lovely inn lost in peaceful hills on the Somerset Levels – a great base for a night or two of affordable luxury. Outside, cockerels crow, cows graze and glorious views from the beer garden drift downhill for a couple of miles – a perfect spot for a pint in summer. Inside, you'll find friendly natives, sofas in front of an open fire and a timber-framed bar, where one airy room rolls into another giving a sense of space and light. There are beamed ceilings, tongue-and-groove panelling, logs piled high in the alcoves. Bedrooms – some big, some huge – are just the ticket. They come with whitewashed walls, cast-iron beds, varnished floors, power showers or double-ended baths. One has a daybed, others have sofas, another has a private courtyard. Delicious food comes from the kitchen, perhaps half a pint of Atlantic prawns, West Country lamb with dauphinoise potatoes, orange and mango cheesecake; in summer you can eat in a courtyard garden. There are local stables if you want to ride and great walking, so bring your boots. Five berths for camper vans wait above the beer garden, too.

| Rooms | 4 doubles, 1 twin/double: £75–£125. |
|---|---|
| Meals | Lunch & dinner £5–£35. |
| Closed | Never. |
| Directions | M5 junc. 25, then south on A358. On dual carriageway, right, signed West Hatch. Follow signs to RSPCA centre up hill for two miles. Signed on left. |

Dionne Walsh
Farmers Arms
West Hatch,
Taunton, TA3 5RS

| Tel | +44 (0)1823 480980 |
|---|---|
| Email | farmersarmswh@gmail.com |
| Web | www.farmersarmssomerset.co.uk |

## Luttrell Arms

You get a triple whammy here: spectacular Dunster Castle, its beautiful estate village and this mediaeval coaching inn on the high street – the view from the terrace across to the castle is candy for your eyes. Inside, a recent refurbishment has brought in a warm style. You'll find a beautiful restaurant with papered walls, an attractive sitting room for afternoon tea, an open fire in the high-ceilinged bar, then a boot bar for sleeping dogs and a game of cribbage. There are a couple of terraces for lunch in the sun, sofas on a veranda that overlooks a tiny courtyard. Bedrooms are scattered about, some with village views, others overlooking the estate. Four are huge with grand four-posters, two sitting under a 500-year-old hammer beam roof. Others have period furniture, pretty wallpapers, perhaps a small private terrace; simpler rooms are smaller, but have good beds. Tasty food spans the spectrum, from a posh burger in the bar to smoked haddock chowder, braised shin of beef and chocolate and raspberry tart in the restaurant. Cliff tops and wild moors wait for fabulous walking. *Minimum stay: 2 nights at weekends*

| | |
|---|---|
| Rooms | 4 doubles, 20 twin/doubles, 4 four-posters: £140-£195. Singles from £100. |
| Meals | Lunch from £4.95. Bar meals from £10.95. Dinner, 3 courses, about £30. Sunday lunch from £15.95. Afternoon tea £12.95. |
| Closed | Rarely. |
| Directions | M5, juncs. 23 or 24, then A39 west for Minehead. Right onto A396 for Dunster. On left in village. |

Becca Way
Luttrell Arms
36 High Street,
Dunster, TA24 6SG

| | |
|---|---|
| Tel | +44 (0)1643 821555 |
| Email | enquiry@luttrellarms.co.uk |
| Web | www.luttrellarms.co.uk |

## Cross Lane House

A medieval farmhouse in a National Trust village, where a 500-year-old bridge sweeps you across to ancient woodland. Outside, a cobbled courtyard leads up to a hay barn that's open on one side – not a bad spot for breakfast in good weather. Inside, original panelling is the big architectural draw, but Max and Andrew's lovely design gives a warm country-house feel, making this an intimate bolthole in which to linger. You'll find a sitting room packed with beautiful things – books galore, a wood-burner, sofas and armchairs to take the strain. There's a spy hole in the panelling, some ancient graffiti, too, then a pretty dining room with candles and low ceilings for nicely priced food, perhaps scallops with wild garlic, chicken wrapped in prosciutto, lemon tart with amaretto cream. Bedrooms upstairs are deeply satisfying: lovely beds, bowls of fruit, timber frames, super bathrooms. One is smaller, two are bigger, the family suite comes with a separate bedroom for children (or adults). Expect Roberts radios, Cowshed oils, a sofa if there's room. Exmoor waits. The road passes quietly at night. *Minimum stay: 2 nights at weekends.*

| | |
|---|---|
| Rooms | 3 doubles, 1 suite for 3: £110–£195. Dinner, B&B from £89 per person. |
| Meals | Lunch from £6 (Thur-Sat). Dinner £29. Sunday lunch £18–£24. |
| Closed | Rarely. |
| Directions | A39 west from Minehead. On right after 5 miles, 1 mile before Porlock. |

Max Lawrence & Andrew Stinson
Cross Lane House
Allerford,
Minehead, TA24 8HW
Tel      +44 (0)1643 863276
Email    max@crosslanehouse.com
Web      www.crosslanehouse.com

## The Oaks Hotel

Where else can you hire an MGB convertible in which to explore beautiful Exmoor? It's no surprise to discover that this hotel is an old school charmer. Tim and Anne do it all themselves, practising the art of old-fashioned hospitality with great flair: they stop to chat, carry bags, ply you with tea and cake on arrival. Their Edwardian house sits above the village, wrapped up in a beautiful garden, with views of hill and sea. Inside, logs smoulder on the hall fire while hot coals glow in the sitting room. There's a snug bar, parquet flooring, floral fabrics, masses of books. Spotless bedrooms, all with sea views, are deeply comfy. Most are big, all are colourful, the price with dinner is a steal. You get bowls of fruit, crisp white linen, fluffy bathrobes and Roberts radios; most have sofas, while beds are turned down every evening. As for dinner, Anne whisks up four-course feasts, perhaps cheese soufflé, smoked haddock mousse, guinea fowl with prunes and brandy, rhubarb and apple crumble. Exmoor, the coast and Dunster Castle all wait – don't miss the tiny villages marooned in the hills.

|  |  |
|---|---|
| Rooms | 1 double, 6 twin/doubles: £155–£175. Dinner, B&B from £115 per person. |
| Meals | Dinner, 4 courses, £37.50. |
| Closed | November–April. |
| Directions | A39 west to Porlock. Keep left down hill into village and hotel on left after 200m. |

Anne & Tim Riley
The Oaks Hotel
Porlock, TA24 8ES

| | |
|---|---|
| Tel | +44 (0)1643 862265 |
| Email | info@oakshotel.co.uk |
| Web | www.oakshotel.co.uk |

## Netherstowe House

Netherstowe is to hotels what Björk is to music – very different, utterly charming, a true original. It's quirky, too – part Ritz hotel, part curiosity shop – and it's full of surprises, not least its peculiar location on the edge of a 1970s housing estate. If that puts you off, don't let it – the house is hidden by beech hedging and once up the drive, you forget the outside world. Staff come to meet you and usher you inside, where gently eccentric interiors mix country-house style with 19th-century colonial overtones. You'll find varnished wood floors, roaring fires, tropical plants erupting from urns, the odd cabinet full of curios. Bedrooms are every bit as flamboyant with beautiful beds, cool colours, old armoires and chic bathrooms; several have free-standing baths. In contrast, contemporary courtyard apartments are utterly uncluttered. They have sofabeds for children and proper kitchens, but breakfast is included and the hotel is yours to roam. As for the food, choose from steaks in the cellar bistro or posh food above, perhaps cured salmon, roast guinea fowl, white chocolate panna cotta.

| | |
|---|---|
| Rooms | 7 doubles, 1 twin: £105–£159. 1 suite for 2: £195. 8 apartments for 4: £130. |
| Meals | Lunch from £19.95. Dinner, 3 courses, about £30. |
| Closed | 26 December to 2 January. |
| Directions | A38 northeast from Birmingham towards Burton on Trent. Left for Lichfield at A5192. Over two r'bouts, past Lidl, down hill, right at traffic lights into Netherstowe Lane. 1st left and drive on right. |

Ben Heathcote
Netherstowe House
Netherstowe Lane,
Lichfield, WS13 6AY

| | |
|---|---|
| Tel | +44 (0)1543 254270 |
| Email | info@netherstowehouse.com |
| Web | www.netherstowehouse.com |

## The Packhorse Inn

The rise of the cool country inn continues apace and the most recent member to join the club is the Packhorse, a beautifully renovated country pub that was rescued from abject neglect. These days it's a small-scale pleasure dome — striking interiors, ambrosial food, bedrooms and bathrooms that elate — yet it remains a village local with a lovely bar that welcomes all. The downstairs is open plan with a fire that burns on two sides and the odd armchair to take the strain. You'll find varnished floorboards, beautiful art, low-hanging lamps at the cool little bar. Chic bedrooms have beautiful beds, cashmere throws, walk-in showers, perhaps a double-ended bath in the room. Back downstairs irresistible food waits, maybe truffled goat's cheese with quince and figs, Suffolk venison and kidney pudding, plum tarte tatin with fruit-cake ice-cream. There's a terrace for good weather and a private dining room turns into a very cool meeting room. This is prime horse-racing country three miles east of Newmarket (the peerless Frankel is at stud nearby). Cambridge and Bury St Edmunds are also close.

| | |
|---|---|
| Rooms | 6 doubles, 2 twin/doubles: £125–£175. Singles from £85. Extra beds for children £10. |
| Meals | Lunch from £6. Dinner, 3 courses, about £35. |
| Closed | Never. |
| Directions | A14, junc. 38, then north onto A11. Take 1st exit east on B1085. Through Kentford and into Moulton. Left at green and on left. |

Philip Turner
The Packhorse Inn
Bridge Street, Moulton,
Newmarket, CB8 8SP

| | |
|---|---|
| Tel | +44 (0)1638 751818 |
| Email | info@thepackhorseinn.com |
| Web | www.thepackhorseinn.com |

## The Great House

Lavenham is a Suffolk gem, a medieval wool town trapped in aspic. The Great House stands across the market place from the Guildhall, its Georgian façade giving way to airy 15th-century interiors, where timber frames and old beams mix with contemporary colours and varnished wood floors. The poet Stephen Spender and his brother Humphrey – famous artist and photographer – once lived here and the house became a meeting place for artists, but these days it's the ambrosial food that draws the crowd. French to its core – the cheese board must qualify as one of the best in Britain – so dig into something delicious, perhaps venison, pistachio and sultana terrine, sea bass served with olives and white wine, then tarte tatin with cinnamon ice-cream. Fabulous bedrooms – all recently refurbished in lavish style – come with delicious bed linen, suede sofas, coffee machines, and robes in magnificent bathrooms. Four are huge, but even the tiniest is a dream. One has a regal four-poster, another has a 14th-century fireplace in its bathroom. All come with an array of gadgets: hi-fi, surround-sound, flat-screen TV... *Minimum stay: 2 nights at weekends.*

| | |
|---|---|
| Rooms | 4 doubles, 1 twin/double: £95–£195. Dinner, B&B from £115 per person. |
| Meals | Breakfast £12–£17. Lunch from £19.50 (not Mon/Tue). Dinner £35 (not Sun/Mon). À la carte only Sat night. |
| Closed | First 4 weeks in January; 2 weeks in summer. |
| Directions | A1141 to Lavenham. At High Street 1st right after The Swan or up Lady Street into Market Place. On-site parking. |

Régis & Martine Crépy
The Great House
Market Place,
Lavenham, CO10 9QZ

| | |
|---|---|
| Tel | +44 (0)1787 247431 |
| Email | info@greathouse.co.uk |
| Web | www.greathouse.co.uk |

## The Swan at Lavenham Hotel & Spa

This medieval inn has never looked better. It's a spectacular tangle of ancient timbers and sagging beams, yet its interiors shine brightly. Fires roar, ceilings soar and the loveliest staff weave through the mix delivering sinful plates of afternoon tea or cocktails before supper. Potter about and find a minstrel's gallery in the vaulted dining room, a fabulous old bar that was a favourite haunt of WWII airmen, then a courtyard garden, where you can stop for a glass of Pimm's in summer. As if that wasn't enough, a chic spa has recently been added with six treatment rooms, a sauna and steam room, then a vitality pool on the terrace; sheer bliss. As for the bedrooms, they're all lovely, some vast with four-posters and timber-framed walls, others more contemporary with cool colours and sofas. All have comfy beds, crisp white linen, fancy bathrooms and fluffy robes; beds are turned down during dinner. There's an open-plan brasserie for lighter bites, then a 14th-century hall for weddings. As for Lavenham, it's one of the best preserved medieval towns in the land. Bury St Edmunds is close, too. *On-site parking available. Ask about special offers.*

| | |
|---|---|
| Rooms | 32 twin/doubles, 2 four-posters: £185–£360. 10 suites for 2: £290–£360. 1 single: £105. Dinner, B&B from £245–£420 per room. |
| Meals | Lunch, 2 courses, from £16.95. Dinner, 3 courses £39.95. Brasserie, 2 courses, from £16. |
| Closed | Never. |
| Directions | In village. |

Ingo Wiangke
The Swan at Lavenham Hotel & Spa
High Street,
Lavenham, CO10 9QA

| | |
|---|---|
| Tel | +44 (0)1787 247477 |
| Email | info@theswanatlavenham.co.uk |
| Web | www.theswanatlavenham.co.uk |

## The Bildeston Crown

A 15th-century village inn with lots of character, plenty of style and some very good food. Outside, there's a terrace overlooking the village, then a small courtyard behind for a pint in the sun. Inside, timber frames, sagging ceilings and heavy beams are all original, but a contemporary feel runs throughout with bold colours, comfy sofas and big art on the walls. There's an open fire in the pretty bar, a good spot for afternoon tea, but the big draw here is the restaurant with Suffolk lamb, Red Poll beef and Nedging pork all from the fields around you; vegetables come from local gardens, too. A couple of menus run side by side: one for dishes like fish pie or chargrilled steak, then another for more complex food, perhaps rabbit terrine wrapped in Parma ham, boeuf bourguignon with dauphinoise potatoes, tarte fine with toffee ice cream; don't miss the roast rib of beef on Sundays. Upstairs, lovely bedrooms wait. One has a four-poster, another comes in black with a funky bath, all have robes in good bathrooms. Bury St Edmunds, medieval Lavenham and the Suffolk coast are close.

| | |
|---|---|
| Rooms | 10 doubles, 1 twin: £100–£195. Singles from £70. |
| Meals | Lunch from £6.50. Bar meals from £12.50. Dinner, 3 courses, £27–£45. Tasting menu £65. Sunday lunch from £17. |
| Closed | Never. |
| Directions | A12 junc. 31, then B1070 to Hadleigh. A1141 north, then B1115 into village & on right. |

Hayley & Chris Lee
The Bildeston Crown
104 High Street,
Bildeston, IP7 7EB

| | |
|---|---|
| Tel | +44 (0)1449 740510 |
| Email | reception@thebildestoncrown.com |
| Web | www.thebildestoncrown.com |

## The Crown

The Crown is all things to all men, a lovely country pub, a popular local restaurant, a small boutique hotel, a cool little bolthole in Constable country. It sits in a pretty village with long views from its colourful terrace over the Box Valley, not a bad spot for a glass of Pimm's after a day exploring the area. It dates to 1560 and has old beams and timber frames, though interiors have youthful good looks: warm colours, tongue-and-groove panelling, terracotta-tiled floors, a fancy wine cellar behind a wall of glass. You'll find rugs and settles, the daily papers, leather armchairs in front of a wood-burner. Four ales wait at the bar, 30 wines come by the glass and there's seasonal food that will make you smile, perhaps mussel chowder, steak and kidney pie, steamed orange pudding with marmalade ice-cream. Airy bedrooms are hidden away at the bottom of the garden, all exemplary with super bathrooms, excellent beds, lovely linen and a dash of colour. All have armchairs or sofas, three have French windows that open onto private terraces with fine views. A great place to eat, sleep and potter.

| | |
|---|---|
| Rooms | 10 doubles: £135–£225.<br>1 suite for 2: £195–£245.<br>Singles from £95.<br>Extra bed/sofabed available £10–£30 per person per night. |
| Meals | Lunch & dinner £5–£30. |
| Closed | Rarely. |
| Directions | North from Colchester on A134, then B1087 east into Stoke-by-Nayland. Right at T-junction; pub on left. |

Richard Sunderland
The Crown
Park Street, Stoke-by-Nayland,
Colchester, CO6 4SE
Tel      +44 (0)1206 262001
Email    info@crowninn.net
Web      www.crowninn.net

## Kesgrave Hall

This Georgian mansion sits in 38 acres of woodland and was built for an MP in 1812. It served as home to US airmen during WWII, becoming a prep school shortly after. Refurbished in 2008, it was an instant hit with locals, who love the style, the food and the informal vibe, and despite its country-house good looks, it is almost a restaurant with rooms, the emphasis firmly on the food. Find wellington boots in the entrance hall, high ceilings in the huge sitting room, stripped boards in the humming bistro and doors that open onto a terrace in summer. Excellent bedrooms have lots of style. One is huge and comes with a faux leopard-skin sofa and free-standing bath. The others might not be quite as wild, but they're lovely nonetheless, some in the eaves, others in beautifully refurbished outbuildings. Expect warm colours, crisp linen, good lighting and fancy bathrooms. Back downstairs tasty bistro food flies from the kitchen, perhaps goat's cheese panna cotta, cottage pie with red cabbage, pear tart with rosemary and vanilla ice-cream. Suffolk's magical coast waits.

| | |
|---|---|
| Rooms | 10 doubles, 7 twin/doubles: £130-£230. 6 suites for 2: £275-£300. |
| Meals | Breakfast £10-£16. Lunch & dinner, 3 courses, £25-£30. |
| Closed | Never. |
| Directions | Skirt Ipswich to the south on A14, then head north on A12. Left at 4th r'bout; signed right after 0.25 miles. |

Oliver Richards
Kesgrave Hall
Hall Road, Kesgrave,
Ipswich, IP5 2PU

| | |
|---|---|
| Tel | +44 (0)1473 333741 |
| Email | reception@kesgravehall.com |
| Web | www.milsomhotels.com |

## The Crown at Woodbridge

This cool little hotel in the middle of Woodbridge slopes down Quay Street, its rainbow of pastel colours now a landmark in town. Inside, open-plan interiors flood with light courtesy of a glass ceiling. A Windermere skiff hangs above the bar, you find painted panelling, comfy sofas, slate floors and a wood-burner roaring in the fireplace. Dining rooms sprawl, one in red, another in pale olive; you get leather banquettes, contemporary art, the odd window seat. Beautiful bedrooms upstairs vary in size, but all have the same smart feel: cool colours, duck down duvets, padded headboards, Hypnos beds. You'll find panels of entwined willow, pitchforks hanging on the wall, super bathrooms that go the whole hog. Back downstairs, Luke Bailey's rustic food is the big draw, perhaps potted shoulder of venison with walnuts and sloe jelly, steamed mussels in white wine and garlic, toffee apple tart with vanilla ice-cream. As for breakfast, everything is brought to your table: poached fruits, flagons of juice, the best sausages in Suffolk. Don't miss Snape Maltings, Sutton Hoo or the Aldeburgh food festival in October.

| | |
|---|---|
| Rooms | 8 twin/doubles: £100–£160. 2 family rooms for 4: £120–£160. Singles from £95. |
| Meals | Lunch & dinner £6–£30. Sunday lunch from £12.50. |
| Closed | Never. |
| Directions | A12 north from Ipswich, then B1438 into town. Pass station & left into Quay St. On right. |

|  | Garth Wray |
|---|---|
| | The Crown at Woodbridge |
| | Thoroughfare, |
| | Woodbridge, IP12 1AD |
| Tel | +44 (0)1394 384242 |
| Email | info@thecrownatwoodbridge.co.uk |
| Web | www.thecrownatwoodbridge.co.uk |

Entry 194  Map 4

## The Crown & Castle

Orford is unbeatable, a sleepy Suffolk village blissfully marooned at the end of the road. River, beach and forest wait, as does the Crown & Castle, a fabulous English hostelry where the art of hospitality is practised with great flair. The inn stands in the shadow of Orford's 12th-century castle. The feel is warm and airy with stripped floorboards, open fires, eclectic art and candles at night. Rooms come with Vi-Spring beds, super bathrooms, lovely fabrics, the odd armchair. Four in the main house have watery views, the suite is stunning, the garden rooms big and light, the courtyard rooms (the latest addition) utterly sublime. All have crisp white linen, TVs, DVDs and digital radios. Wellington boots wait at the back door, so pull on a pair and explore Rendlesham Forest or hop on a boat and chug over to Orfordness. Ambrosial food awaits your return, perhaps seared squid with coriander and garlic, slow-cooked pork belly with a shellfish broth, crushed pistachio meringue with a chocolate ice-cream sundae. A great place to wash up for a few lazy days. Sutton Hoo is close. Very dog-friendly. *Minimum stay: 2 nights at weekends. Children over 8 welcome.*

| | |
|---|---|
| Rooms | 18 doubles, 2 twins: £115–£195. 1 suite for 2: £240–£270. |
| Meals | Lunch from £8.50. À la carte dinner around £35. |
| Closed | Rarely. |
| Directions | A12 north from Ipswich, A1152 east to Woodbridge, then B1084 into Orford. Right in square for castle. On left. |

**David & Ruth Watson**
**The Crown & Castle**
**Orford,**
**Woodbridge, IP12 2LJ**
Tel        +44 (0)1394 450205
Email     info@crownandcastle.co.uk
Web       www.crownandcastle.co.uk

## Wentworth Hotel

The Wentworth has the loveliest position in town, the beach literally a pebble's throw from the garden, the sea rolling east under a vast sky. Inside, fires smoulder, clocks chime and seaside elegance abounds. It's all terrifically English, with vintage wallpapers, kind local staff and an elegant bar that opens onto a terrace garden. The restaurant looks out to sea, spilling onto a sunken terrace in summer for views of passing boats. Delicious English fare is the order of the day: stilton soup, breast of guinea fowl, lemon posset with raspberries and shortbread. The hotel has been in the same family since 1920 and old-fashioned values mix harmoniously with interiors that are refreshed often to keep things sparkling. Spotless bedrooms are deeply comfy, those at the front have huge sea views (and binoculars). Expect warm colours, wicker armchairs, padded headboards and comfortable beds. Bathrooms, all refurbished, are excellent. Sofas galore in the sitting room, but you may want to spurn them to walk by the sea. Joyce Grenfell was a regular. The Snape Maltings are close. *Minimum stay: 2 nights at weekends.*

| | |
|---|---|
| Rooms | 24 twin/doubles: £140–£220. 4 singles: £85–£119. Darfield House – 7 doubles: £140–£205. Dinner, B&B from £79 per person. |
| Meals | Bar meals from £5. Lunch from £12. Dinner, 2-3 courses, £21–£26.50. |
| Closed | Never. |
| Directions | A12 north from Ipswich, then A1094 for Aldeburgh. Past church, down hill, left at x-roads; hotel on right. |

Michael Pritt
Wentworth Hotel
Wentworth Road,
Aldeburgh, IP15 5BD

| | |
|---|---|
| Tel | +44 (0)1728 452312 |
| Email | stay@wentworth-aldeburgh.com |
| Web | www.wentworth-aldeburgh.com |

## The Brudenell Hotel

The Brudenell stands bang on the beach in one of England's loveliest seaside towns. It makes the most of its view: a dining terrace at the front runs the length of the building; a glass-fronted restaurant swims in light; an elegant sitting room looks the right way. The hotel mixes a contemporary style and an informal feel. You'll find coastal art, sunny colours, driftwood sculptures on display. Beautiful bedrooms come in different shapes and sizes. Those at the back look onto open country and river marsh, those at the front have hypnotic views of sea and sky. A chic style runs throughout: seaside colours, good fabrics, blond wood furniture, sofas if there's room; bathrooms are excellent. Back downstairs the open-plan brasserie is the hub of the hotel. It serves good comfort food with lots of fish on the menu, but you can always grab a burger or a steak if that's what you want. Try crispy fried goat's cheese, Harwich crab tart, sticky toffee pudding with clotted cream. Elsewhere, there are beach towels, deckchairs or golf up the road at Thorpeness, and on clear nights the starry sky will amaze you. *Minimum stay: 2 nights at weekends.*

| | |
|---|---|
| Rooms | 12 doubles, 30 twin/doubles: £150-£325. 2 singles: £80. |
| Meals | Lunch from £5. Dinner, 3 courses, about £30. |
| Closed | Never. |
| Directions | A1094 into Aldeburgh. Right at T-junction, down high street, last left in village before car park & yacht club. |

Peter Osborne
The Brudenell Hotel
The Parade,
Aldeburgh, IP15 5BU

Tel     +44 (0)1728 452071
Email   info@brudenellhotel.co.uk
Web    www.brudenellhotel.co.uk

## The Westleton Crown

This is one of England's oldest coaching inns, with 800 years of continuous service under its belt. It stands in a village two miles inland from the sea at Dunwich, with Westleton Heath running east towards RSPB Minsmere nature reserve. Inside, stripped floors, smouldering fires, exposed brickwork and ancient beams sweep you back two hundred years. Weave about and find nooks and crannies in which to hide, flames flickering in open fires, a huge map on the wall for walkers. You can eat wherever you want, there's a conservatory breakfast room with fine local photography, then a colourful terraced garden for barbecues in summer. Fish comes straight off the boats at Lowestoft, local butchers provide local meat, perhaps wild rabbit and ham hock, spiced sea bass with curried cockles, coconut panna cotta with roasted pineapple. Bedrooms are scattered about (Will and Kate loved theirs!), some in the main house, others in converted stables. Expect lime whites, comfy beds, crisp linen, flat-screen TVs. Pretty bathrooms come courtesy of Fired Earth, some with claw-foot baths. Aldeburgh and Southwold are close. *Minimum stay: 2 nights at weekends.*

| | |
|---|---|
| Rooms | 26 doubles, 2 twins: £95–£180. |
| | 3 suites for 2: £185–£215. |
| | 2 family rooms for 4: £160–£180. |
| | 1 single: £90–£100. |
| Meals | Lunch & bar meals from £5.50. |
| | Dinner from £11.95. |
| | Sunday lunch from £14.95. |
| Closed | Never. |
| Directions | A12 north from Ipswich. Right at Yoxford onto B1122, then left for Westleton on B1125. On right in village. |

Gareth Clarke
The Westleton Crown
The Street, Westleton,
Saxmundham, IP17 3AD

| | |
|---|---|
| Tel | +44 (0)1728 648777 |
| Email | info@westletoncrown.co.uk |
| Web | www.westletoncrown.co.uk |

## The Anchor

The Anchor is one of those lovely places that has resisted the urge to be precious. This is a cool little seaside inn where relaxed informality reigns; kids are welcome, staff are friendly, dogs fall asleep in the bar. You're 500 yards from the sea with a terrace that fills with locals in summer and lawns that run off towards the water. Inside, beautiful simplicity abounds – Cape Cod meets English country local. You get books everywhere, beautiful art, roaring fires, a happy vibe. The big draw is Sophie's lovely food. Game and venison come from local estates, fish and seafood from nearby waters, samphire and sea kale are foraged along the coast. Bedrooms fit the mood perfectly. Those in the house are warm and homely; the suites in the garden are big and airy with sofas inside and terraces that overlook nearby dunes. Don't miss dinner, perhaps fish soup, game ravioli, chocolate fondant with caramel ice cream. You wash it all down with Mark's legendary collection of bottled beers and fancy wines. There are festivals by the score – don't miss Latitude or Folk East. Starry skies amaze. Unmissable.

| | |
|---|---|
| Rooms | 9 doubles, 1 single/double: £95–£150. |
| Meals | Lunch from £5.25. |
| | Sunday lunch, 2 courses, £20. |
| | Dinner, 3 courses, about £30. |
| Closed | Christmas Day. |
| Directions | From A12 south of Southwold, B1387 to Walberswick. |

**Mark & Sophie Dorber**
The Anchor
Main Street, Walberswick,
Southwold, IP18 6UA

| | |
|---|---|
| Tel | +44 (0)1502 722112 |
| Email | info@anchoratwalberswick.com |
| Web | www.anchoratwalberswick.com |

## The Swan House

The Swan House is a magical place – quirky, intimate, deeply beautiful. Once a 16th-century tavern, it's now a 21st-century pleasuredome that sits opposite a 14th-century church with the river Waveney passing below. In summer life spills onto the pedestrianised Walk; in winter you sink into sofas in front of the fire. Interiors are perfect: timber frames, ancient walls, beamed ceilings, striking colours. It's a tiny place which adds to its charm. A movie plays in the front hall every day, you get fresh flowers and lovely art everywhere. One restaurant comes in red with pretty rugs and logs in the alcove; the other doubles as a gallery and has a fine oval table. Faultless bedrooms mix low ceilings, contemporary panelling, creaky floorboards and piles of books. Two have open fires, one a mezzanine for children, another a small balcony; all have magnificent bathrooms. Breakfast is extraordinary, one delicious course after another: Irish tea loaf, hams and cheese, plates of fruit, the full cooked works. Dinner is equally splendid: fresh mussels, confit of duck, amaretto ice-cream. One of the best. *Minimum stay: 2 nights at weekends. Children over 6 welcome.*

| | |
|---|---|
| Rooms | 4 doubles: £90–£145. |
| | 1 family room for 4: £140–£165. |
| Meals | Lunch from £6. |
| | Dinner, table d'hôte, £14.90–£19.90; |
| | à la carte, £25–£35. |
| | Sunday lunch from £14. |
| Closed | Rarely. |
| Directions | In centre of town at foot of clock |
| | tower. Car parks nearby. |

**Roland Blunk & Carmela Sabatini**
The Swan House
By the tower,
Beccles, NR34 9HE
Tel      +44 (0)1502 713474
Email    info@swan-house.com
Web      www.swan-house.com

## Hurtwood Hotel

The Surrey Hills are stunning – forest walks, rolling pasture, spectacular views, mountain bike trails. It's an area that remains inexplicably undiscovered, yet it's only an hour from London. As for the Hurtwood, it sits in a pretty village surrounded by wooded hills. It was built by Forte in anticipation of a railway line that never appeared. Caroline recently came home after 20 years in Australia, bought the place, refurbished in style, now it shines. Downstairs, the breakfast room opens onto a terrace, where you can eat in good weather accompanied by bird song. Upstairs, nicely priced rooms have comfort and style with good beds, crisp linen, spotless bathrooms, the odd sofabed. Those at the front flood with light and have views over the village to peaceful hills. Back downstairs, Robi and Lorenzo's fantastic Italian food waits in the restaurant. There's a bar and terrace for pre-dinner drinks, then irresistible food, perhaps tagiolini with fresh Devon crab, ravioli with scallops and prawns, guinea fowl with grapes and Vin Santo. The tasting menu is a steal, you'll think you're in the Tuscan hills. A treat.

| Rooms | 10 doubles, 3 twin/doubles: £85–£115. Extra beds: children £10, adults £15. |
|---|---|
| Meals | Lunch from £5.50. Bar meals from £9.50. Dinner, 3 courses, £25–£35. Tasting menu £31.50. |
| Closed | Never. |
| Directions | A25 east from Guildford, then south, in Shere for Ewhurst. Over railway bridge after 500m, then left into Hook Lane for Peaslake. On right at end of village. |

Caroline Darbishire
Hurtwood Hotel
Walking Bottom, Peaslake,
Guildford, GU5 9RR

| Tel | +44 (0)1306 730514 |
| Email | hurtwoodhotel@mail.com |
| Web | www.hurtwoodhotel.co.uk |

## The Barn at Roundhurst

A 17th-century threshing barn on a small farm lost in deep country. Inside, you find a spectacular space, one huge room that's open to its rafters, with equally beautiful timber frames on display. Other than that, it's all deliciously contemporary, with a cool little fire that throws out the heat, leather sofas, beautiful sculpture, soft lighting and cow hide rugs. Upstairs, there's an honesty bar, then a library for books and maps, playing cards and poker chips! Chic rooms spiral around a pretty courtyard to one side of the barn, most with private terraces. You get boarded floors, blond wood furniture, smart fabrics, the odd exposed beam. Gorgeous bathrooms have white robes, walk-in showers and underfloor heating; most have baths, too. Food is on tap with cold platters – cheese, ham, salads and bread – available every day, then a table d'hôte menu from Thursday to Saturday, perhaps fig and goat's cheese tart, rack of local lamb, Cointreau panna cotta. Good dining pubs are a short drive, great local walking starts from the front door. Petworth and Goodwood are both close.

| | |
|---|---|
| Rooms | 8 twin/doubles: £130–£200. Extra beds £20–£30. |
| Meals | Picnics by arrangement. Dinner: cold platters £10.50; 4-course set menu (Thur-Sat) £40. |
| Closed | Rarely. |
| Directions | A3, A283 south for Petworth, then right for Haslemere on B2131. Left into Jobson's Lane, then 1st right. Keep left and on left after 1 mile. |

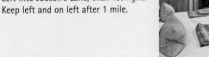

The Bookings Team
The Barn at Roundhurst
Lower Roundhurst Farm,
Jobson's Lane, Lurgashall, GU27 3BN
Tel        +44 (0)1428 642535
Email      bookings@thebarnatroundhurst.com
Web        www.thebarnatroundhurst.com

## Park House Hotel & Spa

A blissful pocket of rural Sussex. Park House sits in 12 acres of glorious English gardens with quilted fields circling the grounds and the South Downs rising beyond. Potter about outside and find a croquet lawn, a grass tennis court and a six-hole golf course that slips into the country. Fine shrubberies burst with colour while wellington boots wait at the front door for long country walks. You may prefer to stay put; the newest addition is a fabulous spa. It comes with a very swanky indoor pool to go with its outside partner, four treatment rooms, a sauna and steam room, then a proper gym and a terraced bar for lazy afternoons. As for the house, it's just as good. Beautiful interiors abound mixing country-house style with contemporary colours. The pavilion bar overlooks the gardens, you breakfast in the conservatory or out on the terrace, there are flagstones in reception, the daily papers in the sitting room, great food in the dining room. Gorgeous bedrooms are the final luxury: heavenly beds, big country views, fancy bathrooms, iMac TVs. Exceptional. *Minimum stay: 2 nights at weekends.*

| | |
|---|---|
| Rooms | 6 doubles, 10 twin/doubles: £108–£192. 4 family rooms for 4: £222–£318. 1 cottage for 2-4: £250–£315. |
| Meals | Lunch from £23.95. Afternoon tea £19.95. Dinner from £30. |
| Closed | Rarely. |
| Directions | South from Midhurst on A286. At sharp left bend, right (straight ahead), signed Bepton. Hotel on left after 2 miles. |

Rebecca Coonan
Park House Hotel & Spa
Bepton,
Midhurst, GU29 0JB

| | |
|---|---|
| Tel | +44 (0)1730 819020 |
| Email | reservations@parkhousehotel.com |
| Web | www.parkhousehotel.com |

## Halfway Bridge Inn

Sam's gorgeous inn wasn't quite as lovely when he took over the reins a few years ago, but after pouring in love and money in equally large amounts, the place now shines. It sits back from the A272, with Goodwood to the south for the races, Petworth to the east for antiques and the South Downs all around for exhilarating walking. Step inside to find a smart, cosy world of original wood floors, whitewashed walls, smouldering fires, the odd mind-your-head beam. It's a deeply pretty place, small but certainly sweet, with snug rooms giving a Dickensian feel, albeit with a 21st-century makeover. Spin round to the bar and find three local ales, 25 wines by the glass, the daily papers and beautifully upholstered bar stools; there's a door onto the terrace for lunch in summer. Big stylish bedrooms wait across the lane in an old stone barn, where old and new mix beautifully — smart bathrooms and lovely furniture amid beams and panelled walls. As for the food, it's a big draw with the locals, perhaps Cornish scallops with tiger prawns, cannon of lamb with a mead-scented jus, a prune and armagnac tart. *Minimum stay: 2 nights at weekends.*

| | |
|---|---|
| Rooms | 6 doubles: £140–£175.<br>1 suite for 2: £190–£230.<br>Singles from £85. Extra bed/sofabed<br>available £30 per person per night. |
| Meals | Lunch & dinner £14.50–£28.<br>Bar meals £6.50–£12.50. |
| Closed | Never. |
| Directions | On A272 halfway between Midhurst &<br>Petworth. |

Sam Bakose
Halfway Bridge Inn
Halfway Bridge,
Petworth, GU28 9BP
Tel       +44 (0)1798 861281
Email    enquiries@halfwaybridge.co.uk
Web     www.halfwaybridge.co.uk

## The Crab & Lobster

This tiny arrowhead of land south of Chichester is something of a time warp, more 1940s than 21st century. The Crab & Lobster is older still – 350 years at the last count. It sits on Pagham Harbour, a tidal marsh that teems with preening birds. Outside, you find a smart whitewashed exterior and a small garden for views across fields of sheep to the water. Inside, flagged floors, whitewashed walls, a fire at one end, a wood-burner at the other. There's a lovely alcove with banquette seating, candles flicker in the evening, in summer you decant onto the back terrace for lunch in the sun. Upstairs, four super rooms come in duck-egg blue with crisp white linen, flat-screen TVs and gorgeous little bathrooms. Three have views of the water, one is up in the eaves and has a telescope to scan the high seas. There's much to explore: Bosham, where King Canute tried to turn back the waves; Fishbourne, for its Roman palace; the Witterings, for miles of beach and dunes. Don't forget dinner, perhaps Selsey crab cakes with chilli jam, fillet of pork with a calvados cream, caramelised plum tart. *Minimum stay: 2 nights at weekends.*

| | |
|---|---|
| Rooms | 4 doubles: £160-£195. |
| | 1 cottage for 4: £250-£280. |
| | Singles from £90. Extra bed/sofabed |
| | available £30 per person per night. |
| Meals | Bar meals from £6.50. |
| | Lunch from £11.95. |
| | Dinner, 3 courses, £35. |
| | Sunday lunch, 2 courses, £26. |
| Closed | Never. |
| Directions | Mill Lane is off B2145 Chichester to |
| | Selsey road, just south of Sidlesham. |

Sam Bakose
The Crab & Lobster
Mill Lane, Sidlesham,
Chichester, PO20 7NB
Tel      +44 (0)1243 641233
Email    enquiries@crab-lobster.co.uk
Web      www.crab-lobster.co.uk

## The Royal Oak Inn

This pretty inn sits in a sleepy Sussex village with the South Downs rising above and the coast at the Witterings waiting below. Inside, an attractive rusticity prevails: stripped floors, low ceilings and the odd racing print (the inn was once part of the Goodwood estate). There's a small bar for a pint in front of an open fire, but these days it's a mostly dining pub, the restaurant spreading itself far and wide, through the conservatory and out onto the terrace in summer. A small army of chefs conjure up irresistible food, perhaps Selsey crab mousse with a Vermouth foam, roast guinea fowl with a prune terrine, whisky Mac jelly with cinnamon oats. Elegant bedrooms are sprinkled about, some in garden cottages, others upstairs. All come in contemporary style with smart fabrics, leather armchairs, comfy beds and good bathrooms. CD players, plasma screens, and DVD libraries keep you amused. Staff are attentive, complimentary newspapers arrive with breakfast. The South Downs are all about, Goodwood is a mile up the road, Chichester Theatre and Bosham are close. *Minimum stay: 2 nights at weekends.*

| | |
|---|---|
| Rooms | 2 doubles, 3 twin/doubles: £110–£190. 3 suites for 2–4: £180–£280. Singles from £85. |
| Meals | Lunch from £7.95. Dinner, 3 courses, about £35. Sunday lunch from £25. |
| Closed | Never. |
| Directions | From Chichester A286 for Midhurst. First right at first mini roundabout into E. Lavant. Down hill, past village green, over bridge, pub 200 yds on left. Car park opposite. |

Charles Ullmann
The Royal Oak Inn
Pook Lane, East Lavant,
Chichester, PO18 0AX

| | |
|---|---|
| Tel | +44 (0)1243 527434 |
| Email | rooms@royaloakeastlavant.co.uk |
| Web | www.royaloakeastlavant.co.uk |

## The Bull

This 16th-century inn on the South Downs has lots to offer – a cracking bar, four fancy bedrooms, tasty local food and an excellent array of ales and craft beers from across the globe. Step inside and it's like travelling back to Dickensian England. Light is rationed on aesthetic grounds, beams sag, fires roar and happy locals gather for a pint of Bedlam, the pub's own brew. You can eat wherever you want – meat from Sussex farms, game from local estates, fish from short-range boats – perhaps scallops with black pudding, roasted sausages with onion gravy, chocolate bread and butter pudding. Upstairs, four stylish bedrooms have recently been refurbished (two larger, two above the bar), with four more coming soon. Expect Farrow & Ball colours, chic fabrics, old-style radiators and comfy beds. Bigger rooms have sofas, you might find timber frames, a cow-hide rug or a low beamed ceiling. All have digital radios, flat-screen TVs and smart little bathrooms. Bring walking boots and mountain bikes and scale the Ditchling Beacon for big views. Brighton and Gatwick are close, don't miss Sunday lunch. *Minimum stay: 2 nights at weekends.*

| | |
|---|---|
| Rooms | 3 doubles, 1 twin/double: £100–£160. |
| Meals | Lunch from £5. |
| | Dinner, 3 courses, £25–£35. |
| | Sunday lunch from £14. |
| Closed | Never. |
| Directions | Leave A23 just north of Brighton for Pyecombe. North on A273, then west for Ditchling on B2112. In centre of village at crossroads. |

Dominic Worrall
The Bull
2 High Street, Ditchling,
Hassocks, BN6 8TA

| | |
|---|---|
| Tel | +44 (0)1273 843147 |
| Email | info@thebullditchling.com |
| Web | www.thebullditchling.com |

## The Griffin Inn

A proper inn, posh with a hint of scruffiness, a community local that draws a devoted crowd. You get open fires, 400-year-old beams, oak panelling and prints on the walls. There's a lively bar, an attractive restaurant and a club room for racing on Saturdays. In summer, life spills onto a pretty terrace for local meat cooked in a wood-fired oven. There are weekend barbecues, too, and deckchairs scattered across the lawns for ten-mile views over Pooh Bear's Ashdown forest to Sheffield Park. Bedrooms are nicely-priced and full of country-inn elegance: uneven floors, the odd four-poster, lovely old furniture and free-standing baths. Rooms in the coach house are quieter, those in Griffin House quieter still. Some in the main house have timber frames, all have robes and colourful art. Back downstairs, seasonal menus do the trick, perhaps rabbit gnocchi, local pheasant, dark chocolate tort with honey ice cream; breakfast sausages are divine. The pub has three cricket teams that travel the world in pursuit of glory – you may find them in the bar on a summer evening after a hot day in the field. *Minimum stay: 2 nights bank holiday weekends.*

| | |
|---|---|
| Rooms | 6 doubles, 7 four-posters: £85–£145. Singles £70–£80 (Sun-Thur). |
| Meals | Bar meals from £6.50. Dinner, 3 courses, £30–£40. |
| Closed | Christmas Day. |
| Directions | From East Grinstead A22 south, right at Nutley for Fletching. On for 2 miles into village. |

Nigel & James Pullan
The Griffin Inn
Fletching,
Uckfield, TN22 3SS

Tel     +44 (0)1825 722890
Email   info@thegriffininn.co.uk
Web     www.thegriffininn.co.uk

## Chilverbridge House

Nick and Nina's stunning 17th-century farmhouse stands in seven lovely acres overlooking the South Downs; you'll find sweeping lawns, an iris-fringed pond and access to Arlington Reservoir and Nature Reserve. As for the once-dilapidated Old Granary and Coach House, a magical restoration has produced four gorgeous bedrooms, a big hit with the Glyndebourne set. They come in fine style with balconies or private patios onto the garden. You get beautiful beds, goose down duvets and plump pillows, then Colefax & Fowler fabrics, delicious antiques and lots of high-tech gadgetry. Bathrooms are the best, all with baths, walk-in showers and thick bathrobes. In summer, you breakfast like a king on the terrace with views of the Long Man of Wilmington At other times you eat at linen-clothed tables by the fire in the low-ceilinged dining room. Beachy Head, Cuckmere Haven and Pevensey Castle all wait, as do the South Downs for magical walking. Come by train, Nick will pick you up from the village station. A brilliant bolthole with a raft of good restaurants waiting close by. *Over 12s welcome in high season.*

| | |
|---|---|
| Rooms | 3 doubles, 1 twin/double: £120–£200. Low season £25 singles discount (Sun-Thurs). |
| Meals | Restaurants within 1 mile. Dinner, 3 courses, £45 by arrangement. |
| Closed | Rarely. |
| Directions | A27 west from Polegate for Brighton. After two miles, right at r'bout for Berwick Station. 1st right, 1st left, on right. |

Nick & Nina Keats
Chilverbridge House
Chilver Bridge Road,
Arlington, BN26 6SB
Tel        07748 395327
Email     chilverbridge@chilverbridgehouse.com
Web      www.chilverbridgehouse.com

## Wingrove House

If you need proof that small hotels are infinitely lovelier than their big brothers, here's the evidence. This gorgeous bolthole stands at the end of a pretty village with an ancient church on one side and the South Downs Way passing on the other. At the front a small walled garden leads up to a stone terrace, a great spot to linger in summer; in winter you grab a sofa in front of the wood-burner and roast away in the cool little sitting room bar (wood floors, interesting art, chic colonial feel). Upstairs, delicious bedrooms have smart fabrics, vibrant colours, iPod docks and fancy bathrooms. Two at the front open onto a veranda, the biggest at the back overlooks the churchyard (the bells rarely chime). There's lots to do. Great walks start from the front door with Cuckmere Haven, Friston Forest and Beachy Head all within range, so work up an appetite, then return to feast on excellent local food, perhaps potted South Coast crab, Sussex lamb with garlic and rosemary, French lemon tart with local raspberry sorbet. Come by train and Nick will pick you up from the station. Brilliant.

| | |
|---|---|
| Rooms | 5 doubles: £95–£200. |
| Meals | Lunch from £10 (Sat & Sun only). Dinner, 3 courses, £28–£32. |
| Closed | Rarely. |
| Directions | M23, A23, then A27 east from Brighton. Past Berwick, then south at r'bout for Alfriston. In village on left. |

Nicholas Denyer
Wingrove House
High Street, Alfriston,
Polegate, BN26 5TD
Tel        +44 (0)1323 870276
Email    info@wingrovehousealfriston.com
Web      www.wingrovehousealfriston.com

### The Tiger Inn

The Tiger sits on a village green that has hardly changed in 50 years and in summer life spills onto the terrace to soak up an English sun. It's all part of a large estate that hugs the coast from Beachy Head to Cuckmere Haven with Birling Gap in between; some of the best coastal walking in the south lies on your doorstep. Back at the inn a fabulous renovation has breathed new life into old bones. Downstairs has bags of character with low beams, stone floors, ancient settles and a roaring fire. Beer brewed on the estate pours from the tap, so try a pint of Legless Rambler before digging into hearty food – Beachy Head beer-battered catch of the day, sausage and mash with a sweet onion gravy, treacle tart with vanilla ice-cream. Five country-house bedrooms are the big surprise. Find beautiful fabrics, padded bedheads, funky bathrooms, the odd beam. Beds are dressed with lambswool throws, warm colours hang on the walls. Back outside, white cliffs wait, as do the South Downs. Finally, Arthur Conan Doyle knew the village and a blue plaque on one of the cottages suggests Sherlock Holmes retired here.

| | |
|---|---|
| Rooms | 4 doubles, 1 twin: £110–£120. |
| Meals | Lunch from £4.95. Dinner, 3 courses, £20–£30. |
| Closed | Never. |
| Directions | West from Eastbourne on A259. Left in village. Parking on right near village hall. |

Janice Avis
The Tiger Inn
The Green, East Dean,
Eastbourne, BN20 0DA

Tel     +44 (0)1323 423209
Email   tiger@beachyhead.org.uk
Web     www.beachyhead.org.uk

## Belle Tout Lighthouse

A fine old lighthouse atop a white cliff with stunning views in every direction. To your left, Beachy Head, to your right, Birling Gap – it's a magical position with the South Downs rolling down into the English Channel. As for the lighthouse, it dates to 1832. It was once moved 57 feet back to stop it crumbling into the sea and it featured prominently in the BBC's production of *The Life and Loves of a She-Devil*. It re-opened in 2010 after a splendid renovation as a lovely little B&B hotel. Bedrooms are rather wonderful: not huge, but all have windows that bring the outside in. You get white walls to soak up the light, fantastic views of rolling hills, pretty fabrics, lovely linen, the odd exposed brick wall; shower rooms are small but sweet, one room has a bath. Ian's legendary breakfasts are served on high with views of sea and cliff. There's a wood-burner in the sitting room, where guests gather each night before climbing up to explore the lantern. Good food waits in the village: a lovely pub and an excellent Thai restaurant. Magnificent walking waits. *Minimum stay: 2 nights. Over 15s welcome.*

| | |
|---|---|
| Rooms | 6 doubles: £145–£220. Singles from £101.50. |
| Meals | Pub/restaurant within 1 mile. |
| Closed | Christmas & New Year. |
| Directions | A259 to East Dean, then south for Beachy Head. Keep left at Birling Gap and on right above sea. |

Ian Noall
Belle Tout Lighthouse
Beachy Head Road, Beachy Head,
Eastbourne, BN20 0AE

| | |
|---|---|
| Tel | +44 (0)1323 423185 |
| Email | info@belletout.co.uk |
| Web | www.belletout.co.uk |

## Strand House

As you follow the Royal Military Canal down to miles of sandy beach, bear in mind that 600 years ago, you'd have been swimming in the sea. This is reclaimed land and Strand House, built in 1425, originally stood on Winchelsea Harbour. Outside, you find wandering wisteria, colourful flowerbeds and a woodland walk that leads up to the village. Inside, medieval interiors have low ceilings, timber frames and mind-your-head beams. There are reds and yellows, sofas galore, a wood-burner in the sitting room, an honesty bar from which to help yourself. It's a home-spun affair: Hugh cooks breakfast, Mary conjures up tasty meals at weekends. Attractive bedrooms are warm and colourful. One has an ancient four-poster, some have wonky floors, all have comfy beds and compact shower rooms. Airy rooms in the cottage have more space, and the suite, with its balcony and views across the fields, is a treat. The house, once a work house, was painted by Turner and Millais. Local restaurants wait: Webb's Fish Café, The Globe in Rye, a Michelin star at the Curlew in Odium. Dogs are very welcome. *Minimum stay: 2 nights, weekends & high season.*

| | |
|---|---|
| Rooms | 6 doubles, 1 twin/double: £80–£150. 1 suite for 4: £180. 5 triples: £80–£150. Singles from £60. Dogs £7.50. |
| Meals | Dinner, 3 courses, £34.50, Fri & Sat, on request. |
| Closed | Rarely. |
| Directions | A259 west from Rye for 2 miles. House on the left at foot of hill, opposite Bridge Inn pub. |

Mary Sullivan & Hugh Davie
Strand House
Tanyards Lane, Winchelsea,
Rye, TN36 4JT

| | |
|---|---|
| Tel | +44 (0)1797 226276 |
| Email | info@thestrandhouse.co.uk |
| Web | www.thestrandhouse.co.uk |

## Jeake's House

Rye is utterly gorgeous, one of those lovely English country towns that's been around for centuries, but has never lost its looks. The same is true of Jeake's House. It's spent 300 years on this steep cobbled street in the old town accruing a colourful past as a wool store, a school, and the home of American poet Conrad Potter Aiken. Inside: timber frames, ancient beams and small smartly carpeted corridors that weave along to cosy bedrooms, the latter generously furnished, deeply comfortable and excellent value for money. Some have four-posters, all have rich fabrics, one has a telly concealed in the wood-burner. The galleried dining room – once an old Baptist chapel, now painted deep red – is full of busts, books, clocks and mirrors – a fine setting for a full English breakfast. There's also a lovely cosy honesty bar, where a fire burns in winter. Outside, you'll find art galleries, antiques shops, old churches and river walks. All this would be blossom in the wind without Jenny, whose natural friendliness has created a winning atmosphere. Don't miss it. *Children over 8 welcome.*

| Rooms | 7 twin/doubles; 1 double with separate bath: £90–£116. 3 four-poster suites for 2: £126–£140. Singles from £79. |
|---|---|
| Meals | Restaurants within walking distance. |
| Closed | Never. |
| Directions | From centre of Rye on A268, left off High St onto West St, then 1st right into Mermaid St. House on left. Private car park, £3 a day for guests. |

Jenny Hadfield
Jeake's House
Mermaid Street,
Rye, TN31 7ET

| Tel | +44 (0)1797 222828 |
|---|---|
| Email | stay@jeakeshouse.com |
| Web | www.jeakeshouse.com |

## The George in Rye

Rye is beautiful, old England trapped in aspic. It was a Cinque Port, Henry James lived here and the oldest church clock in England chimes at the top of the hill. The George stands on its cobbled high street right in the thick of things. Built in 1575 from reclaimed ships' timbers, its exposed beams and panelled walls remain on display. Inside, old and new mix beautifully – expect Jane Austen in the 21st century. There's a roaring fire in the bar, screen prints of the Beatles on the walls in reception, a sun-trapping courtyard for lunch in summer. Beautiful bedrooms come in all shapes and sizes (a couple are small), but chic fabrics, Frette linen and Vi-Spring mattresses are standard, as are good books, fine bathrooms, white robes and cashmere covers on hot water bottles. Some are huge with zinc baths in the room, one has a round bed. You eat in the George Grill, an open kitchen on display, perhaps Provençal fish soup, grilled rib-eye with hand-cut chips, gooseberry soufflé with bay leaf ice cream. Walk it off by following the river down to the sea. *Mapp and Lucia* was filmed in the town.

| | |
|---|---|
| Rooms | 8 doubles, 21 twin/doubles: £135–£195. 5 suites for 2: £295–£325. Singles from £95. |
| Meals | Lunch & dinner from £6–£35. |
| Closed | Never. |
| Directions | Follow signs up hill into town centre. Through arch; hotel on left, below church. 24-hour parking 5 minutes down hill. |

Alex & Katie Clarke
The George in Rye
98 High Street,
Rye, TN31 7JT

| | |
|---|---|
| Tel | +44 (0)1797 222114 |
| Email | stay@thegeorgeinrye.com |
| Web | www.thegeorgeinrye.com |

## The Gallivant

This cute seaside restaurant with rooms stands across the road from Camber Sands, its five miles of pristine beach the best in the south. Kite surfers, beach cricketers and sun worshipers all gather and at low tide vast tracts of land appear, making it a great place to walk. As for the Gallivant, it's a quirky little pad, a boutique motel with fantastic food. The restaurant, recently refurbished, has a cool New England feel with seaside colours, comfy sofas and a wood-burner that burns on both sides. Uncluttered bedrooms – some big, some small – have lots of style: the best linen, Hypnos beds, driftwood furniture. Two in the main house open onto private terraces, four outside are perfect for families, all have good bathrooms, digital radios and flat-screen TVs (and a DVD library). But it's the food that takes the biscuit, much sourced within 30 miles: porridge for breakfast, fish soup for lunch, afternoon tea 'on the house', then a good dinner, perhaps Rye Bay scallops, salt marsh lamb, caramelised banana with toffee sauce. Visiting chefs – Tom Aikens, Mitch Tonks – come up to cook, too. *Minimum stay: 2 nights at weekends.*

| | |
|---|---|
| Rooms | 18 doubles, 2 doubles with terraces: £105–£185. |
| Meals | Lunch from £12.50. Dinner, 3 courses, about £30. |
| Closed | Rarely. |
| Directions | A259 east from Rye, then B2075 for Camber & Lydd. On left after 2 miles. |

Mark O'Reilly
The Gallivant
New Lydd Road, Camber,
Rye, TN31 7RB

| | |
|---|---|
| Tel | +44 (0)1797 225057 |
| Email | enquiries@thegallivant.co.uk |
| Web | www.thegallivant.co.uk |

Entry 216  Map 4

## The Howard Arms

The Howard stands on Ilmington Green, five miles south of Stratford-upon-Avon. It was built at roughly the same time as Shakespeare wrote *King Lear* and little has changed since. It's a lovely country inn and comes with original fixtures and fittings: polished flagstones, heavy beams, mellow stone walls, a crackling fire. Outside, roses ramble on golden stone walls, while a pretty garden waits at the back. Good food comes as standard, perhaps ham hock terrine with homemade piccalilli, marinated duck breast with bok choi, apple tarte tatin with mascarpone cream; there's fish and chips and a good burger, too. Elsewhere, you find oils on walls, books on shelves, settles in alcoves, beautiful bay windows. A colourful dining room floods with light courtesy of fine arched windows that overlook the green. Bedrooms in the main house have a charming old-world feel, garden rooms are more contemporary with excellent bathrooms. You can walk across fields to Chipping Campden; Simon de Montfort once owned this land. The village church dates to the 11th century and has Thompson mice within.

| Rooms | 5 doubles, 3 twin/doubles: £95-£145. Singles from £85. |
|---|---|
| Meals | Lunch from £4.50. Bar meals from £9.50. Dinner, 3 courses, £25-£30. |
| Closed | Never. |
| Directions | From south take A429 Fosse Way through Moreton-in-Marsh. After 5 miles left to Ilmington. |

|  | Robert Jeal |
|---|---|
|  | The Howard Arms |
|  | Lower Green, Ilmington, |
|  | Shipston-on-Stour, CV36 4LT |
| Tel | +44 (0)1608 682226 |
| Email | info@howardarms.com |
| Web | www.howardarms.com |

## The Bell Alderminster

A lively inn on the Alscot estate with gardens that run down to a small river – rugs and picnic hampers are available, so you can decamp in good weather. There's a pretty courtyard terrace, too, with wicker armchairs and sofas, not a bad spot for a pint of home-brewed ale. Inside, you find that happy mix of old and new – low beamed ceilings and exposed brick walls, then cool colours and the odd sofa. There are armchairs in front of the fire, a cute sail-shaded conservatory, live music on the last Friday of the month. There's good food, too, with lamb and beef straight from the estate; you might find duck liver pâté, sea bream with saffron, caramel and chocolate cheesecake. Bedrooms are scattered about, some in the main house, a new batch in the converted barn that flanks the terrace. They vary in size (two are small), but all have comfort and style with smart fabrics, crisp linen and sofas or armchairs if there's room. The suites are enormous with exposed beams and fabulous bathrooms. A road passes to the front, quietly at night. Stratford waits up the road for all things Shakespeare.

| | |
|---|---|
| Rooms | 5 doubles, 2 twins: £95–£140. 2 suites for 2: £145–£165. Singles from £70 (Sun-Thur). |
| Meals | Lunch from £4.75. Bar meals from £7. Dinner, 3 courses, about £25. Sunday lunch from £13.95. |
| Closed | Never. |
| Directions | On A3400 in Alderminster. |

Chris Swain
The Bell Alderminster
Shipston Road, Alderminster,
Stratford-upon-Avon, CV37 8NY
Tel    +44 (0)1789 450414
Email  info@thebellald.co.uk
Web   www.thebellald.co.uk

## Methuen Arms Hotel

The Methuen has always changed with the times. It started life as a 14th-century nunnery, turned into a coaching inn and brewery in 1608, had a Georgian facelift in the late 1700s, then became a boutique hotel in 2010. It's a lovely little place – cosy and stylish with some gorgeous food. It sits on the edge of the village, with an avenue of trees around the corner leading up to Corsham Court, an Elizabethan pile. As for the hotel, there's a beautiful courtyard at the back where you can eat in summer, a restaurant that opens onto the garden, a locals' bar where the main currency is gossip, then a sitting-room bar where you can sink into an armchair in front of the wood-burner and enjoy a pint of Otter. Chic bedrooms are scattered about. You'll find warm colours, padded bedheads, good art, Roberts radios. There are robes in fine bathrooms, four of which have claw-foot baths, one of which is in the bedroom. Don't miss the excellent food, perhaps cream of shallot soup, monkfish wrapped in Parma ham, chocolate mousse with caramelized oranges. Sunday lunch draws a crowd. Bath is close.

| | |
|---|---|
| Rooms | 11 doubles, 2 twin/doubles: £140–£175. 1 family room for 4: £150–£220. Singles from £90. |
| Meals | Lunch from £5.95. Early supper £18.50–£21.50. Sunday lunch from £18.50. Dinner, 3 courses, about £30. |
| Closed | Never. |
| Directions | M4 junc. 17, then A350 south & A4 west. B3353 south into Corsham. On left. |

**Martin & Debbie Still**
Methuen Arms Hotel
2 High Street,
Corsham, SN13 0HB

| | |
|---|---|
| Tel | +44 (0)1249 717060 |
| Email | info@themethuenarms.com |
| Web | www.themethuenarms.com |

## Timbrell's Yard

Those lovely people at the Draco Pub Co. have been doing what they do so well – opening another of their small-scale pleasuredomes. Their latest inn stands close to the bridge in Bradford-on-Avon with beautiful views across the river to the churchyard. Outside, a terrace at the front catches the sun, with this 18th-century listed building standing grandly behind. It's a lovely spot, good enough for Samuel Spode to paint; a copy of his work hangs in the restaurant, the real thing waits in the town's museum. Inside, you get that winning combination of stylish rooms, lovely food and well-kept ales, with cakes and coffee available all day. You'll find stripped floors, hanging lamps, exposed stone walls, then sofas in front of an open fire. Helpful staff weave about, delivering food that makes you smile, perhaps Dorset crab on toast, pork belly with sea salt crackling, vanilla panna cotta with rhubarb jelly. Bedrooms are beautiful. Eleven have river views, two have baths in the room, mezzanine suites have window seats where you can watch the river pass. Bathrooms are predictably divine.

| | |
|---|---|
| Rooms | 14 doubles: £95–£145. |
| | Extra beds for children £20. |
| Meals | Lunch and dinner £5–£35. |
| Closed | Never. |
| Directions | A363 south into Bradford-on-Avon. Over bridge and 1st right. |

Jon Hutchings
Timbrell's Yard
49 St Margaret's Street,
Bradford-on-Avon, BA15 1DE

| | |
|---|---|
| Tel | +44 (0)1225 869492 |
| Email | info@timbrellsyard.com |
| Web | www.timbrellsyard.com |

## The Muddy Duck

In 1125 Cluniac monks founded a monastery in the village; this venerable building was their sleeping quarters. It turned into an alehouse in the 19th-century to satisfy the miners who dug Bath stone from under these hills. These days, it's a gorgeous old inn with an ancient wisteria gracing the stone courtyard at the front, then a smart terraced garden with views across open farmland behind. Inside, old and new mix gracefully: wooden floors, the odd beam and half-panelled walls, then red leather bar stools, armchairs in front of the fire and low-hanging lamps in the restaurant. The bar plays host to a colourful cast of farmers and shoot parties, who come for a pint of Butcombe and some great food. Three bedrooms in the house vary in size. All have warm colours, comfy beds and robes in good bathrooms, but the suite is huge with a sofa in front of an open fire and a claw-foot bath in the room. Two new suites wait beyond the car park with smart bathrooms, snug sitting rooms and small terraces, too. Don't miss the food, perhaps grilled sardines, local duck, honey panna cotta. Bath is close.

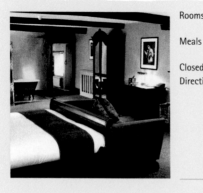

| Rooms | 2 doubles: £95-£150. |
| | 3 suites for 2: £195. |
| Meals | Lunch from £4.95. |
| | Dinner, 3 courses, about £30. |
| Closed | Never. |
| Directions | M4 junction 18, then A46/A4 to Bathford. South on A363 for two miles, then left for Monkton Farleigh. Left at x-roads and on left. |

Charlie Lavender
The Muddy Duck
Monkton Farleigh,
Bradford-on-Avon, BA15 2QH

| Tel | +44 (0)1225 858705 |
| Email | dishitup@themuddyduckbath.co.uk |
| Web | www.themuddyduckbath.co.uk |

## The Beckford Arms

A country-house inn on the Fonthill estate. You sweep in under the Triumphal Arch, which seems appropriate – this is one of the loveliest inns in the land. Outside, in the garden, you find hammocks in the trees and parasols on the terrace, then a church spire soaring beyond. Georgian interiors are no less lovely, a mix of original features and 21st-century style. There's a drawing room with facing sofas in front of a roaring fire; a restaurant with a wall of glass that opens onto the terrace; a bar with parquet flooring for an excellent local pint. Potter about and chance upon the odd chandelier, roaming wisteria and a rather grand mahogany table in the private dining room. Bedrooms are small but perfectly formed with prices to match: white walls, the best linen, sisal matting, good bathrooms. If you want something bigger try the pavilions on the estate; former guests include Byron and Nelson, though we doubt they had it so good. As for the food, it's lovely stuff, perhaps Brixham clam chowder, whole lemon sole, chocolate and Cointreau delice with blood orange sorbet.

| | |
|---|---|
| Rooms | 7 doubles, 1 twin/double: £95–£120. 2 pavilions for 2: £175–£195. |
| Meals | Dinner about £30. |
| Closed | Never. |
| Directions | On the road between Tisbury & Hindon, 3 miles south of A303 (Fonthill exit). |

Charlie Luxton
The Beckford Arms
Fonthill Gifford, Tisbury,
Salisbury, SP3 6PX

| | |
|---|---|
| Tel | +44 (0)1747 870385 |
| Email | info@beckfordarms.com |
| Web | www.beckfordarms.com |

## Howard's House

In a gorgeous English village, a wormhole back in time, this Grade-II listed house dates from 1623 and comes with fine gardens in front of fields that sweep uphill to a ridge of old oak. You can walk straight out, so bring your boots. Inside, airy country-house interiors come with exquisite arched windows, flagstones in reception and the odd beam. Deep sofas, fresh flowers and the morning papers wait in the sitting room, where a fire crackles on cold days. When the sun shines, doors open onto a very pretty terrace for breakfasting. Elegant bedrooms mix old and new to great effect. They're not overly plush, but deeply comfortable with warm colours, mullioned windows, bowls of fruit and a sofa if there's room. Expect oak headboards, pretty fabrics, robes in good bathrooms. Spin downstairs for dinner – perhaps fillet of sea bass with parsnip purée, Scottish beef with roasted shallots, apple crème caramel with a calvados jelly – then climb back up to find your bed turned down. Salisbury, Stonehenge and the gardens at Stourhead are all close.

| | |
|---|---|
| Rooms | 6 doubles, 1 twin/double: £190. 1 four-poster: £210 1 family room for 4: from £190. Singles from £120. |
| Meals | Lunch from £7.95. Dinner: set menu £27-£32.50; à la carte £36-£45; 6-course tasting menu £65. |
| Closed | Rarely. |
| Directions | A30 from Salisbury, B3089 west to Teffont. There, left at sharp right-hand bend following brown hotel sign. Entrance on right after 0.5 miles. |

Noele Thompson & Simon
Greenwood
Howard's House
Teffont Evias, Salisbury, SP3 5RJ
Tel     +44 (0)1722 716392
Email   enq@howardshousehotel.co.uk
Web    www.howardshousehotel.co.uk

## Russell's

A cool little restaurant with rooms in the middle of one of England's prettiest villages. It stands on the green, flanked by posh shops, a great little base in the Cotswolds. Its airy interiors have a contemporary feel with whitewashed walls and a smart bar for the odd cocktail. In summer, you decant onto the terraces, one at the back, one at the front, so follow the sun. Bedrooms are lovely, you don't need to splash out to get something good. Smaller rooms have all the kit: beautiful fabrics, lovely beds, perhaps a walk-in shower or a claw-foot bath. There's good art, waffled bathrobes, gadgetry galore (flat-screen TVs, DVD players, iPod docks). The magnificent four-poster suite has a cross-beamed cathedral ceiling and exposed stone walls, then a spa bath and shower for two. Back downstairs, lovely food awaits (Jay Rayner loved his), perhaps Cornish crab cocktail, rack of local lamb, blood orange soufflé with chocolate ice cream. Don't miss the Gordon Russell Design Museum next door; the hotel was his showroom. J.M. Barrie, Vaughan Williams and Edward Elgar all lived in the village. Brilliant. *Pets by arrangement.*

| | |
|---|---|
| Rooms | 4 doubles, 2 twin/doubles: £120–£245. 1 suite for 2: £245–£300. |
| Meals | Lunch, 2 courses, from £18. Sunday lunch from £24. Dinner, 3 courses, about £40 (not Sun night). |
| Closed | Rarely. |
| Directions | A44 from Oxford & Evesham, then B4632 from Cheltenham. In centre of Broadway on High Street. |

Andrew Riley
Russell's
20 High Street,
Broadway, WR12 7DT
Tel        +44 (0)1386 853555
Email    info@russellsofbroadway.co.uk
Web      www.russellsofbroadway.co.uk

## Brocco on the Park

Sheffield is a friendly city, an arty hub that's full of surprises, a fact ably demonstrated by this stunning small hotel. It sits amid leafy streets, with a smart park to the front, then hills beyond that ripple over to the Peak District. Picasso stayed here when he attended the World Peace Congress in 1950, though things have changed a little since – a recent refit has turned this into a small-scale pleasuredome. Downstairs, there's a Scandi feel in the café/kitchen, with joggers and dog walkers swapping the park for delicious smoothies or a slice of cake. Bedrooms are divine, as good as they look. Expect the best white linen, smart neutral colours, the coolest bathrooms with robes and organic oils. A vast window in one room opens to frame the view; another has a free-standing bath; all are named after birds, their colours reflected in the fabrics. Back downstairs, tasty food waits at night, perhaps cauliflower and pistachio fritters, rib-eye steak with wild mushrooms, spiced plum crumble with vanilla ice cream. Don't miss the Millennium Gallery, the Winter Garden or the cool streets around you.

| | |
|---|---|
| Rooms | 6 doubles, 2 twin/doubles: £75–£220. Extra bed/sofabed available £35 per person per night. |
| Meals | Breakfast from £2. Lunch from £7. Sunday lunch from £16. Dinner from £12. Not Sunday nights. |
| Closed | Rarely. |
| Directions | Leave ring road to southwest at Waitrose, signed Castleton A625. After 1.5 miles, at 1st r'bout, take last exit. Hotel on left. |

AWARD
WINNER

Favourite
newcomer

Tiina Carr
Brocco on the Park
92 Brocco Bank,
Sheffield, S11 8RS

| | |
|---|---|
| Tel | +44 (0)114 266 1233 |
| Email | hello@brocco.co.uk |
| Web | www.brocco.co.uk |

## The Grange Hotel

York Minster, the oldest Gothic cathedral in northern Europe, is utterly imperious, its Great East Window the largest piece of medieval stained glass in the world. It stands less than half a mile from the front door of this welcoming Regency townhouse – a ten-minute stroll after your bacon and eggs. Inside, country-house elegance runs throughout: marble pillars in the flagged entrance hall, an open fire in the morning room and a first-floor drawing room that opens onto a small balcony. Bedrooms come in different shapes and sizes with smart fabrics, period colours and good bathrooms. The bigger rooms have high ceilings, perhaps a four-poster bed, but new rooms in the eaves are lovely too. York racecourse brings a happy crowd to the bar, you'll find an airy elegance and some rather fancy food in the Ivy Restaurant, then a vaulted brasserie with red banquettes for simpler dishes, perhaps French onion soup, boeuf bourguignon, chocolate fondant with chocolate chip ice-cream. Castle Howard for all things *Brideshead* and the North York Moors for exhilarating walking are both close.

| | |
|---|---|
| Rooms | 11 doubles, 18 twin/doubles, 3 four-posters: £137–£235. 1 suite for 2: £284. 3 singles: £123. |
| Meals | Lunch from £16.50. Dinner from £29.95. |
| Closed | Never. |
| Directions | South into York from ring road on A19. On right after two miles, 500 yards north of York Minster. |

Jackie Millan
The Grange Hotel
1 Clifton,
York, YO30 6AA
Tel       +44 (0)1904 644744
Email    info@grangehotel.co.uk
Web      www.grangehotel.co.uk

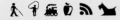

Entry 226   Map 6

## Fantinos

Sleepy Sowerby flows into Thirsk – a refreshingly un-twee market town on the edge of the Dales and Moors. On Sowerby's leafy main street is Fantinos, a simple but smart Italian restaurant-with-rooms clad in Virginia creeper. Drive into the central courtyard to find stables on the right and the restaurant straight ahead, fronted by a terrace with bistro tables, a super sunny spot for a pint of Yorkshire's best. As for the bedrooms, they're divided between stables and house. One sports a black leather headboard, two have accent walls, and the fanciest, Alfa Romeo, large and light in oatmeals and soft greens, faces the courtyard. Vintage suitcases stand in the fireplace and the bathroom (a roll top tub, a powerful shower) is a luxurious place for a soak. The billets in the stables are much smaller, and welcome dogs, as they should: Thirsk is, after all, the 'gateway to the Dales'. Best of all is the restaurant, furnished with pale wood tables and a log-fired oven for all to see. Tuck into risotto, linguine, penne, pizza, Italian clams and 28-day aged sirloin steak – chef-patron Sean is a passionate cook.

| | |
|---|---|
| Rooms | 5 doubles: £85–£125. Dogs £10 per stay. |
| Meals | Lunch from £5. Dinner from £15. |
| Closed | Never. |
| Directions | A1(M), junc. 49, then A168 east for 7 miles. Left into Sowerby and on left opposite green. |

Sean Lockyear
Fantinos
Front Street, Sowerby,
Thirsk, YO7 1JF

| | |
|---|---|
| Tel | +44 (0)1845 523655 |
| Email | info@fantinos.co.uk |
| Web | www.fantinos.co.uk |

## The Black Swan at Oldstead

This delicious restaurant with rooms stands in peaceful hills close to Byland Abbey. It's owned by a family of farmers, who don't just grow their own food, they cook it, too – rather well judging by the Michelin star in the kitchen. You potter up the lane, leave the world behind, then find the lap of luxury. Downstairs, the front bar has lots of character – flagged floors, bay windows, a crackling fire for colder days. In summer, you decant onto the front lawn and listen to the locals: birds, cattle, sheep, pheasants. Bedrooms are scattered about. Four behind the main house have private terraces, oak armoires, beautiful beds, fancy bathrooms (one has a copper bath). Those in the village in a Georgian house have an uncluttered feel with airy colours, the odd antique, gorgeous bathrooms. As for the food, some of which is foraged, you eat from a nine-course tasting menu that changes every day, perhaps asparagus with hazelnuts, trout and squid with radishes, chicken and wild garlic lollipops, then a cocktail of local honey and elderflower. The Moors are on your doorstep, York is down the road. Perfect.

| | |
|---|---|
| Rooms | 5 doubles, 2 four-posters: £230-£410. Price includes dinner for 2. |
| Meals | Lunch from £32 (Sat/Sun only). Dinner, 5 courses included in price; 9-course tasting menu, £25 extra per person; non residents £55/£80 respectively. |
| Closed | First 2 weeks in January. |
| Directions | A19 from Thirsk; left to Thirkleby & Coxwold, then left for Byland Abbey; follow signs left for Oldstead. |

The Banks Family
The Black Swan at Oldstead
Oldstead,
York, YO61 4BL

| | |
|---|---|
| Tel | +44 (0)1347 868387 |
| Email | enquiries@blackswanoldstead.co.uk |
| Web | www.blackswanoldstead.co.uk |

Entry 228   Map 6

## The Talbot Hotel

A 17th-century hunting lodge on the Fitzwilliam estate, not far from Castle Howard. It stands on the edge of town with Malton's streets on one side and big views over field and river on the other. Inside, two fires burn in the drawing room, you find fresh flowers, lovely art, the daily papers and cavernous sofas. There's a bar that drops down to an airy conservatory, then a country-house restaurant as well as a private dining room. It's headed up by TV chef James Martin and regulars love the excellent Yorkshire produce, perhaps local wood pigeon with parsnip purée, beef with wild garlic, buttermilk panna cotta with Yorkshire rhubarb. Lovely bedrooms have smart floral fabrics, pale wool carpets and botanical prints on the walls. Bigger rooms have sofas, several have the view, bathrooms are gorgeous and come with robes. You're well positioned for York, the Moors, coastal walks and Castle Howard. Malton, a historic market town, holds a popular farmers' market every other Saturday and a fabulous food festival in May. The hotel has a cookery school, too, with a focus on Yorkshire game and seafood. *Minimum stay: 2 nights at weekends.*

| | |
|---|---|
| Rooms | 23 doubles: £145–£225.<br>1 suite for 2, 2 suites for 4: £295–£325.<br>Dinner, B&B from £110 per person. |
| Meals | Bar meals from £7.50.<br>Dinner, 3 courses, about £35.<br>Sunday lunch from £20. |
| Closed | Rarely. |
| Directions | A64 north from York, then B2148 into Malton. Keep right in town and on right after half a mile. |

David Macdonald
The Talbot Hotel
45-47 Yorkersgate,
Malton, YO17 7AJ

| | |
|---|---|
| Tel | +44 (0)1653 639096 |
| Email | reservations@talbotmalton.co.uk |
| Web | www.talbotmalton.co.uk |

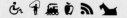

## The White Swan Inn

A dreamy old inn that stands on Market Place, where farmers set up shop on the first Thursday of the month. The exterior is 16th century and flower baskets hang from its mellow stone walls. Inside, you find a seriously pretty world: stripped floors, open fires, a tiny bar, beautiful windows. The restaurant is at the back – the heart and soul of the inn – with delicious food flying from the kitchen, perhaps Whitby fishcakes, rack of spring lamb, glazed lemon tart with blood-orange sorbet. Excellent bedrooms are scattered about. Those in the main house have padded bedheads, delicious linen, Osborne & Little fabrics and flat-screen TV/DVDs; bathrooms have robes and Bath House oils. Rooms in the courtyard tend to be bigger and come in crisp contemporary style with black-and-white screen prints, mohair blankets and York stone bathrooms. You'll also find the Bothy here, a cool little residents' sitting room, with a huge open fire and cathedral ceilings. The moors are all around: fabulous walking, Castle Howard and Whitby all wait. *Minimum stay: 2 nights at weekends.*

| | |
|---|---|
| Rooms | 14 doubles, 4 twin/doubles: £149–£179. 3 suites for 2: £149–£189. Singles from £115. Dinner, B&B from £105 per person. Extra bed/sofabed available £20 per person per night. |
| Meals | Lunch from £5.25. Dinner, 3 courses £25–£35. Sunday lunch from £12.95. |
| Closed | Never. |
| Directions | From North A170 to Pickering. Entering town left at traffic lights, then 1st right into Market Place. On left. |

Catherine Feather
The White Swan Inn
Market Place,
Pickering, YO18 7AA

| | |
|---|---|
| Tel | +44 (0)1751 472288 |
| Email | welcome@white-swan.co.uk |
| Web | www.white-swan.co.uk |

## Estbek House

A super find on the Whitby coast. This is a quietly elegant restaurant with rooms ten paces from the beach at Sandsend. It's small, intimate and very welcoming. Tim cooks brilliantly, David talks you through his exceptional wine list and passes on the local news. Cliffs rise to the north, the beach runs away to the south, East Row Beck river passes directly opposite, ducks waddle across the road. There's a terrace at the front for drinks in summer and a small bar on the lower ground, where you can watch Tim at work in his kitchen. Upstairs, two dining rooms swim in seaside light and come with stripped floors, old radiators and crisp white tablecloths. Grab a window seat for watery views and dig into fresh Whitby crab with avocado and mango salad, local lamb with rhubarb compote, apricot tarte tatin. Bedrooms – bigger on the first floor, smaller on the second – have painted panelling, crisp white linen, colourful throws and shuttered windows. Breakfast is delicious – David's mum makes the marmalade. There are cliff walks, the moors to discover and you can follow the river upstream to Mulgrave Castle.

| | |
|---|---|
| Rooms | 4 doubles, 1 twin/double: £125–£150. Dinner, B&B from £80 per person. |
| Meals | Dinner, 3 courses, about £35. |
| Closed | Occasionally. |
| Directions | North from Whitby on A174 to Sandsend. On left in village by bridge. |

**David Cross & Tim Lawrence**
Estbek House
East Row, Sandsend,
Whitby, YO21 3SU

| | |
|---|---|
| Tel | +44 (0)1947 893424 |
| Email | info@estbekhouse.co.uk |
| Web | www.estbekhouse.co.uk |

## Broom House at Egton Bridge

As lovely a place to stay on the moors as you could hope for. You wind your way in – up dale, down hill – with a carpet of purple heather in late summer and a golden fleece of bracken in autumn. As for this attractive house, it sits on the edge of a pretty village, with fine views of Esk Dale from the garden terrace. Inside, airy interiors are stylish and comfortable, the perfect tonic after a day in the hills. Downstairs, there's a sitting room with garden views, then a dining room for Michael's delicious breakfasts – Whitby kippers, Glaisdale bacon, smoothies from garden strawberries. In summer, you decant onto the terrace for birdsong with your bacon and eggs. Stylish rooms have warm colours, comfy beds, white cotton, perhaps a sofa or doors onto the terrace. All have fine bathrooms, one with a free-standing bath. By day you explore the moors, spin over to Whitby or try a leg of the coast-to-coast path, which passes outside. At night you follow the river into the village for dinner at one of its pubs. You couldn't be in better hands – Michael and Georgina look after you in style. Pure bliss.

| | |
|---|---|
| Rooms | 7 doubles, 1 twin: £90–£150. Singles from £75. |
| Meals | Two good pubs in village. |
| Closed | Christmas. |
| Directions | Leave A171 for Egton. Thru' village to Egton Bridge, under bridge, then right into Broom House Lane. Under bridge and on right. |

Georgina & Michael Curnow
Broom House at Egton Bridge
Broom House Lane, Egton Bridge,
Whitby, YO21 1XD

| | |
|---|---|
| Tel | +44 (0)1947 895279 |
| Email | mw@broom-house.co.uk |
| Web | www.broom-house.co.uk |

## Judges Country House Hotel

This fine old country house is English to its core. It stands in 26 acres of attractive gardens with lawns that sweep down to a small river and paths that weave through private woods. Inside, you find a world that carries you back to grander days. There's an elegant entrance hall that floods with light, a sitting room bar in racing green, then a golden drawing room where doors open to a pretty terrace for lunch in summer. Wander about and find fires primed for combustion, the daily papers laid out in reception, an elegant staircase that rises towards a glass dome. Country-house bedrooms are full of colour. You get bowls of fruit, beautiful beds, gorgeous linen, garden flowers. Bigger rooms have sofas, all have robes in super bathrooms. Back downstairs, there's serious food in the restaurant, perhaps lobster with cardamon and mango, duck with chicory and orange, warm chocolate cake with caramelised banana. If that's not enough, come home early for afternoon tea in front of the fire. The Dales and the Moors are close, while Fountains Abbey and Castle Howard are both within striking distance.

| Rooms | 14 twin/doubles, 3 four-posters: £130–£220. 2 suites for 2: £160–£220. 2 singles: £99–£110. Dinner, B&B from £102.50 per person. |
|---|---|
| Meals | Lunch from £16.95. Dinner, 3 courses, £37.50. |
| Closed | Never. |
| Directions | A1(M), then A19 for Middlesbrough. Left onto A67, through Kirklevington, hotel signed left. |

**Tim Howard**
Judges Country House Hotel
Kirklevington Hall, Kirklevington,
Yarm, TS15 9LW

| Tel | +44 (0)1642 789000 |
| Email | enquiries@judgeshotel.co.uk |
| Web | www.judgeshotel.co.uk |

## The Coach House at Middleton Lodge

You'll think you've washed up at a beautiful country house in Tuscany or Provence. These gorgeous stone barns were crumbling a few years ago, now they're home to one of the loveliest boutique hotels in the north. In summer, life spills onto the courtyard for lunch in the sun, afternoon tea, or cocktails before dinner. Step through the arched glass doors and find a spectacular restaurant open to the rafters, where contemporary design mixes with rustic bricks and mortar. There's a funky bar, an open fire, the odd leather sofa to take the strain. Rooms are equally lovely: chic fabrics, Roberts radios, bath robes, beds for insomniacs to fall asleep in. Five open onto a terrace, one is huge, most have cross beams, claw-foot baths, then a sofa or chaise longue. The food is exceptional, some grown on the estate, much from Yorkshire, perhaps pigeon with praline and pear, roast hake with a clam chowder, toffee chocolate with honeycomb ice cream. You're on a 200-acre estate with the Dales to the west and the Moors to the east. There's the Lodge, too, one of the best wedding venues in the North.

| | |
|---|---|
| Rooms | 9 doubles: £155–£185. Singles from £135. |
| Meals | Lunch from £5.50. Sunday lunch from £12.50. Dinner, 3 courses, £30–£35. Not Mon or Tue mid-October to mid-March. |
| Closed | Rarely. |
| Directions | Leave A1 at Scotch Corner and head east to Middleton Tyas. Left in village onto Kneeton Road. Right after 1 mile; left after 300 yards; hotel signed on right. |

James & Rebecca Allison
The Coach House at Middleton Lodge
Middleton Tyas,
Richmond, DL10 6NJ

Tel        +44 (0)1325 377977
Email      info@middletonlodge.co.uk
Web        www.middletonlodge.co.uk/coach-house

Favourite
newcomer

## Hack & Spade

A great little base in the northern Dales. First, there's this untouched village high on the hill with big views north. Then, there's the Hack and Spade, half chic B&B, half friendly restaurant with rooms. It started life in 1806 as an ale house. Bedrooms are gorgeous – if you want to indulge your pleasure receptors, this is a good place to do it. Downstairs, there's an attractive sitting room with big sofas, stone walls, tartan carpets and lots of books. You'll find warm colours and a wood-burner in the stylish dining room, where Jane serves lovely local food from Thursday to Saturday, perhaps peat-smoked salmon, pork with apple and cider, warm raspberry and almond tart. As for the bedrooms, expect chic design, lots of comfort and fabulous bathrooms. All have padded bedheads, smart fabrics and good lighting; a couple have sofas, those at the back have big country views. Bathrooms don't hold back: two have free-standing baths, all have robes and walk-in power showers. Fabulous walking waits. Don't miss Richmond on market days or the Bowes Museum in Barnard Castle. *Children over 7 welcome.*

| | |
|---|---|
| Rooms | 4 doubles, 1 twin/double: £120–£130. |
| Meals | Dinner (Thurs-Sat) about £30. |
| Closed | Rarely. |
| Directions | A66 west at Scotch Corner for 2 miles, then left for Ravensworth and Kirby Hill. Through Ravensworth, up hill, left for Whashton at staggered x-roads. On left in village. |

Jane & Andy Ratcliffe
Hack & Spade
Whashton,
Richmond, DL11 7JL

| | |
|---|---|
| Tel | +44 (0)1748 823721 |
| Email | jane@hackandspade.com |
| Web | www.hackandspade.com |

## The White Bear Hotel

At five o'clock on a Friday evening there's only one place to be in Masham: the tap room at the White Bear, home of Theakston's beer. The great and the good gather to mark the end of the week, the odd pint is sunk, the air is thick with gossip. Interior design is 1920s trapped in aspic – red leather, polished brass, a crackling fire. But there's more here – a country-house dining room for lovely food; a handsome bar with stripped boards; a flower-filled terrace for lunch in the sun. Bedrooms are lovely, a touch of 21st-century luxury. They occupy the old Lightfoot brewery and come in contemporary style with good fabrics, warm colours, excellent beds and fancy bathrooms. Some have views across town, the vast suite is open to the rafters and worth splashing out on. There's a courtyard for guests, a sitting room, too; staff will bring drinks if you want privacy and peace. Delicious food waits in the restaurant, perhaps shellfish soup, steak and ale pie, treacle sponge pudding. Tours of the brewery are easily arranged, with a pint of your choice at the end. The Dales are all around.

| | |
|---|---|
| Rooms | 13 twin/doubles: £120. |
| | 1 suite for 2: £200–£220. |
| Meals | Lunch from £4.95. |
| | Dinner, 3 courses, about £30. |
| Closed | Never. |
| Directions | North from Ripon on A6108. |
| | In Masham up hill (for Leyburn). |
| | Right at crest of hill. Signed. |

|  |  |
|---|---|
| | Sue Thomas |
| | The White Bear Hotel |
| | Wellgarth, Masham, |
| | Ripon, HG4 4EN |
| Tel | +44 (0)1765 689319 |
| Email | sue@whitebearmasham.co.uk |
| Web | www.thewhitebearhotel.co.uk |

## The Burgoyne Hotel

Reeth is one of those English throwbacks, a beautiful village in the Dales that's hardly changed in 200 years. It was mentioned in the Domesday Book, has the finest grouse moors in the land and its sweeping views over Swaledale stretch for miles. The Burgoyne looks out over it all – afternoon tea in the garden on a sunny day is hard to beat. Inside, an elegant past lives on: a smart drawing room with a crackling fire where you gather for drinks before dinner; a restaurant in racing green where you feast on delicious Yorkshire food; country-house bedrooms full of comfort, with warm colours, good beds, white linen, a sofa if there's room. You'll find pine shutters, cushioned window seats, a four-poster in the old snooker room; all but one has the view. The food is old-school, but utterly delicious, perhaps pheasant and venison terrine, Dover sole with brown shrimps, lemon tart with raspberry sorbet. Best of all are Julia and Mo, who run the place with unstinting kindness. There are maps for walkers, fishing can be arranged, a market passes on Fridays. Richmond is close, too. A delight.

| | |
|---|---|
| Rooms | 4 doubles, 1 twin, 1 four-poster; 2 doubles, 1 twin, each with separate bathroom: £130–£190. 1 suite for 2: £210. Singles from £112.50. Extra beds for children under 13: £25. Dogs: £10 a night. |
| Meals | Dinner: 2 courses, £27; 4 courses, £40. |
| Closed | Midweek in January (Mon-Thur). |
| Directions | From Richmond A6108, then B6270 to Reeth. Hotel on north side of village green. |

**Julia & Mo Usman**
The Burgoyne Hotel
Reeth,
Richmond, DL11 6SN

Tel     +44 (0)1748 884292
Email   enquiries@theburgoyne.co.uk
Web     www.theburgoyne.co.uk

## The Angel Inn

This cute little drover's inn has an old-school feel and sits in a tiny hamlet that's surrounded by glorious country — views stretch across fields of sheep to Rylstone Fell. Outside, there's a terrace for lunch in the sun, inside you find locals gossiping over a pint of Hetton pale ale in the half-panelled bar. It's all very cosy — beamed ceilings, mullioned windows, exposed stone walls, even a working Yorkshire range. There's colourful art on the walls, nooks and crannies to hide away in. The feel is bright and breezy, especially in the dining room, where you dig into delicious food, perhaps seafood parcels with a lobster sauce, chargrilled local beef, a legendary sticky toffee pudding; there's Yapas, too — tapas Yorkshire style! Rooms are scattered about. The suites across the lane have a more traditional feel (half testers, window seats, papered walls, the odd claw-foot bath); those next door in Sycamore House are more contemporary (stylish fabrics, big beds, a sofa if there's room). All have robes in good bathrooms. Jazz bands play at summer barbecues, glorious walks wait.

| | |
|---|---|
| Rooms | 9 doubles: £150-£175. |
| | 5 suites for 2: £175-£200. |
| | Singles from £125. Extra beds £25. |
| Meals | Lunch from £7.50. |
| | Bar meals from £15.95. |
| | Dinner, 3 courses, £35-£55. |
| | Sunday lunch £24.50. |
| Closed | Christmas Day & 1 week in January. |
| Directions | North from Skipton on B6265. Left at Rylstone for Hetton. In village. |

Juliet Watkins
The Angel Inn
Hetton,
Skipton, BD23 6LT

Tel     +44 (0)1756 730263
Email   info@angelhetton.co.uk
Web    www.angelhetton.co.uk

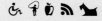

## The Traddock

A northern outpost of country-house charm, beautiful inside and out. It's a family affair and those looking for a friendly base from which to explore the Dales will find it here. You enter through a wonderful drawing room — crackling fire, pretty art, the daily papers, cavernous sofas. Follow your nose and find polished wood in the dining room, panelled walls in the breakfast room, then William Morris wallpaper in the sitting room bar, where you can sip a pint of Skipton ale while playing a game of Scrabble. Bedrooms are just the ticket, some coolly contemporary, others deliciously traditional with family antiques and the odd claw-foot bath. Those on the second floor are cosy in the eaves, all have fresh fruit, homemade shortbread and Dales views. Elsewhere, a white-washed sitting room that opens onto the garden and a rug-strewn restaurant for fabulous local food, perhaps Whitby crab, slow-roasted pork, raspberry and white chocolate soufflé. Spectacular walks start at the front door, there are cycle tracks and some extraordinary caves — one is bigger than St Paul's. Brilliant. *Minimum stay: 2 nights at weekends March — November.*

| | |
|---|---|
| Rooms | 8 doubles, 1 twin/double, 2 family rooms for 4: £95–£165. 1 single: £85–£100. Extra bed/sofabed available £15 p.p.p.n. Dinner, B&B from £78 per person. |
| Meals | Lunch from £9.50. Dinner, 3 courses, around £30. |
| Closed | Never. |
| Directions | 0.75 miles off the A65, midway between Kirkby Lonsdale & Skipton, 4 miles north-west of Settle. |

Paul Reynolds
The Traddock
Austwick,
Settle, LA2 8BY
Tel    +44 (0)15242 51224
Email  info@thetraddock.co.uk
Web    www.thetraddock.co.uk

Old favourite

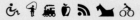

# Channel Islands

Photo: White House Hotel,
enry 240

## White House Hotel

Herm is unique, a tiny island run benignly by the 40 souls lucky enough to live on it. They keep things blissfully simple: no cars, no TVs, just a magical world of field and sky, a perfect place to escape the city. A coastal path rings the island; high cliffs to the south, sandy beaches to the north, cattle grazing the hills between. You get fabulous views at every turn — shimmering islands, pristine waters, yachts and ferries zipping about. There are beach cafés, succulent gardens, an ancient church, even a tavern. Kids love it, so do parents, and the self-catering cottages are extremely popular. As for the hotel, it lingers happily in an elegant past, a great spot from which to enjoy the island. You'll find open fires, delicious four-course dinners, a tennis court, a pool to keep you cool. Spotless bedrooms are scattered about, some in the village's colour-washed cottages, others with balconies in the hotel. Several come in contemporary style with fancy bathrooms, but most are warmly traditional as befits the setting. Expect pretty colours, padded headboards and watery views.

| | |
|---|---|
| Rooms | 28 twin/doubles, 5 family rooms for 2, 5 family rooms for 4: £138–£208. 2 singles: £64–£84. 20 cottages for 2–6: £273–£1,288 per week. Singles from £69. |
| Meals | Lunch from £5. Dinner, 4 courses, £28.50. |
| Closed | November to Easter. |
| Directions | Via Guernsey. Trident ferries leave from the harbour at St Peter Port 8 times a day in summer (£11 return). |

Siôn Dobson Jones
White House Hotel
Herm Island, GY1 3HR

| | |
|---|---|
| Tel | +44 (0)1481 750075 |
| Email | hotel@herm.com |
| Web | www.herm.com |

## The Georgian House

Holly's family have been holidaying in Alderney for more than 30 years, now she's come back to take over this treasure of a hotel. Along with her charming young team, she's turned it into the beating heart of the island. Step off the cobbled high street straight into a traditional, cosy bar; grab a bite here or something more extravagant in the light-strewn dining room that opens out to the pretty garden. Vegetables and salad come from their own allotment, the butter is vivid yellow and meat and fish is as local as can be: try the divine head-to-toe pork dish (great for sharing) or a zingy chilli squid. Upstairs four quaint bedrooms, all en suite, are pretty and pristine with locally made soaps and views across the road to the town. The 100-seater cinema opposite shows art house films on reels, during the interval you wander over to The Georgian for a drink. The hotel is packed with locals and visitors alike, and rightly so; there are barbecues, bands, taster evenings, and a blissful atmosphere. Old forts and stunning beaches wait, so hire bikes and explore the island. And book early.

| | |
|---|---|
| Rooms | 2 doubles, 2 twin/doubles: £70-£95. Singles from £45. |
| Meals | Light lunch from £6. Dinner, 3 courses, £25-£30. |
| Closed | Mid-January to mid-March. |
| Directions | Sent on booking. Airport pick-ups. |

Holly Fisher
The Georgian House
Victoria Street, GY9 3UF
Tel      +44 (0)1481 822471
Email    info@georgianalderney.com
Web      www.georgianalderney.com

# Scotland

Photo: The Airds Hotel &
Restaurant, entry 245

## The Creggans Inn

If you're looking for a small hotel in a great position with lovely rooms and excellent food, you'll find it here. There's a little history, too – the inn was once owned by the real James Bond. Sir Fitzroy Maclean was one of a cast of characters on whom Ian Fleming based his hero; the fact the Royal Navy send their big ships into Loch Fyne is purely coincidental. These days, life at the inn is decidedly restful. Views from the front stretch for miles, the loch eventually giving way to the distant peaks of the Kintyre peninsular. Inside, an airy elegance abounds. There's a first-floor sitting room with big views; a locals' bar which doubles as the clubhouse for the shinty team; then picture windows in the smart restaurant, where you dig into super food while watching the sun set, perhaps Ramsay haggis with whisky sauce, pot roast chicken with a thyme jus, bread and butter pudding with honey glazed figs. Comfy bedrooms have lots of style: warm colours, pretty fabrics, delicate wallpapers, robes in sparkling bathrooms; most have loch views. Castles and gardens, golf and boat trips wait.

| | |
|---|---|
| Rooms | 4 doubles, 9 twin/doubles: £120–£180. 1 suite for 2: £160–£220. Singles from £85. Dinner, B&B from £80 per person. |
| Meals | Lunch from £4.25. Bar meals from £10.95. Dinner, 3 courses, about £30. |
| Closed | Never. |
| Directions | From Glasgow, A82 to Tarbert, A83 towards Inverary for 13 miles, then left on A815 to Strachur (10 miles). Hotel on left before village. |

Archie & Gillian MacLellan
The Creggans Inn
Loch Fyne, Strachur,
Cairndow, PA27 8BX

| | |
|---|---|
| Tel | +44 (0)1369 860279 |
| Email | info@creggans-inn.co.uk |
| Web | www.creggans-inn.co.uk |

## The Manor House

A 1780 dower house for the Dukes of Argyll – their cottage by the sea. Built of local stone, it sits high on the hill with long views over Oban harbour to the Isle of Mull. It's a smart and proper place, not one to bow to fads of fashions, with sea views from the terrace, a roaring fire in the drawing room, beautiful tiles in the entrance hall, an elegant bay window in the bar, then a half-panelled dining room for excellent food. Some bedrooms are on the small side, but all are pretty with warm colours, fresh flowers, crisp linen, bowls of fruit and piles of towels in good bathrooms; those that look seaward have binoculars with which to scour the horizon. Try Loch Fyne kippers for breakfast, seafood risotto for lunch and, if you've room, roast saddle of lamb with shepherds' pie for dinner; there's excellent home baking, too. Ferries leave for the islands from the bottom of the hill – you can watch them sail from the hotel garden. There's a computer for guests to use, afternoon tea can be arranged, and you can watch the sun set from McCaig's Tower overlooking Oban. *Over 12s welcome.*

| | | |
|---|---|---|
| Rooms | 9 doubles, 2 twins: £120-£235.<br>Dinner, B&B from £87.50 per person. | |
| Meals | Lunch from £4.25.<br>Dinner, 4 courses, £42. |  |
| Closed | Christmas. | |
| Directions | In Oban follow signs to ferry.<br>Hotel on right 0.5 miles after ferry<br>turn-off, signed. | |

Gregor MacKinnon
The Manor House
Gallanach Road,
Oban, PA34 4LS

| | |
|---|---|
| Tel | +44 (0)1631 562087 |
| Email | info@manorhouseoban.com |
| Web | www.manorhouseoban.com |

## The Pierhouse

The position here is unbeatable. You're at the end of the road, on the shores of Loch Linnhe, with views across to Lismore and rising mountains beyond. As for the Pierhouse – well, shipwrecked sailors would refuse rescue. Outside, there's a sun-trapping terrace from which to watch the odd boat chug past while digging into langoustines fresh from the waters around you. Interiors are just as good. Glass walls frame the view, there's a smart bar for a wee dram, a white-washed snug with sofas in front of a wood-burner, then, a restaurant for some of the best seafood on the west coast. Chic rooms have a wing to themselves, so expect deep peace. Those at the front have the view, all have an uncluttered Scandi feel with warm colours, padded bedheads, smart fabrics and robes in sparkling bathrooms. You get bowls of fruit, a sofa if there's room, crisp linen on comfy beds. There's lots to do: the ferry across to Lismore for fine walking, Ben Nevis, magical Ardnamurchan. As for the food, come back for oysters, scallops, lobster Thermidor or a rib-eye steak; the seafood platters are out of this world.

| | |
|---|---|
| Rooms | 4 doubles, 4 twin/doubles: £90–£195. 2 suites for 2: £145–£225. Extra beds: children aged 2-12 £30, 12+ £40. |
| Meals | Lunch from £4.95. Bar meals from £12.50. 3-course à la carte dinner £30–£50. |
| Closed | Christmas & Boxing Day. |
| Directions | A82 north for Fort William, then A828 south for Oban. Right for Port Appin after 12 miles. At end of road. |

AWARD
WINNER

Favourite
newcomer

Nick & Nikki Horne
The Pierhouse
Port Appin,
Appin, PA38 4DE
Tel        +44 (0)1631 730302
Email     reservations@pierhousehotel.co.uk
Web      www.pierhousehotel.co.uk

## The Airds Hotel & Restaurant

This smart country-house hotel on the Appin peninsular stands above Loch Linnhe with views across the water to the Morvern Mountains. It started life in 1750, an inn for passengers taking the paddle steamers up to the Caledonian canal. These days, it's one of the loveliest places to stay on the West Coast, its whitewashed exterior giving no hint of the wonders within. You enter through a small conservatory, then find yourself in a world of smouldering fires, freshly cut flowers, beautiful wallpapers and sofas by the dozen. Bedrooms pack a lovely punch – warm colours, smart fabrics, Frette linen for Vi-Spring beds, sparkling marble bathrooms with Italian robes. Those at the front have the view, bigger rooms have sofas, some at the back have terraces, all spoil you rotten. Best of all is the ambrosial food, perhaps seared scallops with pickled cauliflower, lemon sole with parsley mousse, banana soufflé with passion fruit ice-cream. Outside, there's a garden for croquet and afternoon tea with views of water and mountains. The loveliest staff look after you all the way. Brilliant.

| | |
|---|---|
| Rooms | 8 twin/doubles: £305–£375. 3 suites for 4 with sofabed: £395–£455. Price includes dinner for 2. 1 self-catering cottage for 5: £795–£915 per week. |
| Meals | Lunch from £7. Dinner, 5 courses, included; non-residents £55. Tasting menu £75. Sunday lunch £18.95. |
| Closed | Mon & Tue November – January. |
| Directions | A82 north for Fort William, then A828 south for Oban. Right for Port Appin after 12 miles. On left after 2 miles. |

**Shaun & Jenny McKivragan**
The Airds Hotel & Restaurant
Port Appin,
Appin, PA38 4DF

| | |
|---|---|
| Tel | +44 (0)1631 730236 |
| Email | airds@airds-hotel.com |
| Web | www.airds-hotel.com |

## Bealach House

Good food, a lovely welcome and a fine position in Salachan Glen make this a great place to stay when travelling up the west coast. You follow a track through the forest to the only house in the valley. Sheep graze, birds sing, rivers run – other than that you won't hear a thing. Jim and Hilary had a dining pub in the Yorkshire Dales before coming north for a quieter life. Outside, eight acres of gardens have big valley views. Inside, tea and homemade cake is served in front of the wood-burner on colder days or out on the terrace when the sun shines. Bedrooms upstairs aren't huge, but two have room for a sofa and all have warm colours, comfy beds, decanters of sherry and excellent power showers (one has a bath, too). After a hearty breakfast – local eggs, home-made bread – you can climb Ben Nevis, drive up to Loch Ness or take the ferry across to Mull. After which Hilary's food works wonders, perhaps smoked salmon, local venison, chocolate soufflé with a white chocolate sauce (bring your own wine). You can walk from the front door, on clear nights stars fill the sky. *Over 14s welcome.*

| | |
|---|---|
| Rooms | 2 doubles, 1 twin: £90–£110. Singles from £65. |
| Meals | Dinner £25–£30. |
| Closed | Mid-October to mid-February. |
| Directions | A828 south from Fort William for Oban. Signed left, through gate, 2 miles south of Duror. Follow signs up track for 1 mile to house. |

**Jim & Hilary McFadyen**
Bealach House
Salachan Glen, Duror,
Appin, PA38 4BW

| | |
|---|---|
| Tel | +44 (0)1631 740298 |
| Email | enquiries@bealachhouse.co.uk |
| Web | www.bealachhouse.co.uk |

## The Colonsay

Another fabulous Hebridean island, a perfect place to escape the world. Wander at will and find wild flowers in the machair, a golf course tended by sheep and huge sandy beaches across which cows roam. Wildlife is ever present, from a small colony of wild goats to a rich migratory bird population; the odd golden eagle soars overhead, too. At low tide the sands of the south give access to Oronsay. The island's 14th-century priory was one of Scotland's finest and amid impressive ruins its ornate stone cross still stands. As for the hotel, it brims with an easy style – airy interiors, stripped floors, fires everywhere, friendly staff. There's a locals' bar for a pint (and a brewery on the island), a pretty sitting room packed with books, a dining room for super food, a decked terrace for drinks in the sun. Bedrooms have local art, warm colours, lovely fabrics and the best beds; some have sea views, all have good bathrooms. Spin around on bikes, search for standing stones, lie in the sun and stare at the sky. There's a festival in May for all things Colonsay. Wonderful.

| | | |
|---|---|---|
| Rooms | 4 doubles, 3 twins: £85–£150. 1 family room for 4: £105–£140. 1 single: £75–£80. |  |
| Meals | Lunch from £4.50. Packed lunch £7. Bar meals from £11.50. Dinner, 3 courses, about £25. | |
| Closed | November, January (after New Year) & February. | |
| Directions | Calmac ferries from Oban or Kennacraig (not Tue) or Hebridean Airways (Tue & Thur). Hotel on right, half a mile up road from jetty. | |

|  |  |
|---|---|
| | Jane Howard The Colonsay Scalasaig, Isle of Colonsay, PA61 7YP |
| Tel | +44 (0)1951 200316 |
| Email | hotel@colonsayestate.co.uk |
| Web | www.colonsayestate.co.uk |

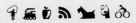

## Tiroran House

The setting is magnificent – 17 acres of gardens rolling down to Loch Scridian. Otters and dolphins pass through, buzzards and eagles glide above, red deer visit the garden. As for this 1850 shooting lodge, you'll be hard pressed to find a more comfortable island base, so it's no surprise to discover it was recently voted 'Best Country House Hotel in Scotland' for the second year in a row. There are fires in the drawing rooms, fresh flowers everywhere, games to be played, books to be read. Airy bedrooms hit the spot: crisp linen, beautiful fabrics, the odd chaise longue; some have watery views, all have silence guaranteed. You eat in a smart dining room with much of the delicious food from the island or waters around it, perhaps mussel and oyster broth, saddle of lamb with carrot purée, chocolate tort with vanilla ice cream. You're bang in the middle of Mull with lots to do: Tobermory, the prettiest town in the Hebrides; Calgary and its magical beach; day trips to Iona and its famous monastery; cruises to Staffa and Fingal's Cave. Come back for afternoon tea – it's as good as the Ritz.

| Rooms | 5 doubles, 5 twin/doubles: £175-£220. |
|---|---|
| Meals | Dinner, 4 courses, £48. |
| Closed | Rarely. |
| Directions | From Craignure or Fishnish car ferries, A849 for Bunessan & Iona car ferry. Right onto B8035 for Gruline. After 4 miles left at converted church. House 1 mile further. |

Hotel of the Year
Scotland

Laurence & Katie Mackay
Tiroran House
Tiroran,
Isle of Mull, PA69 6ES
Tel      +44 (0)1681 705232
Email    info@tiroran.com
Web      www.tiroran.com

Entry 248   Map 8, 10

## Glengorm Castle

Few places defy overstatement, but Glengorm does so with ease. It stands in 5,000 acres at the top of Mull with views that stretch across the sea to Coll and the Uists, Barra and Rhum. Directly in front the land falls away, rolls over lush pasture, then tumbles into the sea. Sheep and cattle graze – Tom wins prizes for his cows. Despite the grandeur, this is a family home with children and dogs pottering about. You feel immediately at ease. First you bounce up a four-mile drive, then you step into a vast hall, where sofas wait in front of the fire and big art hangs on the walls. An oak staircase sweeps you up to wonderful country-house rooms; three have the view, all have warm colours, antique furniture and excellent bathrooms. Elsewhere, a panelled library for guests to use with a selection of whiskies 'on the house', then a vast kitchen garden, coastal paths, even a swimming hole. Breakfast is a feast – grab the table by the window. There's a farm shop, a café and a deli, too, even guided wildlife walks and a hide from which to spot otters. Good restaurants wait in Tobermory.

| | |
|---|---|
| Rooms | 3 doubles, 1 four-poster; 1 twin/double with separate bath: £130–£210. Tower Rooms: 1 apartment for 4: from £250 per night. |
| Meals | Restaurants 5 miles. |
| Closed | Castle closed Christmas & New Year. |
| Directions | North to Tobermory on A848. Straight over roundabout (not right for town). Over x-roads after half a mile and straight ahead for four miles to castle. |

**Tom & Marjorie Nelson**
Glengorm Castle
Tobermory,
Isle of Mull, PA75 6QE

| | |
|---|---|
| Tel | +44 (0)1688 302321 |
| Email | enquiries@glengormcastle.co.uk |
| Web | www.glengormcastle.co.uk |

## Knockinaam Lodge

Lawns run down to the Irish sea, roe deer come to eat the roses, sunsets turn the sky red. This beautiful hunting lodge is one of the loveliest country-house hotels in the land. There's a Michelin star in the dining room, 150 malts in the panelled bar and a level of service you rarely find in such far-flung corners of the realm. There's history, too. Churchill once stayed and you can sleep in his room, then climb into the deepest of baths and read his books. Immaculate interiors abound: gorgeous bedrooms, faultless bathrooms, a morning room where the scent of fresh flowers mingles with wood smoke. You'll find beautiful art, the daily papers, games and books galore. Outside, cliff walks lead over to Portpatrick, peregrine falcons circle on high, bluebells carpet the hills in spring. When it's stormy, waves crash all around. There's golf on the coast at Portpatrick, then Luce Bay for miles of sand. John Buchan knew the house and described it in *The Thirty-Nine Steps* as the house to which Hannay fled. Remote, beguiling, utterly spoiling – grand old Knockinaam is simply unmissable.

| Rooms | 4 doubles, 5 twin/doubles: £290–£440. 1 family room for 4: £350–£420. Price includes dinner for 2. |
|---|---|
| Meals | Lunch, by arrangement, £32.50–£40. Dinner, 5 courses, included; non-residents £67.50. |
| Closed | Never. |
| Directions | From A77 or A75 pick up signs to Portpatrick. West from Lochans on A77, then left after 2 miles, signed. Follow signs for 3 miles to hotel. |

David & Sian Ibbotson
Knockinaam Lodge
Portpatrick,
Stranraer, DG9 9AD

Tel     +44 (0)1776 810471
Email   reservations@knockinaamlodge.com
Web     www.knockinaamlodge.com

## Cavens

The Solway Firth is a magical spot, a patch of heaven most ignore, so you'll mostly have it to yourself. You swoop down from Dumfries through glorious country, then crest a hill and there it is, vast tracts of tidal sands with a huge sky above. It's a magnet for birdlife, the rich pickings of low tide too tempting to refuse. As for this 1752 shooting lodge, it stands in 20 acres of sweeping lawns, native woodlands and sprawling fields. Inside, elegant interiors come as standard. Two lovely sitting rooms are decked out with busts and oils, golden sofas, smouldering fires, a baby grand piano; in summer, you slip onto the terrace for afternoon tea. Country-house bedrooms have garden views, period furniture, bowls of fruit. One is smaller, others big with room for sofas. One has a stunning bathroom, another has an en suite sun-room. Back downstairs, there's an honesty bar for pre-dinner drinks, then Angus's delicious food in the smart restaurant, perhaps scallops with lime and Vermouth, Galloway pork in a mustard sauce, lemon panna cotta. There are gardens aplenty and golf at spectacular Southerness.

| | |
|---|---|
| Rooms | 4 doubles, 1 twin: £100-£190. Extra bed/sofabed available £30 per person per night. |
| Meals | Dinner: 3-course market menu £25; 3-course à la carte about £35. Packed lunch available. |
| Closed | Rarely. |
| Directions | From Dumfries A710 to Kirkbean (12 miles). Signed in village on left. |

Jane & Angus Fordyce
Cavens
Kirkbean,
Dumfries, DG2 8AA
Tel       +44 (0)1387 880234
Email     enquiries@cavens.com
Web       www.cavens.com

## Trigony House Hotel

A small, welcoming, family-run hotel with good food, nicely priced rooms and a lovely garden, where you may spot red squirrels. The house dates to 1700, a shooting lodge for the local castle. Inside, you find Japanese oak panelling in the hall, a wood-burner in the pretty sitting room and an open fire in the dining room, where doors open onto the terrace for dinner in summer. Adam cooks lovely rustic fare, perhaps goats' cheese tart, loin of roe venison, chocolate brownie cheesecake with chocolate ice cream; there's a small, organic kitchen garden that provides much for the table in summer. Bedrooms vary in size, but not style — all have pretty fabrics, summer colours and good bathrooms. Some are dog-friendly, one has a conservatory/sitting room that opens onto a private lawn, there's a film library downstairs for your TV. After a full cooked breakfast, head west for the Southern Upland Way or the spectacular country between Moniaive and the Galloway Forest. Don't miss Drumlanrig Castle up the road for its gardens, walking trails and excellent mountain bike tracks.

| | |
|---|---|
| Rooms | 4 doubles, 4 twin/doubles: £85–£130. 1 suite for 2: £155. Dinner, B&B from £82.50 per person. |
| Meals | Lunch from £5. Dinner £25–£35. |
| Closed | 24–26 December. |
| Directions | North from Dumfries on A76; through Closeburn; signed left after 1 mile. |

Adam & Jan Moore
Trigony House Hotel
Closeburn,
Thornhill, DG3 5EZ

Tel     +44 (0)1848 331211
Email   trigonyhotel@gmail.com
Web     www.trigonyhotel.co.uk

## Ardmor House

A very friendly B&B bang in the middle of fashionable Leith. The house dates to 1890 and was once a doctor's surgery. These days, there's a small rose garden at the front, then softly chic interiors within. Robin runs a relaxed ship and goes out of his way to make your stay special. Bedrooms have lots of style: high ceilings, padded bedheads, iPod docks, crisp white linen. You'll find robes for compact shower rooms, then colourful fabrics and cool art on the walls. Downstairs, delicious treats wait for breakfast: croissants and muffins, smoked salmon and scrambled eggs, the full cooked works; there's locally roasted coffee and lovely homemade jams, too. After which, stroll north past trendy shops and bars to the coast. Cafés wait on the Water of Leith, you can board the royal yacht Britannia for afternoon tea on its top deck. Buses whizz you into the heart of this beautiful city: to Hollyrood, the castle or the Meadows on sunny days. Stay local at night for great food and cool bars – try the Compass for good pub grub, La Favorita for pizza round the corner or The Kitchin for a Michelin star.

| Rooms | 2 doubles, 1 twin/double: £95–£170. |
|---|---|
| | 1 family room for 3: £110–£170. |
| | 1 single: £65–£95. |
| Meals | Restaurants on your doorstep. |
| Closed | Rarely. |
| Directions | From A702 ring road, north on A1 to Leith. South on A900 for a mile and on right. |

**Robin Jack**
Ardmor House
74 Pilrig Street,
Edinburgh, EH6 5AS

| | |
|---|---|
| Tel | +44 (0)131 554 4944 |
| Email | info@ardmorhouse.com |
| Web | www.ardmorhouse.com |

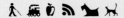

## 21212

A smart restaurant with rooms in Edinburgh's East End with Holyrood Palace, the Botanic Gardens and lovely Leith all close. Paul left his Michelin star down south, bought this Georgian townhouse, spent a fortune turning it into a 21st-century pleasuredome, then opened for business and won back his star. The house stands at the top of a hill with long views north towards the Firth of Forth. Inside, contemporary splendour waits. High ceilings and vast windows come as standard, but wander at will and find a chic first-floor drawing room, cherubs on the wall, busts and statues all over the place, even a private dining pod made of white leather. Stunning bedrooms have enormous beds, cool colours, fat sofas and iPod docks. Those at the front have the view, all have robes in magnificent bathrooms. As for the restaurant, the kitchen is on display behind a wall of glass and the food it produces is heavenly stuff, perhaps sea bass with cashew nuts, pork with pistachio and onion mustard, lemon curd cheese cake tart with melon juice. Princes Street and its lovely gardens are a short stroll. *Minimum stay: 3 days at New Year.*

| | |
|---|---|
| Rooms | 4 doubles: £95–£295. |
| Meals | Lunch from £22. Dinner £55–£70. Not Sun or Mon. |
| Closed | Rarely. |
| Directions | A720 ring road, then A702/A7 into town. Right at T-junc. at Balmoral Hotel, then immediately left with flow. Right at second r'bout and 1st right. On right. |

Paul Kitching & Katie O'Brien
21212
3 Royal Terrace,
Edinburgh, EH7 5AB
Tel      +44 (0)131 523 1030
Email    reservations@21212restaurant.co.uk
Web      www.21212restaurant.co.uk

## 23 Mayfield

A great base for all things Edinburgh. Built in 1868, this Victorian villa was once home to a coffee merchant and stands in the shadow of Arthur's Seat. Outside, much prized, off-street parking waits. Inside, you find original fireplaces, ornate ceilings and a stained-glass window on the landing. Ross has added Victorian colours, newspapers on poles, gilt-framed pictures that hang on chains – but best of all is breakfast, served in winter with candelabra on every table. You'll find chesterfield sofas in the sitting room, then old movies playing on the television. Bedrooms offer modern comforts: excellent beds, travertine bathrooms, bold colours, perhaps a panelled wall. You get iPod docks, Bose CD players, the family suite has a Nintendo Wii. There's good art throughout, a hot tub in the garden, you can jump on a bus and whizz into town. Breakfast is excellent: porridge with honey, free-range eggs, marshmallow pancakes, Stornoway black pudding with the full cooked works. Ross also has an apartment for six in the centre of town if you need more space. *Minimum stay: 2 nights at weekends.*

| | |
|---|---|
| Rooms | 3 twin/doubles,<br>3 four-posters: £80–£170.<br>1 family room for 4: £80–£190.<br>1 triple: £80–£175. Singles from £70. |
| Meals | Restaurants within half a mile. |
| Closed | 24-26 December. |
| Directions | A720 bypass, then north onto A722<br>for Edinburgh. Right onto A721 at<br>T-junction with traffic lights. Over<br>x-roads with main flow, under railway<br>bridge, on right. |

Ross Birnie
23 Mayfield
23 Mayfield Gardens,
Edinburgh, EH9 2BX

| | |
|---|---|
| Tel | +44 (0)131 667 5806 |
| Email | info@23mayfield.co.uk |
| Web | www.23mayfield.co.uk |

## 94DR

Close to Holyrood and Arthur's Seat, this super-friendly designer B&B is not only popular for its contemporary style, but for Paul and John, who treat guests like friends and make sure you see the best of their city. A traditional Victorian exterior gives no hint of the chic interiors that wait within. You'll find original floor tiles and ornate ceilings, but other than that it's a clean sweep of modern splendour: deep charcoal downstairs; pure white above. There's a sitting room with iPads in case you want to book a restaurant, then an honesty bar, an espresso machine and lots of handy guide books. Upstairs, stylish, well-priced bedrooms wait. Some are big with claw-foot baths, others smaller with walk-in power showers. All come with comfy beds, bathrobes, beautiful linen and fine contemporary art. The family suite (two rooms) has bunk beds and a PlayStation for kids. Delicious breakfasts are served in a conservatory overlooking the back garden, a memorable feast orchestrated by Paul, with lively conversation that travels the world. Majestic Edinburgh is yours to explore. *Minimum stay: 2 nights at weekends.*

| | |
|---|---|
| Rooms | 3 doubles: £100–£145. |
| | 2 suites for 2: £125–£200. |
| | 1 family room for 4: £125–£190. |
| | Singles from £80. |
| Meals | Restaurants on your doorstep. |
| Closed | 2–15 January. |
| Directions | A720 to Sheriff Hall roundabout then A7 for 1 mile. |

John MacEwan & Paul Lightfoot
94DR
94 Dalkeith Road,
Edinburgh, EH16 5AF

| | |
|---|---|
| Tel | +44 (0)131 662 9265 |
| Email | stay@94dr.com |
| Web | www.94dr.com |

## The Bridge Inn at Ratho

This lovely inn sits in a small village directly above the Union Canal. Footpaths head west into the country, you can hire bikes and follow the tow path into Edinburgh, or jump on the pub's canal boat for a Sunday lunch cruise. If all that sounds too strenuous, then plonk yourself down on the terrace and watch the odd boat chug past while sipping a pint of good ale. Inside, the view is weather-proofed by big windows in the dining room. An easy style runs throughout. You'll find wood-burners, smart colours, a whisky bar, the odd sofa. In summer, there are barbecues on Friday nights, an ice cream shed in the garden, even a small festival in May with live bands and lots of beer. Rooms aren't huge, but hit the spot. They're stylish and comfy with smart beds and crisp linen. All but one has the view, three have walk-in power showers, one has a claw-foot bath. The airport is ten minutes away, but you're not on the flight path, so peace reigns. Finally, don't miss nearby Jupiter Artland in summer, a wonderland of beautiful things. Children and dogs are very welcome.

| | |
|---|---|
| Rooms | 3 doubles, 1 twin/double: £80–£120. Singles from £65. |
| Meals | Lunch & dinner £5–£35. Sunday lunch £12.95. |
| Closed | Christmas Day. |
| Directions | West from A720 (Edinburgh ring road) on A71. Right at x-roads after 3 miles, signed Ratho. Right in village and inn on left above canal. |

**Graham & Rachel Bucknall**
The Bridge Inn at Ratho
27 Baird Road,
Ratho, EH28 8RA

Tel      +44 (0)131 333 1320
Email   info@bridgeinn.com
Web    www.bridgeinn.com

## The Ship Inn

There are few inns where you can sit on the terrace and watch a game of cricket on the beach below. And it's not beach cricket as you know it: Mark Waugh, Viv Richards and Wasim Akram have all played here. The Ship doubles as the pavilion… and the venue for post-match celebrations, no doubt. As for this quirky bolthole, it's as good as any in the land. Graham and Rachel bought it recently and have refurbished in fine style. Outside, on sunny days, you decant onto the terrace for lunch in the sun and gaze across the water to Edinburgh's hills. Inside, a warm contemporary design mixes with roaring fires, smart wallpapers and the odd stone wall. Sofas and armchairs are scattered about, staff weave through the throng delivering delicious food, perhaps fish and seafood from local waters, lamb and beef from nearby farms, sinful puddings you can't resist. Rooms have a cool, uncluttered style: airy colours, crisp linen, comfy beds, fancy bathrooms with walk-in showers; those at the front have the view. St Andrews waits for golf, Dundee for Captain Cook's boat, the Discovery. A perfect place.

| | |
|---|---|
| Rooms | 6 doubles: £80–£140. Singles from £70. Extra beds £15, cots free. |
| Meals | Lunch & dinner £5–£35. Sunday lunch £12.95. |
| Closed | Christmas Day & 2 weeks in January. |
| Directions | A917 east into Elie. In village, right after small green, onto Stenton Row. Straight ahead and on left. |

Graham & Rachel Bucknall
The Ship Inn
The Toft,
Elie, KY9 1DT

| | |
|---|---|
| Tel | +44 (0)1333 330246 |
| Email | info@shipinn.scot |
| Web | www.shipinn.scot |

## 15 Glasgow

This is a smart Glasgow address – bang in the middle of town, yet beautifully insulated from it. The house, grand Victorian, stands on an attractive square with communal gardens in the middle. Inside, the feel is distinctly contemporary, though you still get a couple of Corinthian pillars in the original tiled entrance hall. Shane and Laura spent a year renovating, and while technically you're in a B&B, the interiors here are a match for any boutique hotel. Downstairs there's a vast sitting room with a couple of sofas in front of a fire. Bedrooms upstairs are no less generous. Those at the back are large, the suites at the front are huge. All come with king-size beds, crisp white linen, handmade bedheads and robes in seriously fancy bathrooms. Suites have a few added extras: big sofas, beautiful windows, one has a double-ended bath overlooking the square. Breakfast is brought to you whenever you want. As for Glasgow, you'll find great restaurants nearby: the Finnieston for seafood and gin cocktails, the Gannet for a flat-iron steak, Ben Nevis for a wee dram and live folk music most nights.

| | |
|---|---|
| Rooms | 2 doubles, 1 twin/double: £99–£135. 2 suites for 2: £129–£165. Singles from £89. |
| Meals | Restaurants on your doorstep. |
| Closed | Never. |
| Directions | West into Glasgow on M8. Exit at junc. 18 for Charing X (outside lane), then double back at lights. 1st left, 1st left, 1st left (really). Follow square round to house. |

**Shane & Laura McKenzie**
15 Glasgow
15 Woodside Place,
Glasgow, G3 7QL

| | |
|---|---|
| Tel | +44 (0)141 332 1263 |
| Email | info@15glasgow.com |
| Web | www.15glasgow.com |

Entry 259   Map 8

## The Lime Tree

Quite a few hotels have art galleries, few secure a Matisse exhibition! David, a mountain guide and artist, somehow managed to fill a room with the great man's work. Then, when the Royal Geographical Society came to town, he planted a full-scale replica of Ernest Shackleton's boat on the lawn. These days, he's just finished marking out an epic three-week walk from Fort William up the coast to Cape Wrath – you can plan your own adventures from his lovely map room in the hotel. As for this Macintosh manse, it dates to 1850, though the lime tree itself was planted in 1700, the year the town was settled. Inside, a small, quirky world of stripped floors, open fires and beautiful windows for views of Loch Linnhe. Airy bedrooms are good for the price. Expect white linen, comfy beds, blond wood furniture, neat little bathrooms. There's a rustic bistro for tasty food, perhaps seafood soup, boeuf Bourguignon, Bakewell tart with vanilla ice-cream. Ben Nevis is close, but if you want to do more than walk, climbing, cragging, mountain biking and kayaking can all be arranged.

| | |
|---|---|
| Rooms | 4 doubles, 1 twin: £70-£130. |
| | 4 family rooms for 4: £80-£120. |
| | Singles from £60. |
| | Extra beds in family rooms: under 11s £10, everyone else £25. |
| Meals | Dinner, 3 courses, £25-£30. |
| Closed | Rarely. |
| Directions | North to Fort William on A82. Hotel on right at 1st roundabout in town. |

**David Wilson**
The Lime Tree
Achintore Road,
Fort William, PH33 6RQ

| | |
|---|---|
| Tel | +44 (0)1397 701806 |
| Email | info@limetreefortwilliam.co.uk |
| Web | www.limetreefortwilliam.co.uk |

## Kilcamb Lodge Hotel & Restaurant

Another beautiful West Coast setting with Loch Sunart at the end of the garden and Glas Bheinn rising beyond. Kilcamb – a barracks during the Jacobite uprising – has a bit of everything: a drawing room with an open fire; an elegant dining room for good food; a cool little brasserie that's recently been refurbished; a handful of lovely bedrooms in warm country-house style. There's a 12-acre garden that rolls down to the sea, where you can spot otters and seals. Ducks and geese fly over, if you're lucky you'll see eagles. Back inside, there's a stained-glass window on the landing, fresh flowers in the drawing room, driftwood lamps and good books. You can eat in the restaurant or the brasserie, either a five-course tasting menu or something simpler, perhaps a plate of seafood, Highland lamb, iced whisky parfait. Bedrooms have warm colours, some with a contemporary feel, others a smart country-house style. All have good bathrooms, crisp linen and comfy beds. Day trips to Mull are easy to arrange. Don't miss Ardnamuchan or Senna Bay at the end of the road.

| | |
|---|---|
| Rooms | 2 doubles: £190–£275<br>6 twin/doubles: £250–£335.<br>2 suites for 2: £290–£415.<br>Price includes dinner for 2. |
| Meals | Lunch from £7.50. Afternoon tea from £5.50. 3-course dinner included; non-residents about £40.<br>Tasting menu £55. |
| Closed | Jan. Limited opening Nov & Feb. |
| Directions | From Fort William A82 south for 10 miles to Corran for ferry across to Ardgour, then A861 to Strontian. Hotel west of village on left. |

David & Sally Ruthven-Fox
Kilcamb Lodge Hotel & Restaurant
Strontian,
Acharacle, PH36 4HY

| | |
|---|---|
| Tel | +44 (0)1967 402257 |
| Email | enquiries@kilcamblodge.co.uk |
| Web | www.kilcamblodge.co.uk |

## Doune

You arrive by boat – there's no road in – a ferry across to Knoydart, the last great wilderness in Britain. You'll find mountains, sea and beach – a thrilling landscape of boundless peace and ever-changing light. Guillemots race across the water, dolphins and seals come to play, the Sound of Sleat shoots across to Skye. As for Doune, it's a tiny community of happily shipwrecked souls, who rescued this land from ruin; Martin, Jane and Liz look after you with instinctive generosity. The dining room is the hub, pine-clad from top to toe, with a stove to keep you warm and a couple of fiddles for the odd ceilidh. The food is delicious – crab from the bay, roast lamb from the hill, chocolate tart with homemade ice-cream. Bedrooms along the veranda are delightfully simple; pine-clad with mezzanine bunks for children, hooks for clothes, armchairs for watching the weather; compact shower rooms sparkle. The walking is magnificent, boat trips can be arranged, the night sky will astound you. There's a lodge for groups, too. A very special place, miss it at your peril. *Minimum stay: 3 nights.*

| | |
|---|---|
| Rooms | 2 doubles, 1 twin, each with mezzanine bed for children: £90. 1 single with separate shower: £33. Dinner, B&B £75-£85 per person (includes packed lunch). |
| Meals | Dinner £35. |
| Closed | October to Easter. |
| Directions | Park in Mallaig; the boat will collect you at an agreed time. |

Martin & Jane Davies
Doune
Knoydart,
Mallaig, PH41 4PL

Tel       +44 (0)1687 462667
Email   martin@doune-knoydart.co.uk
Web     www.doune-knoydart.co.uk

## Grants at Craigellachie

An old factor's house on the banks of Loch Duich with the Five Sisters of Kintail flaunting their beauty to the south; three are munros, views from the top are spectacular. This is a great little base for Highland flings – quirky, homespun, lovely owners. There's lots to do: Glenelg, Applecross and Skye are on your doorstep, Loch Ness is within easy reach, Dornie Castle (the one on the water you see on TV) is on the other side of the loch. After a day pottering through magical landscapes, come home to this cute restaurant with rooms. It's a tiny operation. Tony and Liz do it all themselves: cook, clean, polish and shine, chat to guests after delicious breakfasts, point you in the right direction. There are four rooms, two in the main house (small but sweet, warm colours, fine for a night), then two out back, smarter altogether with neutral colours, lovely linen, robes in fancy bathrooms. One is a suite (with a small kitchen), both have decked terraces. As for Tony's lovely food, don't expect to go hungry. You might have hand-dived scallops and thyme, Glenelg lamb with rosemary, whisky panna cotta.

| | |
|---|---|
| Rooms | 2 doubles, 1 twin: £105-£148. 1 suite for 2: £155-£185. Singles £67-£120. Dinner, B&B £85-£125 per person. |
| Meals | Dinner, 3 courses, about £35. Not Sun or Mon. |
| Closed | Mid-November to mid-February. |
| Directions | A87 north from Invergarry to Shiel Bridge. Left in village for Glenelg. First right down to Loch Duich. On left in village. |

Tony & Liz Taylor
Grants at Craigellachie
Ratagan, Glenshiel,
Kyle, IV40 8HP

| | |
|---|---|
| Tel | +44 (0)1599 511331 |
| Email | info@housebytheloch.co.uk |
| Web | www.housebytheloch.co.uk |

## The Torridon

It's hard to beat the top of Scotland, the landscapes here feed the soul. Mountains rise, red deer roam, eagles soar, the light changes every minute. This 1887 shooting lodge was built for the Earl of Lovelace and stands in 58 acres that roll down to the shores of Upper Loch Torridon. Inside, sparkling interiors thrill: a huge fire in the panelled hall, a zodiac ceiling in the drawing room, 350 malts in the pitch pine bar. Big windows pull in the view, while canny walkers pour off the hills to recover in style. Bedrooms are hard to fault, some big, others bigger, with a cool, contemporary style running throughout: bold colours, padded headboards, exquisite linen, magnificent bathrooms; one room has a shower in a turret. Outside, a beautiful two-acre kitchen garden provides much for the table, perhaps lovage and courgette soup, then shoulder of lamb with rosemary gnocchi and passion fruit tart with mango mousse. Dan and Rohaise also own the village inn for simpler food and good rooms from £110. Don't miss the free excursions: kayaking, guided walks, abseiling and mountain biking are all on tap. *Pets by arrangement.*

| | |
|---|---|
| Rooms | 10 doubles, 2 twins, 2 four-posters: £230-£465. 4 suites for 2: £465. 1 boathouse for 4: £925-£1,425 per week. Extra bed £40 per night per person. |
| Meals | Lunch from £5.95. Dinner, 5 courses, £60. |
| Closed | January. |
| Directions | A9 to Inverness, A835 to Garve, A832 to Kinlochewe, A896 to Annat (not Torridon). Signed on south shore. |

Daniel & Rohaise Rose-Bristow
The Torridon
Annat,
By Achnasheen, IV22 2EY

| | |
|---|---|
| Tel | +44 (0)1445 791242 |
| Email | info@thetorridon.com |
| Web | www.thetorridon.com |

## Mackay's Rooms

This is the north-west corner of Britain and it's utterly magical: huge skies, sandy beaches, aquamarine seas, cliffs and caves. You drive – or cycle – for mile upon mile with mountains soaring into the heavens and ridges sliding into the sea. If you like big, remote landscapes, you'll love it here; what's more, you'll pretty much have it to yourself. Mackay's – they have the shop, the bunkhouse and the garage, too – is the only place to stay in town, its earthy colours mixing with stone walls, open fires and stripped floors to great effect. Bedrooms (some big, others smaller) are extremely comfy. They come with big wooden beds and crisp white linen, while Fiona, a textiles graduate, has a fine eye for fabrics and upholstery. You also get excellent bathrooms, iPod docks, flat-screen TVs and DVD players. Breakfast sets you up for the day – grilled grapefruit, whisky porridge, venison sausages, local eggs – so head east to the beach, west for great golf or catch the ferry across to Cape Wrath and scan the sea for whales. There's surfing for the brave and the beautiful.

| | |
|---|---|
| Rooms | 6 doubles, 1 twin: £125–£165.<br>Singles from £110.<br>4 self-catering cottages for 2–6:<br>£800–£1,600 per week. |
| Meals | Restaurants in village. |
| Closed | October to May.<br>Cottages open all year. |
| Directions | A838 north from Rhiconich.<br>After 19 miles enter Durness village.<br>Mackay's is on right-hand side<br>opposite memorial. |

Fiona Mackay
Mackay's Rooms
Durine, Durness,
Lairg, IV27 4PN

| | |
|---|---|
| Tel | +44 (0)1971 511202 |
| Email | stay@visitdurness.com |
| Web | www.visitdurness.com |

## Hotel Eilean Iarmain

The most beautiful spot on Skye, simple as that. You're at the end of the road, in a whitewashed hamlet, almost paddling in the Sound of Sleat. Mountains rise, the sea sparkles, the odd fishing boat potters by. If you want deep peace in a magical landscape, you'll find it here. Warm Hebridean interiors fit the mood: tartan carpets, panelled walls, a pine-clad hall. There's an open fire in the sitting room, then an airy restaurant for lovely food, perhaps hand-dived local scallops, Highland lamb and venison, cranachan soufflé with fresh raspberries. Bedrooms are split between the main house (warmly traditional), the garden house (nicely uncluttered) and the old stables (pine-clad suites over two floors); the latter two have gardens overlooking the water. You get the odd half-tester, a turret or two, robes in adequate bathrooms. There's an art gallery, a whisky shop and a popular bar, where the odd ceilidh breaks loose and fiddles fly. It was all the work of Sir Iain Noble, who founded Scotland's Gaelic University here to keep the language and culture of the islands alive. He did a fine job.

| | |
|---|---|
| Rooms | 10 doubles, 2 twin/doubles: £170–£190. 4 suites for 2: £220–£250. Singles from £110. Extra beds for children aged 5–13: £20. Under 5s: free. |
| Meals | Bar meals from £11.95. 3-course à la carte dinner, £35–£40. |
| Closed | Never. |
| Directions | A87 over Skye Bridge, then left after 7 miles onto A851, signed Armdale. Hotel on left after 8 miles, signed. |

Carlotta Graham
Hotel Eilean Iarmain
Isle Ornsay, IV43 8QR
Tel        +44 (0)1471 833332
Email    hotel@eileaniarmain.co.uk
Web      www.eileaniarmain.co.uk

## Viewfield House Hotel

This old ancestral pile stands high above Portree Bay with fine views tumbling down to the Sound of Rassay below. Twenty acres of mature gardens and woodland wrap around you, with croquet on the lawn and a hill to climb for 360° views of peak and sea. As for this grand Victorian factor's house, expect a few aristocratic fixtures and fittings: hunting trophies in the hall, cases filled with curios, a grand piano and open fire in the drawing room, Sanderson wallpaper in the dining room. Family oils hang on the walls, you'll find wood carvings from distant lands and a flurry of antiques, all of which blend grandeur with touches of humour. Upstairs a warren of bedrooms wait. Most are big, some are vast, all come in country-house style with lovely fabrics, crisply laundered sheets and sea views from those at the front. Dive into Skye – wildlife, mountains, sea lochs and castles all wait, as do a couple of distilleries. Suppers are on tap – tomato and basil soup, lamb noisettes, chocolate and almond cake with vanilla sauce; there's Highland porridge for breakfast, too. Fantastic.

| Rooms | 3 doubles, 8 twin/doubles: £130–£150. 2 singles: £58–£75. Dinner B&B from £80 per person. |
| Meals | Dinner, 3 courses, £25. Packed lunch £7. |
| Closed | Mid-October to Easter. |
| Directions | On A87, coming from south, driveway entrance on left just before the Portree filling station. |

Hugh Macdonald
Viewfield House Hotel
Viewfield Road,
Portree, IV51 9EU
Tel       +44 (0)1478 612217
Email    info@viewfieldhouse.com
Web     www.viewfieldhouse.com

## Culdearn House

Grantown is a great base for Highland flings. You can fish the Spey, jump on the whisky trail, check out a raft of castles, even ski in Aviemore. Loch Ness is close, as is Royal Deeside, there's golf everywhere and the walking is divine; in short, expect to be busy. As for Culdearn, it stands in a row of five identical houses that were built in 1860 by Lord Seafield, one for each of his daughters. These days it's a lovely small hotel where William and Sonia look after guests with unstinting kindness. There's an open fire and facing sofas in the smart sitting room, panelled windows and a marble fireplace in the dining room, then stylish bedrooms that offer the sort of comfort you'd want after a day in the hills. You get the comfiest beds, the crispest linen, then decanters of sherry, pretty furniture and spotless bathrooms. Back downstairs, William looks after a tempting wine list and 60 malts, while Sonia whisks up delicious four-course dinners, perhaps West Coast scallops, bramble sorbet, fillet of beef, a walnut and maple syrup parfait. Don't miss the ospreys at Boat of Garten. *Children over 10 welcome.*

| Rooms | 4 doubles, 1 twin/double, 1 twin: £150-£170. Singles £75-£100. Dinner, B&B £100-£125 per person. |
|---|---|
| Meals | Dinner, 4 courses, £45. |
| Closed | Never. |
| Directions | North into Grantown from A95. Left at 30 mph sign & house directly ahead. |

Sonia & William Marshall
Culdearn House
Woodlands Terrace,
Grantown on Spey, PH26 3JU
Tel      +44 (0)1479 872106
Email   enquiries@culdearn.com
Web     www.culdearn.com

## Dalmunzie Castle

Dalmunzie is quite some sight, an ancient hunting lodge lost to the world in one of Scotland's most dramatic landscapes. You're cradled by mountains in a vast valley; it's as good a spot as any to escape the world. Surprisingly, you're not that remote – Perth is a mere 30 miles south – but the sense of solitude is magnificent, as is the view. As for the hotel, you potter up a one-mile drive to find a small enclave of friendly souls. Interiors are just the ticket: warm, cosy and quietly grand. You find sofas in front of open fires, a smart restaurant for delicious Scottish food, a snug bar for a good malt, a breakfast room with a big view. Country-house bedrooms have colour and style. Some are grand, others simpler, several have ancient claw-foot baths and two are in the towers. There's loads to do: fantastic walking, mountain bike trails, royal Deeside, the Highland games at Braemar, even skiing up the road in winter. As for the tricky golf course, it was almost certainly laid out by Alister MacKenzie, who later designed Augusta National; the famous par three at Amen Corner is all but identical to the seventh here.

| | |
|---|---|
| Rooms | 8 doubles, 5 four-posters: £295-£305. |
| | 1 family room for 4: £345. |
| | Tower room – 3 doubles: £345. |
| Meals | Lunch from £6.95. |
| | Packed lunch from £10. |
| | Dinner, 5 courses, £50. |
| Closed | Occasionally in winter. |
| Directions | North from Blairgowrie on A93. |
| | Hotel signed left in Glenshee up |
| | one-mile drive. |

Jamie Webb
Dalmunzie Castle
Spittal O'Glenshee,
Blairgowrie, PH10 7QG
Tel +44 (0)1250 885224
Email reservations@dalmunzie.com
Web www.dalmunzie.com

## Killiecrankie House Hotel

No Highland fling would be complete without a night at Killiecrankie. Henrietta runs the place with great charm and has spent the last five years pouring in love and money; now it shines. Outside, gardens galore: one for roses, another for vegetables, and a fine herbaceous border. Further afield, you'll find much to please: Loch Tummel, Rannoch Moor and magnificent Glenshee, over which you tumble for the Highland Games at Braemar. Return to the indisputable comforts of a smart country hotel: tartan in the dining room, 52 malts at the bar, views at breakfast of red squirrels climbing garden trees. There's a snug sitting room where a fire burns in winter; in summer doors open onto the garden. Delightful bedrooms come in different shapes and sizes. All are smart with pretty linen, warm colours, chic fabrics and lovely views. Dinner is predictably delicious, perhaps pea and mint soup, Highland venison, sticky toffee pudding. There's porridge with cream and brown sugar for breakfast. Castles, hills and distilleries wait. A great wee place with staff who care. *Minimum stay: 2 nights at weekends.*

| | |
|---|---|
| Rooms | 3 doubles, 5 twin/doubles: £230-£280. 2 singles: £115-£140. Price includes dinner. |
| Meals | Lunch from £4.50. Dinner included; non-residents £42. |
| Closed | January/February. |
| Directions | A9 north of Pitlochry, then B8079, signed Killiecrankie. Straight ahead for 2 miles. Hotel on right, signed. |

Henrietta Fergusson
Killiecrankie House Hotel
Killiecrankie,
Pitlochry, PH16 5LG

| | |
|---|---|
| Tel | +44 (0)1796 473220 |
| Email | enquiries@killiecrankiehotel.co.uk |
| Web | www.killiecrankiehotel.co.uk |

## Craigatin House & Courtyard

Craigatin is one of those lovely places where beautiful rooms have attractive prices and hands-on owners go out of their way to make your stay special. It stands peacefully in two acres of manicured gardens on the northern shores of town; good restaurants are a short stroll. Smart stone exteriors give way to warmly contemporary interiors, where beautiful windows flood rooms with light. There are shutters in the breakfast room, which overflows into an enormous conservatory where sofas wait in front of a wood-burner and walls of glass open onto the garden. Big uncluttered bedrooms — some in the main house, others in converted stables — are super value for money. Expect Farrow & Ball colours, comfy beds, crisp white linen, padded bedheads and pretty shower rooms. Breakfast offers the full cooked works and tempting alternatives, perhaps smoked haddock omelettes or apple pancakes with grilled bacon and maple syrup. As for Pitlochry — gateway to the Highlands — it's a vibrant town with lots to do: castles and mountains, lochs and forests, its famous Festival Theatre. You're on the whisky trail, too. *Minimum stay: 2 nights at weekends.*

| | |
|---|---|
| Rooms | 11 doubles, 2 twins: £95–£105. 1 suite for 2: £122. Singles from £85. |
| Meals | Restaurants within walking distance. |
| Closed | Christmas. |
| Directions | A9 north to Pitlochry. Take 1st turn-off for town, up main street, past shops and signed on left. |

**Martin & Andrea Anderson**
Craigatin House & Courtyard
165 Atholl Road,
Pitlochry, PH16 5QL

| | |
|---|---|
| Tel | +44 (0)1796 472478 |
| Email | enquiries@craigatinhouse.co.uk |
| Web | www.craigatinhouse.co.uk |

Entry 271   Map 9

## Torrdarach House

You're high on the hill with big views south and lovely gardens to enjoy. Susanne and Graeme – an Austro-English alliance – stayed here on their holidays, fell in love with the place, then bought it. It was a clever move – the house was recently renovated from top to toe: new bedrooms, new bathrooms, new everything. The result is this friendly, stylish, nicely priced B&B. An airy sitting room looks the right way – there are comfy sofas, a whisky bar and binoculars to scan the hills. Chic bedrooms come in the same happy style: neutral colours, smart fabrics, textured wallpaper, tartan bedheads. You get blond oak furniture, cute leather armchairs, flat-screen TVs and excellent showers. Downstairs, the breakfast room overlooks the garden, so watch out for red squirrels while tucking into porridge with a splash of whisky or the full cooked works. A drying room with safe storage for bikes and golf clubs is on the way, while Graeme is a golf professional and Pitlochry has a good course, so if you need to iron out that slice of yours… Fabulous walking, the Festival Theatre, and the odd distillery wait. *Minimum stay: 2 nights at weekends April – October.*

| | |
|---|---|
| Rooms | 5 doubles, 2 twin/doubles: £94–£109. Singles £84. |
| Meals | Pubs/restaurants 400 yds. |
| Closed | Rarely. |
| Directions | North to Pitlochry on A9. In town, up high street, past shops, then 1st right into Larchwood Road. Up hill, keep left, then right into Golf Course Road. On right. |

**Graeme Fish & Susanne Wallner**
Torrdarach House
Golf Course Road,
Pitlochry, PH16 5AU

| | |
|---|---|
| Tel | +44 (0)1796 472136 |
| Email | info@torrdarach.co.uk |
| Web | www.torrdarach.co.uk |

## Knockendarroch Hotel & Restaurant

This grand old house on a hill was built in 1880, then sold in 1910 for £100! It is also the birthplace of the Pitlochry Festival Theatre, the plays originally performed in the garden. These days it's simply a lovely place to stay with views from the front that shoot across the valley to forested hills. Inside, you find original tiles in the hall, a double sitting room with two fires, a whisky bar for a wee dram, a wallpapered restaurant with views of Ben Vrackie and plenty of original contemporary art. Good paths lead up through forest and moorland for big Highland views, not a bad way to work up an appetite for some very good food, perhaps fillet of hake with chilli and lemongrass, Perthshire lamb with parsnip purée, elderflower panna cotta with pear sorbet. Bedrooms are lovely, it really doesn't matter which you choose, though the big ones at the front do have exceptional views. You'll find comfy beds, smart fabrics, tartan throws and padded headboards, perhaps a cushioned window seat or a sofa if there's room. Two have balconies, most have binoculars to scan the hills. There's a drying room for wet gear, too. *Minimum stay: 2 nights at weekends. Children over 10 welcome.*

| | |
|---|---|
| Rooms | 12 twin/doubles: £140-£195.<br>Dinner, B&B £85-£125.50 per person. |
| Meals | Lunch from £5.<br>Dinner, 3 courses, £25<br>(£42 non-residents). |
| Closed | 20 December to 6 February. |
| Directions | A9 north to Pitlochry. Up high street,<br>then right into Bonnethill Road.<br>Right again into Toberargan Road<br>and on right. |

Struan & Louise Lothian
Knockendarroch Hotel & Restaurant
Higher Oakfield,
Pitlochry, PH16 5HT

| | |
|---|---|
| Tel | +44 (0)1796 473473 |
| Email | info@knockendarroch.co.uk |
| Web | www.knockendarroch.co.uk |

## Kinnaird Estate

A magnificent 1770 mansion set in 6,000 acres of prime Perthshire countryside. The river Tay passes dramatically below, sheep and cattle graze contentedly, paths behind lead into the estate. The house is sublime from top to toe, grand yet welcoming, a place to feel at home. Most beautiful of all is the panelled drawing room with roaring fire, grand piano, beautiful art and sofas galore. The dining room has original murals. You breakfast in the company of the Maharaja of Jaipur (well, his portrait), there's a billiards room with fine views, a snug study, too. Big country-house bedrooms have vast beds, smart wallpapers and colourful fabrics. Those at the front get the view, several have fires, excellent bathrooms come with white robes. The estate owns a couple of world-class fishing beats, so come to try your luck; there's shooting in season, clays, too. Food is delicious (local meat, estate eggs) and you can bring your own wine. Staff are lovely. Five estate cottages tempt you to linger. Fabulous walking and the odd castle wait. House parties are welcome. *Over 12s welcome.*

| | |
|---|---|
| Rooms | 7 twin/doubles: £140–£160. |
| | 1 suite for 2: £180. |
| | Singles from £120. |
| | 5 self-catering cottages for 2–8: |
| | £560–£1,050 per week. |
| Meals | Picnic lunch £10. |
| | Dinner, 3 courses, £35 (not Mon or Tue). |
| Closed | Christmas. |
| Directions | Leave A9 for B898 2 miles north of |
| | Dunkeld. On right after 6 miles. |

Guesthouse Manager
Kinnaird Estate
Dunkeld, PH8 0LB

| | |
|---|---|
| Tel | +44 (0)1796 482440 |
| Email | reservations@kinnairdestate.com |
| Web | www.kinnairdestate.com |

## The Townhouse

Perth stands on the river Tay, an ancient city steeped in history. Robert the Bruce recaptured it from Edward I in 1309, Charles II was crowned up the road at Scone Palace. As for this lovely Georgian townhouse, it stands on South Inch, the city's main park, with the river passing to one side. It's a great base for gentle explorations – Braemar, Stirling, St Andrews, Edinburgh and the Fife coast are all within easy reach. Inside, smart interiors mix old and new to great effect. You'll find fresh flowers, the daily papers, antique furniture and contemporary art. Bedrooms are nicely priced: indulging, comfy, grandly attired. There's lots to catch the eye: curios, porcelain, antiques, good art. You get smart fabrics, huge beds and excellent bathrooms, perhaps a mahogany dresser or an ornate marble fireplace. All of which would be blossom in the wind without David. He ran the seriously cool Hôtel Le Toiny on St Barts for 18 years, and his humorous, helpful and generous way with guests makes him the star of the show. Breakfast is a treat. Good restaurants wait on your doorstep. Scone is two miles north.

| | |
|---|---|
| Rooms | 4 twin/doubles: £85-£125. Singles £65-£75. Extra beds £15. |
| Meals | Restaurants on your doorstep. |
| Closed | Never. |
| Directions | M90, junc. 10, then A912 into Perth. Pick up park on both sides, then left at traffic lights onto Marshall Place. On right. |

**David Henderson & Laurent Moller**
The Townhouse
17 Marshall Place,
Perth, PH2 8AG

| | |
|---|---|
| Tel | +44 (0)1738 446179 |
| Email | info@thetownhouseperth.co.uk |
| Web | www.thetownhouseperth.co.uk |

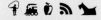

## Barley Bree

A few miles north of Gleneagles, a super little restaurant with rooms that delivers what so many people want: stylish interiors, super food, excellent prices, a warm welcome. This is a small family-run affair. Fabrice is French and cooks sublimely, Alison, a Scot, looks after the wine. As for Barley Bree – whisky soup to you and me – it's an 18th-century coaching inn, its name plucked from a Robert Burns poem. Happy locals and travellers from afar come for fabulous Scottish food that's cooked with French flair, perhaps fennel soup with basil pesto, saddle of venison with piquillo purée, tarte tatin with vanilla ice cream. The restaurant, nicely rustic, has a fire that burns on both sides, while in summer you decant onto a terrace for lunch in the sun. Six comfy rooms have neutral colours, crisp linen, good beds and underfloor heating in neat little shower rooms. The big room, with a claw-foot bath, is well worth splashing out on. There's a sitting room for guests with books, good art, stripped boards and a fire. Don't miss the gardens at Drummond Castle or Innerpeffray Library.

| | |
|---|---|
| Rooms | 6 twin/doubles: £110–£150. Singles from £70. |
| Meals | Lunch from £8. Sunday lunch from £13.50. Dinner, 3 courses, about £40 (not Sun evening, Mon or Tue). |
| Closed | Mon & Tue. Christmas, 7 July to 22 July, 20 October to 23 October, 1 January to 8 January. |
| Directions | A9 north from Dunblane, then A822 for Muthill. In village on left before church. |

Fabrice & Alison Bouteloup
Barley Bree
6 Willoughby Street,
Muthill, PH5 2AB
Tel      +44 (0)1764 681451
Email    info@barleybree.com
Web      www.barleybree.com

## The Royal Hotel

An attractive small hotel, intimate and welcoming with stylish interiors – a country house in the middle of town. Queen Victoria once stayed, hence the name. It stands on the river Earn, its eponymous loch glistening five miles up stream. You're well placed to strike out in all directions: Loch Tay, Pitlochry, The Trossachs and Perth are all close. Those who linger fare well. You get a wall of books in a beautiful sitting room where two fires burn. Newspapers hang on poles, logs tumble from wicker baskets, sofas and armchairs are impeccably upholstered. There's a grandfather clock in the hall, rugs on stripped floors in a country-house bar, then walls festooned with beautiful art. You can eat all over the place, in the bar, in the conservatory or at smartly dressed tables in the elegant dining room, perhaps seared pigeon with a whisky sauce, duck breast with a chilli jam, banoffee pancakes with Drambuie ice cream. Smart homely rooms have padded bedheads, crisp linen, mahogany dressers, gilt-framed mirrors. Bathrooms have robes, one four-poster has a log fire. Drummond Castle Gardens are close.

| Rooms | 5 doubles, 3 twins, 3 four-posters: £150–£190. 1 house for 4 (self-catering, minimum 2 nights low season): £320–£890 per week. |
|---|---|
| Meals | Bar meals from £6.95. Dinner, 3 courses, £25–£30. |
| Closed | Rarely. |
| Directions | A9 north of Dunblane, A822 thro' Braco, left onto B827. Left for town centre, over bridge, hotel on square. |

Teresa Milsom
The Royal Hotel
Melville Square, Comrie,
Crieff, PH6 2DN

| Tel | +44 (0)1764 679200 |
|---|---|
| Email | reception@royalhotel.co.uk |
| Web | www.royalhotel.co.uk |

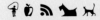

## Creagan House at Strathyre

Creagan is a delight – a small, traditional restaurant with rooms run with great passion by Gordon and Cherry. At its heart is Gordon's delicious food, which draws a devoted crowd, perhaps fillet of brill with plum and damson, local venison with a sloe gin and juniper sauce, then an apple, prune and almond flory with clotted cream. Food is local – meat and game from Perthshire, seafood from west-coast boats – and served on Skye pottery; some vegetables come from the garden. A snug sitting room doubles as a bar, where a good wine list and 50 malt whiskies wait; if you like a dram, you'll be happy here. Bedrooms fit the bill: warm and comfy with smart carpets, pretty colours, flat-screen TVs, a sofa if there's room. Breakfast is a treat; where else can you sit in a baronial dining room and read about the iconography of the toast rack while waiting for your bacon and eggs? No airs and graces, just the sort of attention you only get in small owner-run places. Hens, woodpeckers and red squirrels live in the garden. There are hills to climb, boat trips on lochs, secure storage for bikes. Very dog-friendly.

| | |
|---|---|
| Rooms | 3 doubles, 1 twin, 1 four-poster: £135-£155. Singles from £90-£100. Extra bed/sofabed available £30 per person per night. |
| Meals | Dinner, 3 courses, £37.50. |
| Closed | 28 October to 18 March. |
| Directions | From Stirling A84 north through Callander to Strathyre. Hotel 0.25 miles north of village on right. |

Gordon & Cherry Gunn
Creagan House at Strathyre
Strathyre,
Callander, FK18 8ND

| | |
|---|---|
| Tel | +44 (0)1877 384638 |
| Email | eatandstay@creaganhouse.co.uk |
| Web | www.creaganhouse.co.uk |

## Monachyle Mhor

Monachyle is unique – a designer hotel on a remote hill farm that started life as a B&B. Today it's one of the hippest places to stay in Scotland and it's still run by the same family with the children at the helm. Dick farms, Melanie designs the magical rooms, Tom cooks some of the best food in Scotland. It sits in 2,000 acres of blissful silence at the end of the track with the Trossachs circling around you and Loch Voil shimming below. Sheep graze, buzzards swoop, the odd fisherman tries his luck. Inside, there's a cool little bar, a fire in the sitting room, then a slim restaurant that drinks in the view. Bedrooms ooze 21st-century chic: big beds, cool colours, fabulous design, hi-tech gadgets. Bathrooms are equally good, perhaps a deluge shower in a granite steam room or claw-foot baths with views down the glen. Loft-house suites are enormous, but the smaller rooms are lovely, too. Dinner is a five-course feast with beef, lamb, pork and venison all off the farm. Rob Roy lived in the glen, you can visit his grave. The hotel holds a festival in May – fabulous food and cool Scottish tunes.

| | |
|---|---|
| Rooms | 4 twin/doubles: £195. 5 suites for 2: £265. 1 family room for 4: £195-£265. Courtyard rooms – 5 twin/doubles: £215. |
| Meals | Lunch from £5.50. Dinner £50. Sunday lunch £32. |
| Closed | Two weeks in January. |
| Directions | M9, junc. 11, then B824 and A84 north. Right for Balquhidder 6 miles north of Callander. 5 miles west along road & Loch Voil. Hotel on right, signed. |

Tom Lewis
Monachyle Mhor
Balquhidder,
Lochearnhead, FK19 8PQ

| | |
|---|---|
| Tel | +44 (0)1877 384622 |
| Email | monachyle@mhor.net |
| Web | mhor.net/monachyle-mhor-hotel/ |

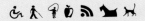

## Mhor 84

The entirely benevolent expansion of the Mhor empire has mastered the Midas touch, turning this old roadside inn into the coolest motel in the land. Outside, the glen shoots down to Loch Voil, with mountains to climb and bike tracks to follow. Inside, chic white minimalism mixes with warm Scottish tradition, a perfect blend of relaxed 21st-century living. There's style and humour in equal measure – boarded floors, tractor seat bar stools, curios hanging on the walls, the odd sofa for afternoon tea. Fires roar, cake stands bulge, happy staff weave through the throng delivering fabulous food that you eat at old school tables – porridge with honey for breakfast, sourdough and hummus for lunch, Scotch rarebit, Tyree lobster and plum crumble for dinner. There's live folk music every Thursday – Ewan MacPherson of Shooglenifty often plays – and a fine selection of malts if you fancy a dram. Simple bedrooms have white walls, contemporary art, small armchairs and honest prices; spotless bathrooms are 1980s originals, all part of the fun. There's a games room, too, with a juke box and pool table.

| | |
|---|---|
| Rooms | 2 doubles, 4 twin/doubles: £70-£80. 1 family room for 4: £80-£110. |
| Meals | Breakfast from £4.50. Lunch from £3.90. Dinner, 3 courses, £35-£30. |
| Closed | Christmas Day. |
| Directions | A84 north from Callander. Through Strathyre, then right after three miles for Kingshouse. In village. |

**Dugald McGarry**
Mhor 84
Balquhidder,
Lochearnhead, FK19 8NY

| | |
|---|---|
| Tel | +44 (0)1877 384646 |
| Email | motel@mhor.net |
| Web | mhor.net/mhor-84-motel/ |

## Cringletie House

Cringletie's splendours are hard to miss. You're wrapped up in 65 acres of beautiful grounds with daffodils that erupt in spring, cows that graze in lush fields and a peaceful walled garden for a game of boules. Pheasants strut, buzzards circle, views roll over nearby hills. As for the house, it dates to 1860, its playful turrets giving it a soft grandeur. Inside, you get the full works: an open fire in the hall, then a fine old staircase that sweeps you up to a striking first-floor dining room that has the feel of an 18th-century gentleman's club; expect panelled walls, vintage wallpapers and a spectacular muralled ceiling. There's a sitting room up here, too — equally grand, with fat sofas in front of the fire. Bedrooms are scattered about. Some downstairs open onto the garden, those at the top have the best views. It doesn't matter which you go for, they're all lovely, with warm colours, crisp linen, comfy beds and excellent bathrooms. Friday night barbecues are held in the walled garden in summer. Take to the hills, follow the Tweed or scoot up to Edinburgh; it's less than an hour by car.

| | |
|---|---|
| Rooms | 12 twin/doubles: £135–£245. |
| | 1 suite for 2: £235–£265. |
| | 1 cottage for 6: £235–£465. |
| Meals | Lunch from £4.50. |
| | Afternoon tea £18.50. |
| | Dinner, 3 courses, £35. |
| | Sunday lunch £22.50. |
| Closed | Two weeks in January. |
| Directions | North from Peebles on A703. |
| | Hotel signed left after two miles. |

Jeremy Osbourne
Cringletie House
Edinburgh Road,
Peebles, EH45 8PL

| | |
|---|---|
| Tel | +44 (0)1721 725750 |
| Email | gm@cringletie.com |
| Web | www.cringletie.com |

## Windlestraw

A small country house with lovely interiors and beautiful views down the Tweed Valley. Hills rise, deer roam, osprey glide through the afternoon sky. John and Sylvia came back from Dubai to do their own thing and have been hard at work presiding over a chic refurbishment. Fires roar, a grand piano waits to be played, there's a sun-trapping terrace for afternoon tea. You find a conservatory sitting room filled with books and curios, a panelled dining room for super food, then binoculars with which to scan the valley — sunsets turn the hills orange. Country-house bedrooms have a warm contemporary style: smart colours, comfy beds, sofas in the bigger rooms, fine views from those at the front. Spotless bathrooms do the trick: one has a claw-foot bath, bigger rooms have robes. Good food waits downstairs, perhaps scallops from Eyemouth, local lamb, an irresistible tarte tatin. There's lots to do: walking, fishing, mountain biking, even kayaking on the Tweed; if you try your hand on Pebbles golf course, the views may well be better than your game! There's a literary festival at Traquair House in August, too.

| | |
|---|---|
| Rooms | 5 doubles, 1 twin: £160–£200. Singles from £105. Dinner, B&B from £120 p.p. Extra beds for children: under 12s £15; 12+ £25. Cots free. |
| Meals | Dinner, 5 courses, £40. |
| Closed | Christmas, January/February. |
| Directions | East from Peebles on A72. Into Walkerburn; house signed left on western flank of town. |

John & Sylvia Matthews
Windlestraw
Galashiels Road,
Walkerburn, EH43 6AA
Tel       +44 (0)1896 870636
Email    stay@windlestraw.co.uk
Web      www.windlestraw.co.uk

## The Buccleuch Arms

The Scottish Borders are often overlooked by people on their sprint north, but these lush lowlands are every bit as beautiful as their highland counterparts. Hills roll, the Tweed flows, a string of ancient towns wait jam-packed with history. And where better to base yourself than this lovely hotel bang in the middle of it all? It sits on the green in this ancient town with hills all around and its 12th-century abbey a short stroll from the front door. Interiors are filled with low-key elegance: stripped boards, painted panelling and a roaring fire in reception; a quirky bistro that opens onto a beautiful garden in summer; a bar at the front for a wee dram and fishermen's tales. Rooms have style, colour and comfort with good beds, pretty fabrics and generous prices. Delicious food waits, too, perhaps crayfish ravioli, local roe deer, sticky toffee pudding. You can fish the Tweed, walk in the hills, play golf on fine courses. There's a literary festival in June and cricket beyond the car park in summer. Floors Castle and Sir Walter Scott's home, Abbotsford, are close. A treat.

| | |
|---|---|
| Rooms | 17 twin/doubles: £80–£130. |
| | 1 family room for 3: £95–£130. |
| | 1 single: £75–£90. |
| Meals | Lunch from £6.50. |
| | Bar meals from £11.50. |
| | Dinner, 3 courses, £25–£40. |
| Closed | Christmas. |
| Directions | In St Boswells, on green, at junction with A68 and B6404. |

Billy & Rachael Hamilton
The Buccleuch Arms
The Green, St Boswells,
Melrose, TD6 0EW

Tel      +44 (0)1835 822243
Email    info@buccleucharms.com
Web      www.buccleucharms.com

## The Allanton Inn

Allanton, population 100. Welcome to the sleepy back of beyond, an untouched corner of the rural idyll that most people skip on their rush north. Well, there's no rush here, just patchwork fields, rolling hills and the river Tweed pottering off to the coast. As for this cute little inn, it's a great base from which to explore. The style is charming, the locals friendly, the prices lovely, the food a treat. It sits on the only street in town with a garden that backs onto open country; in summer you can have lunch in the sun while watching the farmer plough his fields. Inside, home-spun interiors have warmth, style and colour. There's an open-plan feel, the airy bar flowing into a half-panelled restaurant. You'll find a smouldering fire, good art, fresh flowers. Pretty rooms above come with good bathrooms, Farrow & Ball colours, padded bedheads and homemade biscuits. A couple are big, those at the back have the view. Super local food waits downstairs, perhaps hot smoked salmon, rack of local lamb, Tia Maria tiramisu. Local fishing is easy to arrange, there's golf and excellent walking, too.

| | |
|---|---|
| Rooms | 3 doubles, 2 twin/doubles: £75–£95. 1 family room for 4: £100–£130. Singles from £70. |
| Meals | Lunch from £6.75. Dinner, 3 courses, £25–£35. Sunday lunch from £12.50. |
| Closed | Christmas. |
| Directions | West from Berwick on A6105, then left in Churnside onto B6437. On left in village. |

**William & Katerina Reynolds**
The Allanton Inn
Allanton,
By Duns, TD11 3JZ

| | |
|---|---|
| Tel | +44 (0)1890 818260 |
| Email | info@allantoninn.co.uk |
| Web | www.allantoninn.co.uk |

## Scarista House

All you need to know is this: Harris is one of the most beautiful places in the world. Beaches of white sand that stretch for a mile or two are not uncommon. If you bump into another soul, it will be a delightful coincidence, but you should not count on it. The water is turquoise, coconuts sometimes wash up on the beach. The view from Scarista is simple and magnificent: field, ridge, beach, water, sky. Patricia and Tim are the kindest people, quietly inspiring. Their home is island heaven: coal fires, rugs on painted floors, books everywhere, old oak furniture, a first-floor drawing room and fabulous Harris light. Homely bedrooms come in country-house style. The golf club has left a set of clubs by the front door in case you wish to play (the view from the first tee is one of the best in the game). A corncrake occasionally visits the garden. There are walking sticks and wellington boots to help you up the odd hill. Kind local staff may speak Gaelic and the food is exceptional, maybe quail with an armagnac mousse, fillet of Stornoway halibut, orange marmalade tart. A perfect place.

| | |
|---|---|
| Rooms | 2 doubles, 1 twin: £185–£230. |
| | 3 suites for 2: £205–£240. |
| | Singles £125–£155. |
| Meals | Dinner, 3 courses, £43. |
| | Packed lunch £7.50. |
| Closed | Christmas, New Year, |
| | 1 January to 28 February. |
| Directions | From Tarbert A859 south, signed |
| | Rodel. Scarista 15 miles on left after |
| | golf course. W10 bus stops at gate. |

Patricia & Tim Martin
Scarista House
Scarista,
Isle of Harris, HS3 3HX

| | |
|---|---|
| Tel | +44 (0)1859 550238 |
| Email | timandpatricia@scaristahouse.com |
| Web | www.scaristahouse.com |

# Wales

## The Dolaucothi Arms

David and Esther's cute little inn sits in a village deep in rural Carmarthenshire. It's an absolute gem, a testament to beautiful simplicity, with lovely interiors that see no need to abandon their period charm for contemporary design. Instead, you find beautiful Georgian windows, original tiles in the bar, then varnished floorboards in the airy restaurant. It's a little like walking onto the pages of a Jane Austen novel, a touch of old-world charm. Pick up a pint of local ale, sink into a chesterfield sofa and roast away in front of the wood-burner; in summer you decant into the pretty garden for a pint in the sun. Excellent food awaits you – homemade soups and pies, lamb from the Dolaucothi estate, the best local steaks, sticky toffee pudding. Circular walks help you atone, there's a river at the bottom of the garden, then National Trust goldmines to visit in the village. Bedrooms upstairs are a steal with smart colours, woollen throws and sparkling bathrooms; some have garden views, all get decanters of port. Breakfast is a treat. Aberglasney Gardens are within easy reach. Don't miss Sunday lunch.

| | |
|---|---|
| Rooms | 2 doubles: £75-£80. Singles £55. Extra bed/sofabed available £20 per person per night. |
| Meals | Lunch from £5. Dinner, 3 courses, £20. Sunday lunch from £9. |
| Closed | 26 December to 2 January. |
| Directions | A40 toward Llandovery then right turn onto A482 to Lampeter. After 8 miles, you'll see Pumpsaint sign as you enter the village. Pub is on your left. |

David Joy & Esther Hubert
The Dolaucothi Arms
Pumpsaint,
Llanwrda, SA19 8UW

| | |
|---|---|
| Tel | +44 (0)1558 650237 |
| Email | info@thedolaucothiarms.co.uk |
| Web | www.thedolaucothiarms.co.uk |

## Ty Mawr Country Hotel

Pretty rooms, attractive prices and delicious food make this welcoming country house
hard to resist. It sits in a very peaceful spot. You drive over hills, drop into the village,
then wash up at this 16th-century stone house that comes in soft yellow. Outside, a
sun-trapping terrace laps against a trim lawn, which in turn drops into a passing river.
Gentle eccentricities abound: croquet hoops take odd diversions, logs are piled high like
giant beehives, a seat has been chiselled into a tree trunk. Inside, original stone walls and
low beamed ceilings give a warm country feel. There are fires everywhere – one in the
attractive sitting room that overlooks the garden, another in the dining room that burns
on both sides. Excellent bedrooms are all big. You get big beds, warm colours, crisp
linen, good bathrooms. Some have sofas, all are dog-friendly, three overlook the garden.
Back downstairs, the bar doubles as reception, while Welsh art on the walls is for sale.
Steve's cooking is the final treat, perhaps Cardigan Bay scallops, organic Welsh beef,
calvados and cinnamon rice pudding. Top stuff. *Children over 10 welcome.*

| | |
|---|---|
| Rooms | 4 doubles, 2 twin/doubles: £115-£130. Singles £75. Dinner, B&B £80-£88 per person. |
| Meals | Dinner £25-£30. |
| Closed | Rarely. |
| Directions | M4 west onto A48, then B4310 exit, for National Botanic Gardens. 6 miles north to Brechfa. In village centre. |

Annabel & Steve Thomas
Ty Mawr Country Hotel
Brechfa, SA32 7RA

| | |
|---|---|
| Tel | +44 (0)1267 202332 |
| Email | info@wales-country-hotel.co.uk |
| Web | www.wales-country-hotel.co.uk |

## The Cors

A bohemian bolthole, one of the best. Nick is a cook, an artist and gardener, his two lush acres a perfect retreat in summer, so come to sip your Earl Grey while the river potters past. Gunnera, bamboo and tree ferns all flourish, so expect a little green-fingered theatre. Inside, a small, personal world of French inspiration – sit in the bar and be swept back to 1950s Paris. Doors open onto a Victorian veranda where roses and clematis ramble elegantly, perfect for pre-dinner drinks in summer. As for the food, you eat accompanied by cool tunes, with busts and paintings all around – perhaps at the front with garden views, or wrapped up behind in claret reds. It's a feast of local produce with an Italian twist: roasted figs with gorgonzola and Parma ham, Carmarthenshire chicken filled with spinach and mascarpone, then a zesty lemon tart. Bedrooms upstairs have a simple, chic style: rugs on bare boards, vintage William Morris wallpapers, pretty pine, bold colours – perfect for the price. Don't miss Laugharne for all things Dylan Thomas. *Minimum stay: 2 nights in summer.*

| | |
|---|---|
| Rooms | 3 doubles: £80.  Singles from £50. |
| Meals | Dinner, 3 courses, from £35 (Thur-Sat only). Sunday lunch from £17. |
| Closed | 2 weeks in November. |
| Directions | A4066 south from St Clears for Laugharne. In village right at pub. Over bridge and on right. |

Nick Priestland
The Cors
Newbridge Road,
Laugharne, SA33 4SH
Tel      +44 (0)1994 427219
Email   nick@thecors.co.uk
Web     www.thecors.co.uk

## Penbontbren

You're lost in lovely hills, yet only three miles from the sea. Not that you're going to stray far. These gorgeous suites don't just have wonderful prices, they're heaped with comforts, too – this is a great spot to come and do nothing at all. Richard and Huw have thought it all through. You get crockery and cutlery, kettles and fridges, then you're encouraged to bring your own wine or to buy provisions from the farm shop for lunch. As for the suites, expect big beds, super bathrooms, sofas and armchairs in pretty sitting areas, then doors onto semi-private terraces – perfect for lunch in summer. You get iPod docks, flat-screen TVs, robes and White Company lotions, too. The new garden room is a little smaller than the others, but has a big terrace to compensate. Breakfast is served in the main house – the full Welsh works. Beautiful hills, sandy beaches, Cardigan and magical St Davids all wait. Good local restaurants are on hand: lobster from the sea, lamb from the hills. Don't miss The Shed in Porthgain for excellent fish and chips. A great place to unwind with discounts for longer stays. *Minimum stay: 2 nights in high season.*

| | |
|---|---|
| Rooms | 6 suites for 2: £99–£120.<br>Singles from £80.<br>1 self-catering cottage for 7:<br>£700–£1,150 per week. |
| Meals | Restaurants within 3 miles. |
| Closed | Christmas. |
| Directions | A484 from Carmarthen, then B4333<br>for Aberporth and onto A487. |

Richard Morgan-Price & Huw Thomas
Penbontbren
Glynarthen,
Llandysul, SA44 6PE
Tel       +44 (0)1239 810248
Email   contact@penbontbren.com
Web     www.penbontbren.com

AWARD
WINNER

Nicely priced

## Nanteos Mansion

A grand old manor house lost at the end of a one-mile drive, with a small lake, a walled garden and 25 acres of ancient woodland. Views at the front stretch across to nearby hills, four pillars stand at the front door, sofas wait by a wood-burner in the hall. The house dates to 1731, but stands on medieval foundations. It is most famous for the Nanteos Cup – the Holy Grail to you and me – which legend says was carried here by monks from Glastonbury Abbey. A magnificent renovation recently brought the house back to life – electric-shock therapy performed by interior designers. Downstairs, there's a morning room, a sitting-room bar and an elegant restaurant where you dig into Nigel's delicious food, perhaps chilli salt squid, salt marsh lamb, a trio of chocolate puddings. Upstairs, big suites are grand and gracious, some panelled, others with fine wallpaper, but the rooms are lovely, too, with lots of colour, original art and robes in excellent bathrooms. There's loads to do: rivers to fish, mountains to climb, coastal paths to follow. Don't miss the music room (Wagner visited). Brilliant.

| | |
|---|---|
| Rooms | 14 twin/doubles: £180–£300. 1 house for 8: £500. Singles from £130. Dinner, B&B from £125 per person. |
| Meals | Lunch from £7.50. Dinner £33.95–£39.50. Sunday lunch from £22. |
| Closed | Rarely. |
| Directions | Leaving Aberystwyth to the south, take A4120 Devil's Bridge Road, then immediately right onto B4340. House signed left after 1 mile. |

Nigel Jones
Nanteos Mansion
Rhydyfelin,
Aberystwyth, SY23 4LU
Tel        +44 (0)1970 600522
Email   info@nanteos.com
Web     www.nanteos.com

## Ffin Y Parc

If you love art, if beautiful things tickle you pink, if you like big old houses stylishly refurbished with a streak of contemporary flair, then you should cancel whatever you're doing next week and head for Ffin Y Parc. This is a gorgeous country pad – homespun, quirky, a creative bolthole that sits in 14 peaceful acres. Inside it's an exceptional gallery, not any old gallery showing a little local art, but one that curates some of the best Welsh art, with two artists a month on display – in the conservatory café where you scoff your bacon and eggs, in the airy bar where cool tunes play, and in the big sitting room where you sink into armchairs and watch smouldering logs on the fire. Bedrooms upstairs are equally lovely, with beautiful colours, elegant furniture, more fabulous art and some very fancy bathrooms. Two cool stone cottages wait outside if you want to stay a while. Lunch is served in the café: soups, quiche, perhaps a club sandwich, there are light meals in the evening for guests and a restaurant that comes to life at weekends. Snowdon waits.

| | |
|---|---|
| Rooms | 2 doubles, 1 twin/double: £135–£165. 1 suite for 2: £180–£210. 1 self-catering cottage for 2 (short breaks from £295), 1 self-catering cottage for 4 (short breaks from £375): £495–£750 per week. |
| Meals | Lunch from £5.50. |
| Closed | Mon & Tue. January. |
| Directions | A55, junc.19, then A470 south for 10 miles. House signed left 1 mile south of Llanrwst. |

Roland Powell & Ralph Sanders
Ffin Y Parc
Betws Road,
Llanrwst, LL26 0PT

| | |
|---|---|
| Tel | +44 (0)1492 642070 |
| Email | ralph@ffinyparc.co.uk |
| Web | www.ffinyparc.com |

## Escape Boutique B&B

A designer B&B with lovely rooms, attractive prices and some seriously fancy bathrooms. The house stands high on the hill, away from the crowds, a short stroll from the buzz of town and its two-mile beach. This is a 19th-century mill owner's villa and its fine old windows, sparkling wood floors and carved fireplace bear testament to its Victorian roots. Other than that it's a clean sweep of funky interiors. Sam and Gaenor scoured Europe for their eclectic collection of colourful retro furniture that fills the rooms — orange swivel chairs, iconic G-plan sofas, beautiful beds wrapped in crisp white linen. You'll find cow-hide rugs, funky wallpapers, big views from rooms at the front. All come with flat-screen TVs, Blu-ray DVD players and iPod docks. Bathrooms are excellent: one room has a shower for two, another has a copper bath in the room. Downstairs, there's an honesty bar in the sitting room, while delicious breakfasts are served in an attractive dining room. Good food waits in town — the Seahorse for fish, Mamma Rosa for Italian. Great Orme waits above for big views of the bay. *Minimum stay: 2 nights at weekends.*

| | |
|---|---|
| Rooms | 8 doubles, 1 twin/double: £95–£149. Singles from £80. |
| Meals | Restaurants within walking distance. |
| Closed | Christmas. |
| Directions | A55 junc. 19, then A470 for Llandudno. On promenade, head west hugging the coast, then left at Belmont Hotel and house on right. |

Sam Nayar & Gaenor Loftus
Escape Boutique B&B
48 Church Walks,
Llandudno, LL30 2HL

| | |
|---|---|
| Tel | +44 (0)1492 877776 |
| Email | info@escapebandb.co.uk |
| Web | www.escapebandb.co.uk |

## Osborne House

Osborne House – originally the summer residence of a Cheshire brewer – dates to 1850, and was one of the first houses to be built on the promenade. It fell into the hands of Elyse's parents in the mid-1980s, who refurbished from top to toe, turning 23 small rooms into seven enormous suites. They didn't hold back – expect a grand Victorian feel with a dash of Belle Époque. You'll find Corinthian columns, crystal chandeliers, noble portraits on the walls, comfy sofas in front of the fire. Downstairs, there's a sitting room at the front with views of the bay, a bar in the middle for the daily papers, then curtains that open theatrically onto a muralled dining room at the back. Suites are huge – big sitting rooms, brass beds, claw-foot baths and walk-in showers. You'll find rugs on wood floors, ornate marble fireplaces, armchairs and sofas to take the strain; all but one have sea views. Bistro food waits downstairs, perhaps seared scallops, a rib-eye steak, baked toffee and chocolate sponge. There's off-road parking, too, and you can use the pool at the Empire, Osborne House's sister hotel. *Minimum stay: 2 nights at weekends.*

|  |  |
|---|---|
| Rooms | 7 suites for 2: £135–£185. |
|  | Dinner, B&B from £82.50 per person. |
| Meals | Lunch from £5. |
|  | Afternoon tea from £8.50. |
|  | Dinner from £10.95. |
| Closed | 1 week over Christmas |
| Directions | A55, junc. 19, then A470 in Llandudno. At sea, turn left, then right at r'about onto North Parade. On left. |

Elyse Waddy
Osborne House
Promenade, 17 North Parade,
Llandudno, LL30 2LP

| | |
|---|---|
| Tel | +44 (0)1492 860330 |
| Email | sales@osbornehouse.co.uk |
| Web | www.osbornehouse.co.uk |

## The Hand at Llanarmon

Single-track lanes plunge you into the middle of nowhere. All around, valleys rise and fall, so pull on your boots and scale a mountain or bring your bike and hurtle along fantastic trails. Back at The Hand, a 16th-century drovers' inn, the pleasures of a traditional local are hard to miss. A coal fire burns on the range in reception, a wood fire crackles in the front bar, a wood-burner warms the restaurant. Expect stone walls, low beamed ceilings, old pine settles and candles on the mantelpiece. There's a locals' bar for darts and pool, a quiet sitting room for maps and books. Delicious food draws a crowd, so grab a table and dig into something hearty, perhaps duck pakoras with cauliflower purée, steak and ale pie with mashed potatoes, dark chocolate crème brûlée with vanilla ice cream. Jackie and Jonathan recently bought the inn and are full of ideas – a treatment room is coming soon, bedrooms are getting a lovely makeover. One has a claw-foot bath, all are spotless with a cosy country feel. John Ceiriog Hughes, who wrote *Bread of Heaven*, lived in the valley. Special indeed.

| Rooms | 9 doubles, 4 twin/doubles: £90–£128. Singles from £52.50. |
|---|---|
| Meals | Lunch from £4.75. Bar meals from £9.50. Dinner, 3 courses, £25–£30. Sunday lunch from £15. |
| Closed | Rarely. |
| Directions | Leave A5 south of Chirk for B4500. Llanarmon 11 miles on. |

Jackie & Jonathan Greatorex
The Hand at Llanarmon
Llanarmon Dyffryn Ceiriog,
Llangollen, LL20 7LD
Tel       +44 (0)1691 600666
Email     reception@thehandhotel.co.uk
Web       www.thehandhotel.co.uk

## Plas Bodegroes

A glorious house, one of the loveliest places to stay in Wales. It may be far flung, but it's worth every second it takes to get here. Outside, six acres of beautiful gardens include a 200-year-old avenue of beech trees. Inside, a cool elegance roams freely: golden wallpapers, smouldering fires, a quirky bar that appears from thin air. French windows flood the house with light and open on to a veranda that's wrapped in climbing roses. In good weather you take afternoon tea here while watching sheep graze in the fields; it's a little like being in a period drama. Bedrooms are beautiful – chic fabrics, smart beds, crisp linen, super bathrooms – it really doesn't matter which one you get. Some open onto a courtyard, a lovely spot for pre-dinner drinks in the evening sun. As for dinner, you eat in a dining room that doubles as an art gallery, a suitably theatrical spot for Chris's fabulous food, perhaps Nefyn Bay scallops, Welsh mountain lamb, bread and butter pudding with Welsh whisky ice cream. The Llyn Peninsula waits: excellent walking, sandy beaches, towering cliffs. Pure heaven.

| | |
|---|---|
| Rooms | 5 doubles, 2 twin/doubles: £140–£160. 3 suites for 2: £180. Singles from £115. Dinner. B&B £107.50–£127.50 p.p. (min 2 nights). |
| Meals | Sunday lunch £24.50. Dinner £48.50. Not Sun or Mon evenings. |
| Closed | Sunday nights and Mondays. December to February. |
| Directions | From Pwllheli A497 towards Nefyn. House on left after 1 mile, signed. |

Chris & Gunna Chown
Plas Bodegroes
Efailnewydd,
Pwllheli, LL53 5TH
Tel        +44 (0)1758 612363
Email      gunna@bodegroes.co.uk
Web        www.bodegroes.co.uk

Hotel of the Year
Wales

Entry 295   Map 5

## Plas Dinas Country House

The family home of Lord Snowdon dates to the 1600s and stands in 15 rural acres with an avenue of oak sweeping you up to the house. Princess Margaret often stayed and much of what fills the house belongs to the family: striking chandeliers, oils by the score, gilt-framed mirrors – an Aladdin's cave of beautiful things. There's a baby grand piano in the drawing room, where you find a roaring fire and an honesty bar, but potter about and find masses of memorabilia framed on the walls (make sure you visit the private dining room). Bedrooms – some with views across fields to the sea – mix a graceful past with modern design. You get four-posters, period colours, bold wallpapers, a sofa if there's room. A cute room in the eaves has mountain views, all have hot-water bottles, Apple TVs and excellent bathrooms, some with showers, others with free-standing baths. Good food waits in the restaurant, perhaps fishcakes with lime and ginger, lamb shank with a rosemary jus, chocolate tart with white chocolate ice-cream. Snowdon is close, as you'd expect, so bring walking boots and mountain bikes. *Minimum stay: 2 nights on bank holiday weekends.*

| | |
|---|---|
| Rooms | 5 doubles, 5 twin/doubles: £99–£249. |
| Meals | Dinner, 3 courses, £25–£35. |
| Closed | Christmas. |
| Directions | South from Caernarfon on A487. Through Bontnewydd and signed right after half a mile at brow of shallow hill. |

**Neil Baines & Marco Soares**
Plas Dinas Country House
Bontnewydd,
Caernarfon, LL54 7YF

| | |
|---|---|
| Tel | +44 (0)1286 830214 |
| Email | info@plasdinas.co.uk |
| Web | www.plasdinas.co.uk |

## Llwyndû Farmhouse

The view here is fabulous – a clean sweep across Cardigan Bay to the Llyn Peninsula beyond. Below, a ten-mile beach runs north to Harlech Point; behind, the Rhinog mountains rise. As for the farmhouse, it sits high on the hill and dates to 1581. It's a small, homespun world – Peter and Paula do it all themselves – a simple retreat with delicious slow food at the end of the day. Inside, you find thick stone walls, comfy sofas and a wood-burner in the inglenook. Bedrooms are scattered about. Those in the main house have a cosy feel with warm colours, low ceilings, perhaps a four-poster. Those in the outbuildings tend to be a little bigger and have painted stone walls, then ceilings open to the rafters. By day you explore the wonders of Snowdonia – you can climb mountains, take to cycle tracks or merely walk in the hills. By night you return to feast on local delights under ancient beams, perhaps Rhydlewis smoked salmon, Welsh Black steak, apple tarte tatin; if you're still hungry after that, excellent Welsh cheeses wait. Don't miss Portmeirion, or links golf at Harlech and Aberdovey. *Minimum stay: 2 nights.*

| | |
|---|---|
| Rooms | 3 doubles, 2 four-posters: £104–£126. 1 family room for 4: £104–£146. Singles from £52. Dinner B&B from £82 per person. |
| Meals | Dinner £25–£30. |
| Closed | January. |
| Directions | Signed right on A496 2 miles north of Barmouth where street lights stop. |

Peter & Paula Thompson
Llwyndû Farmhouse
Llanaber,
Barmouth, LL42 1RR

| | |
|---|---|
| Tel | +44 (0)1341 280144 |
| Email | intouch@llwyndu-farmhouse.co.uk |
| Web | www.llwyndu-farmhouse.co.uk |

## Penmaenuchaf Hall

This grand old house sits high on the hill with fine views over the Mawddach estuary. It stands in 20 acres of woodlands and formal gardens with daffodils, snowdrops and bluebells running riot in spring and a walled garden that bursts with summer colour. The house has attitude, too. It was built in 1865 for a Bolton cotton merchant, and an open fire crackles in the half-panelled hall, where sofas and armchairs wait. The drawing room is equally grand with mullioned windows that frame the view, cavernous sofas and a grand piano, country rugs on original wood floors. There's an airy restaurant, where French windows open onto a terrace, so eat al fresco in good weather, perhaps seared scallops, Gressingham duck, apple tart and honey ice cream. Bedrooms come in traditional country-house style with big, comfy beds and warm colours. Some are huge, others have balconies or a new bathroom, all have iPod docks and digital radios. Outside, Snowdon waits, there are 13 miles of river to fish and the fabulous mountain biking trails of Coed-y-Brenin for fun at all levels in the forest. *Children over 6 welcome.*

| | |
|---|---|
| Rooms | 7 doubles, 5 twin/doubles, 1 four-poster: £180-£280. 1 family room for 4: £250-£280. Singles from £125. |
| Meals | Lunch from £6. Afternoon tea from £7.90. Dinner, 3 courses, £27.50-£45. |
| Closed | Rarely. |
| Directions | From Dolgellau A493 west for about 1.5 miles. Entrance on left. |

Mark Watson & Lorraine Fielding
Penmaenuchaf Hall
Penmaenpool,
Dolgellau, LL40 1YB

| | |
|---|---|
| Tel | +44 (0)1341 422129 |
| Email | relax@penhall.co.uk |
| Web | www.penhall.co.uk |

## Y Meirionnydd

By day you explore the mighty wonders of Snowdonia, by night you return to this lovely small hotel and recover in style. It's one of those places that delivers just what you want; it's smart without being posh, the welcome is second to none, tasty food hits the spot, the bedrooms are excellent. You're in the middle of a small country town with a terrace at the front, so sit outside in summer and watch the world pass by. Inside, soft colours and warm lighting create a relaxed feel. There's a cute bar with armchairs and games, an airy breakfast room for the full Welsh works, then a smart restaurant cut into the rock, which was once the county jail; the food is somewhat better these days, perhaps game terrine with mustard piccalilli, rump of Welsh lamb with rosemary dumplings, Penderyn Welsh whisky and honey ice cream. Bedrooms upstairs fit the bill nicely. Some are bigger than others, but all have the same style: clean lines, cool colours, big beds, beautiful linen. You get the odd stone wall, an armchair if there's room, then super bathrooms. There's secure storage for bikes, too. *Minimum stay: 2 nights at weekends.*

| | |
|---|---|
| Rooms | 3 doubles, 2 twin/doubles: £99-£125. Singles £65. |
| Meals | Dinner, 3 courses, £25. Not Mondays in low season. |
| Closed | One week at Christmas. |
| Directions | In centre of town on one-way system, off A470. |

Marc Russell & Nick Banda
Y Meirionnydd
Smithfield Square,
Dolgellau, LL40 1ES
Tel    +44 (0)1341 422554
Email  info@themeirionnydd.com
Web    www.themeirionnydd.com

## The Whitebrook

Chris and Kirsty came west to do their own thing, revamping this famous old restaurant with rooms in great style, then winning a Michelin star — all in their first year. It's quite some feat, but no surprise. Chris has a culinary pedigree few can match, including five years with Raymond Blanc at Le Manoir aux Quat'Saisons. As for the house, it sits in a tiny village that's wrapped up in the Wye Valley. Forest rises all around, bluebells carpet the woods in spring, deer amble by in summer. Outside, there's a terrace for lunch in good weather. Inside, a cool, uncluttered elegance runs throughout, a great spot to treat yourself to Chris's ambrosial food. Much is foraged — hogweed, nettles, wild chervil, bitter cress — while most is local with lamb from the valley and beef from Ross. You can eat à la carte or splash out on a seven-course tasting menu, perhaps squab pigeon with rhubarb, Cornish turbot with ground elder, caramelised white chocolate with pink grapefruit. Lovely rooms have colour and style, woollen throws, good beds and fancy bathrooms. Tintern Abbey on the river Wye is close.

| | |
|---|---|
| Rooms | 6 doubles, 2 twin/doubles: £130-£190. |
| Meals | Lunch from £25. |
| | Dinner, 3 courses, £54. |
| | Tasting menu £67. Not Mondays. |
| | Sunday lunch £35. |
| Closed | Mondays. Two weeks in January. |
| Directions | M4 junc. 24, A449/A40 north to Monmouth, then B4293 south. Up hill. After 2.7 miles left for Whitebrook. On right after two miles. |

Chris & Kirsty Harrod
The Whitebrook
Whitebrook,
Monmouth, NP25 4TX
Tel        +44 (0)1600 860254
Email      info@thewhitebrook.co.uk
Web        www.thewhitebrook.co.uk

## The Bell at Skenfrith

The position here is magical: an ancient stone bridge, a river snaking through the valley, glorious hills rising beyond, cows grazing in lush fields. It's a perfect spot, not least because providence blessed it with this chic little inn. Inside, you find a locals' bar for the odd game of rugby, sofas in front of a wood-burner in the sitting room, then an airy restaurant for some very good food. In summer, doors fly open and life spills onto a stone terrace with views of hill and wood – a fine spot for lunch in the sun. Elegant country-house bedrooms brim with light. Some are beamed, most are big, you'll find padded bedheads, Farrow & Ball colours, perhaps a walnut bed or a claw-foot bath in your room. Those at the front have river views, those at the back look onto the hills, some have sofas, all have robes in excellent bathrooms. Seven circular walks start at the front door with maps to show you the way. Delicious food awaits your return, perhaps Welsh rarebit with a poached egg, braised beef brisket with dauphinoise potatoes, apple doughnuts with toffee sauce and mulled cider. *Minimum stay: 2 nights at weekends.*

| | |
|---|---|
| Rooms | 5 doubles, 3 twin/doubles, 3 four-posters: £130–£220. Singles from £75. Dinner, B&B from £85 per person. |
| Meals | Lunch from £5.95. Sunday lunch from £12.95. Dinner, 3 courses, around £35. |
| Closed | Rarely. |
| Directions | From Monmouth B4233 to Rockfield; B4347 north for 5 miles; right on B4521; Skenfrith 1 mile. |

Richard Ireton & Sarah Hudson
The Bell at Skenfrith
Skenfrith,
Abergavenny, NP7 8UH
Tel        +44 (0)1600 750235
Email      enquiries@skenfrith.co.uk
Web        www.skenfrith.co.uk

## Penally Abbey

This beautifully refurbished country-house hotel sits high on the hill with long views over Carmarthen Bay, but you'll turn your back on them for the chic interiors that run through this splendid house. Outside, there's a small courtyard, then five acres of lawns and woodland, where bluebells run riot in spring. Inside, airy interiors reveal cool colours, painted panelling, parquet flooring, the odd Doric column. There's a lovely bar in deep charcoal with fine art on the walls, then a big drawing room with an open fire and huge sea views. Doors in the sun room open onto a graveled terrace, where you can read the papers, dig into afternoon tea, or fall asleep in the sun. Bedrooms have a lovely new look: off-white walls, beautiful beds, crisp white linen, chic fabrics. Big rooms in the main house have vast windows to frame the view, those in the coach house have sublime white marble bathrooms. You eat in style in the restaurant – period colours, grand chandelier – perhaps local crab, sea bass with chilli and ginger, dark chocolate tort with pistachio ice cream. There's fine coastal walking, too.

| | |
|---|---|
| Rooms | 3 doubles, 6 twin/doubles, 2 four-posters: £130–£160. Dinner, B&B from £90 per person. |
| Meals | Lunch from £5. Dinner, 3 courses, £30–£35. Sunday lunch from £12.95. |
| Closed | January. |
| Directions | From Tenby A4139 for Pembroke. Right into Penally after 1.5 miles. Hotel signed above village green. Train station 5-mins walk. |

Melanie & Lucas Boissevain
Penally Abbey
Penally,
Tenby, SA70 7PY

| | |
|---|---|
| Tel | +44 (0)1646 661787 |
| Email | info@penally-abbey.com |
| Web | www.penally-abbey.com |

## Stackpole Inn

This lovely inn sits in a pretty village that's marooned in beautiful country. It's a few miles back from the sea, with Barafundle Bay – one of the finest beaches in Britain – a short walk away. You can pick up the coastal path, too, and follow it round past Stackpole Quay and St Govan's Chapel to the cliffs at Linney Head, then the surfers at Freshwater West. It's pure heaven, one of those sleepy areas you drop into for a couple of days and hardly use your car. As for the Stackpole, it's a great little base – stylish and welcoming with tasty rustic food, perhaps deep-fried whitebait, rib of local beef, almond and hazelnut tart. Outside, the pub is drenched in honeysuckle and there's a small garden to the front for a drop of Welsh ale in summer. Inside, you find low wooden ceilings, exposed stone walls, a hard-working wood-burner and four hand pumps at the slate bar. Super bedrooms have comfy beds, stripped floors, seaside colours and excellent bathrooms. All have sofabeds, two have velux windows for star gazing. Dogs and children are very welcome.

| | |
|---|---|
| Rooms | 2 twin/doubles: £90.<br>2 family rooms for 4: £90–£120.<br>Singles from £60. |
| Meals | Dinner, 3 courses, £25–£30<br>(not Sun October–March).<br>Lunch from £5.<br>Sunday lunch from £9.50. |
| Closed | Rarely. |
| Directions | B4319 south from Pembroke for 3 miles,<br>then left for Stackpole. Through<br>Stackpole Cheriton, up hill, right at<br>T-junction. On right. |

**Gary & Becky Evans**
Stackpole Inn
Stackpole,
Pembroke, SA71 5DF
Tel       +44 (0)1646 672324
Email    info@stackpoleinn.co.uk
Web     www.stackpoleinn.co.uk

## The Grove at Narberth

In the last few years the Grove has emerged as one of the loveliest places to stay in Wales – a cool country-house hotel with one foot in its Georgian past and the other in a contemporary present. It stands deep in Pembrokeshire's beautiful hills with sprawling views to the front and a vast kitchen garden that provides much for the table. Inside, Arts & Crafts interiors come as standard in the main house – an explosion of wood in the entrance hall, a roaring fire in the drawing-room bar, a super-smart restaurant for some of the best food in Wales, perhaps foie gras brulée with pickled rhubarb, spiced red mullet with a squid risotto, chocolate mousse with beetroot sorbet. Gorgeous bedrooms are split between the main house and converted outbuildings. All are divine, some are just bigger than others. Expect beautiful fabrics, cool wallpaper, crisp white linen, delicious beds. Bathrooms are equally spoiling with robes and heated floors, perhaps a claw-foot bath or a walk-in power shower. The coastal path is close, as is Laugharne, where Dylan Thomas lived, and Narberth, a quirky country town. *Minimum stay: 2 nights at weekends.*

| | |
|---|---|
| Rooms | 14 doubles: £190–£270. |
| | 6 suites for 2: £310. |
| | Singles from £160. |
| | Extra bed £30 per child, £50 per adult. |
| Meals | Lunch from £7. Afternoon tea from £9. |
| | Dinner, 3 courses, £54. |
| | 7-course tasting menu £78. |
| Closed | Never. |
| Directions | M4, then A48 & A40 west towards Haverfordwest. At A470 roundabout, take 1st exit to Narberth. Through town, down hill, then follow brown signs to hotel. |

Neil Kedward & Zoe Agar
The Grove at Narberth
Molleston,
Narberth, SA67 8BX

| | |
|---|---|
| Tel | +44 (0)1834 860915 |
| Email | info@thegrove-narberth.co.uk |
| Web | www.thegrove-narberth.co.uk |

## Roch Castle Hotel

The best way to plan your day at this fabulous 12th-century castle is to spin onto the ramparts after breakfast and search for the best weather. This isn't a tricky task, the views are spectacular – west over Newgale beach to St Davids; south over St Brides Bay to Skomer Island, north over rolling country to the Preseli Hills. As for the castle, it was built by a Norman knight and stands in 12 beautiful acres. Recently refurbished, it offers the best of two worlds: 800-year-old bricks and mortar, 21st-century comfort and style. Airy interiors are home to local art, eastern ceramics, the odd tapestry hanging on the wall. Climb the stairs and find a tiny chapel, a smart sitting room, a wood-burner for winter nights, an honesty bar for summer sundowners. Chic bedrooms have comfy beds, warm colours, wood floors and espresso machines. You get robes in good bathrooms; all have power showers, a couple have baths, too. The coastal path waits at nearby Newgale beach (you can surf its waves, too). You'll find good restaurants in Solva and St Davids, or take the whole place and cook for yourselves. Brilliant. *Minimum stay: 2 nights at weekends.*

| | |
|---|---|
| Rooms | 6 doubles: £200–£230. |
| Meals | Restaurants nearby. |
| Closed | Never. |
| Directions | West from Haverfordwest on A487. In Roch, right into village and on right after 600m. |

Wendy Stratton
Roch Castle Hotel
Roch,
Pembroke, SA62 6AQ

| | |
|---|---|
| Tel | +44 (0)1437 729900 |
| Email | stay@rochcastle.com |
| Web | www.rochcastle.com |

## Crug Glas

If you've never been to St Davids, know this: it is one of the most magical places in Britain. It sits in Pembroke's national park, has an imperious 12th-century cathedral, and is surrounded by magnificent coastline that's dotted with cliffs and vast sandy beaches. As for Janet's wonderful retreat, it's part chic hotel, part farmhouse B&B, stylish yet personal, a great place to stay. The house dates from 1120 and sits in 600 acres of arable and grazing land (they rear cattle, grow cereals). Outside, you find lawns and a small copse sprinkled with bluebells, then field and sky, and that's about it. Inside, there's an honesty bar in the sitting room and a Welsh dresser in the dining room, where Janet serves delicious food: homemade soups, home-reared beef, chocolate mousse with clotted cream. Bedrooms are the big surprise: a vast four-poster, a copper bath, old armoires, beautiful fabrics. All have robes in fancy bathrooms, one room occupies much of the top floor, two beautiful suites in an old barn have exposed timbers and underfloor heating. The coast is close.

| | |
|---|---|
| Rooms | 5 doubles, 2 twin/doubles: £150-£190. Singles from £95. |
| Meals | Lunch, 2 courses, from £18. Dinner, 3 courses, £25-£30. Sunday lunch £22.50. Afternoon tea from £12.50. |
| Closed | 22-27 December. |
| Directions | South from Fishguard on A487. Through Croes-goch, then signed right after 2 miles. |

Janet & Perkin Evans
Crug Glas
Solva,
Haverfordwest, SA62 6XX

| | |
|---|---|
| Tel | +44 (0)1348 831302 |
| Email | janet@crugglas.plus.com |
| Web | www.crug-glas.co.uk |

## The Manor Town House

Fishguard is quirky – arty and friendly with a folk festival in May and a jazz festival in August. You'll find great coastal walks, sandy beaches and magical St Davids a few miles south. In short, it's much more than an overnight stop on your way to Ireland and, with a happy vibe waiting at The Manor Town House, hard to resist. Chris and Helen escaped London and have taken to their new world like ducks to water. Inside, you're greeted by a couple of gorgeous sitting rooms – stripped floorboards, cool colours, local art, and crackling fires in winter. One has an honesty bar, you get fresh flowers, lots of books, and comfy sofas from which to plan your day. Homely bedrooms have lots of charm: bold colours, beautiful fabrics, the odd antique, super-comfy beds. Those at the back have sea views, perhaps a sofa or a padded window seat, while compact bathrooms do the trick. Breakfast is a treat, there's a garden for afternoon tea overlooking the harbour, and it's a one-minute stroll up the road to Bar 5 for cocktails and The Lounge at No. 3 for the best food in town. Pembrokeshire awaits. Brilliant. *Minimum stay: 2 nights at weekends in summer.*

| | |
|---|---|
| Rooms | 2 doubles, 3 twin/doubles: £90-£115. 1 single: £70-£85. Extra beds: adult £20, child under 16, £15. |
| Meals | Local restaurants within 100m. |
| Closed | 23-27 December. |
| Directions | M4 west, A48 west, A40 north, then A487 into town. Right at roundabout and on left. Parking close by. |

**Chris & Helen Sheldon**
The Manor Town House
11 Main Street,
Fishguard, SA65 9HG

| | |
|---|---|
| Tel | +44 (0)1348 873260 |
| Email | enquiries@manortownhouse.com |
| Web | www.manortownhouse.com |

## Cnapan Restaurant & Hotel

Cnapan is a way of life — a family affair with two generations at work in harmony. Judith excels in the kitchen, Michael looks after the bar and son Oliver has returned to the fold to help them both. It is a very friendly place that ticks to its own beat with locals popping in to book tables and guests chatting in the bar before dinner. The house is cosy and traditionally home-spun — whitewashed stone walls and old pine settles in the dining room; comfy sofas and a wood-burner in the sitting room; a tiny telly in the bar for the odd game of rugby (the game of cnapan, rugby's precursor, originated in the town). There are maps for walkers, bird books, flower books, the daily papers, too. Spill into the garden in summer for pre-dinner drinks under the weeping willow, then tuck into Judith's delicious food: smoked salmon fishcakes, Preseli lamb, banoffee pie with espresso ice-cream. Comfy bedrooms, warmly simple, are good value for money; half have new showers, half are getting them soon. You're in the Pembrokeshire National Park; beaches and cliff-top coastal walks beckon. *Minimum stay: 2 nights at weekends.*

| | |
|---|---|
| Rooms | 1 double, 4 twin/doubles: £95. 1 family room for 3: £110. Singles from £65. Dinner, B&B from £75 per person. |
| Meals | Dinner £25-£30. |
| Closed | 22 December to 19 March. |
| Directions | From Cardigan A487 to Newport. 1st pink house on right, 300 yds into Newport. |

**Michael, Judith & Oliver Cooper**
Cnapan Restaurant & Hotel
East Street,
Newport, SA42 0SY

Tel        +44 (0)1239 820575
Email      enquiry@cnapan.co.uk
Web        www.cnapan.co.uk

## Llys Meddyg

This cool little restaurant with rooms has a bit of everything: chic bedrooms that pack a punch, super food in a pine-clad restaurant, a cellar bar for cocktails before dinner, a pretty garden for summer. It's a friendly place with happy staff on hand to help, and it draws in the locals, who come for the excellent food, perhaps brown crab brulée with white crab meat, local pheasant with an oriental consommé, caramelized pear with blue-cheese ice-cream. You eat in style with a fire burning at one end of the restaurant and Welsh art hanging on the walls. Chic bedrooms come as standard. They're split between the main house (cool colours, vast beds, funky bathrooms) and the mews behind (rustic, airy and peaceful). All have the same fresh style: Farrow & Ball colours, lovely art, blond oak beds, fluffy white bath robes. In summer, decant into the garden, where a café/bistro opens up for coffee and cake or pizza from a wood-fired oven. Pembrokeshire's coastal path waits for windswept cliffs and sandy beaches. Don't miss St Davids or Laugharne for all things Dylan Thomas. Dogs are very welcome.

| | |
|---|---|
| Rooms | 4 doubles, 4 twin/doubles: £100–£180. 1 suite for 2: £100–£180. Singles from £85. |
| Meals | Lunch from £7. Dinner from £14. |
| Closed | Rarely. |
| Directions | East from Fishguard on A487. On left in Newport towards eastern edge of town. |

**Louise & Edward Sykes**
Llys Meddyg
East Street,
Newport, SA42 0SY

Tel     +44 (0)1239 820008
Email   info@llysmeddyg.com
Web     www.llysmeddyg.com

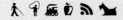

Entry 309   Map 1

## Gliffaes Hotel

A charming country-house hotel that towers above the river Usk as it pours through the valley below. In summer, doors open onto a large terrace, where you can sit in the sun and soak up the view – red kites circle above, sheep graze beyond. You're in 35 peaceful acres of formal lawns and mature woodland. Inside, interiors pack a punch. Afternoon tea 'on the house' is served every day in the panelled sitting room – family portraits hang on the wall, logs crackle in the grandest fireplace. This is a well-known fishing hotel and fishermen often gather in the bar for a quick drink and a tall tale. Eventually, they spin into the restaurant and dig into lovely seasonal food (the hotel is part of the Slow Food Movement), perhaps goat's cheese soufflé, fillet of halibut, lemon tart with passion fruit sorbet. Country-house bedrooms wait above. Expect smart fabrics, warm colours, crisp linen, fresh flowers. Several have river views, a couple have small balconies, one has a claw-foot bath that overlooks the front lawn. Outside, beautiful gardens include a small arboretum of specimen trees. Wonderful. *Minimum stay: 2 nights at weekends.*

| Rooms | 19 twin/doubles: £112–£265. |
|---|---|
| | 4 singles: £100. |
| | Dinner, B&B from £90 per person. |
| Meals | Light lunches from £5. |
| | Sunday lunch £22–£29. |
| | Dinner, 3 courses, £42. |
| Closed | January. |
| Directions | From Crickhowell, A40 west for 2.5 miles. Signed left and on left after 1 mile. |

**James & Susie Suter**
Gliffaes Hotel
Gliffaes Road,
Crickhowell, NP8 1RH

| Tel | +44 (0)1874 730371 |
|---|---|
| Email | calls@gliffaeshotel.com |
| Web | www.gliffaeshotel.com |

## The Felin Fach Griffin

It's quirky, homespun, and thrives on a mix of relaxed informality and colourful style. The low-ceilinged bar resembles the sitting room of a small hip country house, with timber frames, cool tunes and comfy sofas in front of a smouldering fire. Painted stone walls come in blocks of colour, there's live music on Sunday nights, and you dine informally in the white-walled restaurant, with stock pots simmering on an Aga. The food is excellent, perhaps dressed Portland crab, rump of Welsh beef, treacle tart with bergamot sorbet; much of what you eat comes from a half-acre kitchen garden, with meat and game from the hills around you. Bedrooms above have style and substance: comfy beds wrapped in crisp linen, good bathrooms with fluffy towels, Roberts radios, a smattering of books, but no TV unless you ask. Breakfast is served in the dining room; wallow with the papers, make your own toast, scoff the full Welsh. A main road passes outside, but quietly at night, while lanes lead into the hills, so walk, ride, bike, canoe. Hay is close for books galore. Don't miss excellent off-season deals.

| Rooms | 2 doubles, 2 twin/doubles, 2 four-posters: £125–£160. 1 family room for 3: £165. Dinner, B&B from £90 p.p. |
|---|---|
| Meals | Lunch from £7. Dinner, 3 courses, about £30. Sunday lunch from £20. |
| Closed | Christmas Eve & Day (evening). 4 days in January. |
| Directions | From Brecon A470 north to Felin Fach (4.5 miles). On left. |

Charles & Edmund Inkin
The Felin Fach Griffin
Felin Fach,
Brecon, LD3 0UB
Tel        +44 (0)1874 620111
Email    enquiries@felinfachgriffin.co.uk
Web      www.felinfachgriffin.co.uk

## The Lake Country House & Spa

Deep in the silence of mid-Wales, an old-school country house that looks after you well. Fifty acres of lawns, lakes and ancient woodland wrap around you, there's a spa with an indoor pool, treatment rooms and a tennis court by the lake. Sit in a hot tub and watch guests fish for their supper, try your luck on the nine-hole golf course, saddle up nearby and take to the hills. Come home to afternoon tea in the big, elegant drawing room, where an archipelago of rugs warms a brightly polished wooden floor and chandeliers hang from the ceiling. The hotel opened over a hundred years ago and the leather-bound fishing logs date to 1894. A feel of the 1920s lingers. Fires come to life in front of your eyes, grand pianos and grandfather clocks sing their songs, snooker balls crash about in the distance. Dress for a delicious dinner – the atmosphere deserves it – then retire to cosseting bedrooms. Most are suites: those in the house are warmly traditional, those in the lodge softly contemporary. The London train takes four hours and stops in the village. Resident geese waddle.

| | |
|---|---|
| Rooms | 6 twin/doubles: £195. |
| | 24 suites for 2: £240-£260. |
| | Singles from £145. Dinner, B&B |
| | (min. 2 nights) from £122.50 p.p. |
| Meals | Lunch, 3 courses, £22.50. |
| | Dinner, 4 courses, £38.50. |
| Closed | Never. |
| Directions | From Builth Wells A483 west for |
| | 7 miles to Garth. Signed from village. |

Jean-Pierre Mifsud
The Lake Country House & Spa
Llangammarch Wells, LD4 4BS
Tel       +44 (0)1591 620202
Email    info@lakecountryhouse.co.uk
Web      www.lakecountryhouse.co.uk

## Milebrook House Hotel

An old-school country hotel with three acres of gardens that run down to the river Teme. You'll find Wales on one bank and England on the other, so bring your wellies and wade across; the walking is magnificent. The house, once home to writer Wilfred Thesiger, is informally run by two generations of the Marsden family with Beryl and Rodney leading the way. Step inside and enter a world that's rooted in a delightful past: clocks tick, cats snooze, fires crackle, the odd champagne cork escapes its bondage. Beautiful art hangs on the walls, the sitting room is stuffed with books, the bar comes in country-house style and there's food to reckon with in the dining room – perhaps Cornish scallops with a pea purée, rack of Welsh lamb with fondant potatoes, glazed orange tart with mango and praline. A kitchen garden supplies much for the table. You can fish for trout, spot deer in the woods, play croquet on the lawn. Red kite, moorhens, kingfishers and herons live in the valley. Homely bedrooms do the trick, and Presteigne and Ludlow are close.

| | |
|---|---|
| Rooms | 5 doubles, 4 twins: £144. |
| | 1 family room for 3: £172. |
| | Singles from £85. |
| | Dinner, B&B from £114 p.p. |
| Meals | Lunch, 2 courses, £14.95 (not Mon). |
| | Dinner, 3 courses, £32.95. |
| Closed | Rarely. |
| Directions | From Ludlow A49 north, then left at Bromfield on A4113 towards Knighton for 10 miles. Hotel on right. |

Rodney, Beryl & Joanne Marsden
Milebrook House Hotel
Stanage, Knighton, LD7 1LT

| | |
|---|---|
| Tel | +44 (0)1547 528632 |
| Email | hotel@milebrookhouse.co.uk |
| Web | www.milebrookhouse.co.uk |

## Fairyhill

This lovely country house on the Gower sits in 24 acres of beautiful silence with a sun-trapping terrace at the back for lunch in summer. Potter about and find a walled garden, a stream-fed lake, free-range ducks and an ancient orchard. Inside, country-house interiors come fully loaded: smart fabrics, warm colours, deep sofas, the daily papers. There's an open fire in the bar, a grand piano in the sitting room, then delicious food in the restaurant, most locally sourced. Stylish bedrooms hit the spot. Most are big and fancy, a couple are small, but sweet. Some have painted beams, others a sofa or a wall of golden paper. Sparkling bathrooms, some with separate showers, have deep baths, white robes and fancy oils; if that's not enough, there's a treatment room, too. Outside, the Gower waits — wild heathland, rugged coastline, some of the best beaches in the land — so explore by day, then return for a good meal, perhaps scallops with cauliflower and chorizo, Gower lamb with gratin potatoes, baked honey and amaretto cheesecake. The wine list is one of the best in Wales, so don't expect to go thirsty. *Children over 8 welcome.*

| | |
|---|---|
| Rooms | 3 doubles, 5 twin/doubles: £200–£300. Singles £180–£280. Dinner, B&B from £125 p.p. Extra bed £75 p.p. |
| Meals | Lunch from £10. Afternoon tea £20. Dinner £35–£45. Sunday lunch £27.50. |
| Closed | First 3 weeks in January. Mon & Tue, November–March. |
| Directions | M4 junc. 47, A483 south, then A484 west to Gowerton and B4295 for Llanrhidian. Through Oldwalls, 1 mile up on left. |

Andrew Hetherington & Paul Davies
Fairyhill
Reynoldston,
Gower Peninsula, SA3 1BS
Tel   +44 (0)1792 390139
Email  postbox@fairyhill.net
Web   www.fairyhill.net

# Alastair Sawday's

'More than a bed
for the night…'

Britain
France
Ireland
Italy
Portugal
Spain

www.sawdays.co.uk

Self-Catering | B&B | Hotel | Pub | Treehouses, Cabins, Yurts & More

Photo: The Idle Rocks Hotel, entry 26

Quick reference indices

### Wheelchair-accessible

At least one bedroom and bathroom accessible for wheelchair users. Phone for details.

### Children of all ages welcome

These owners have told us that they welcome children of all ages. Please note cots and highchairs may not necessarily be available.

### Channel Islands

### Scotland

### Wales

### Pets

Pets welcome; please let the owner know if you want to bring pets.

### England

Quick reference indices

Quick reference indices

## Pool
Swimming pool on the
premises; use may be by
arrangement.

## Bike

Bikes on the premises to hire or borrow.

## Tennis

Tennis court on the premises; use may be by arrangement.

Quick reference indices

Alastair Sawday has been publishing books for over twenty years, finding Special Places to Stay in Britain and abroad. All our properties are inspected by us and are chosen for their charm and individuality, and with twelve titles to choose from there are plenty of places to explore. You can buy any of our books at a reader discount of 25%* on the RRP.

 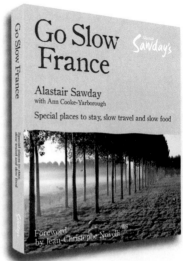

| List of titles: | RRP | Discount price |
| --- | --- | --- |
| British Bed & Breakfast | £15.99 | £11.99 |
| British Hotels and Inns | £15.99 | £11.99 |
| Pubs & Inns of England & Wales | £15.99 | £11.99 |
| Dog-friendly Breaks in Britain | £14.99 | £11.24 |
| French Bed & Breakfast | £15.99 | £11.99 |
| French Châteaux & Hotels | £15.99 | £11.99 |
| Italy | £15.99 | £11.99 |
| Portugal | £12.99 | £9.74 |
| Spain | £15.99 | £11.99 |
| Go Slow England & Wales | £19.99 | £14.99 |
| Go Slow France | £19.99 | £14.99 |

*postage and packaging is added to each order

How to order:
You can order online at: www.sawdays.co.uk/bookshop/
or call: +44(0)117 204 7810

# Join us

## TIME AWAY IS FAR TOO PRECIOUS TO SPEND IN THE WRONG PLACE. THAT'S WHY, BACK IN 1994, WE STARTED SAWDAY'S.

Twenty years on, we're still a family concern – and still on a crusade to stamp out the bland and predictable, and help our guests find truly special places to stay.

If you have one, we do hope you'll decide to take the plunge and join us.

———

*Alastair*   *Toby*

ALASTAIR & TOBY SAWDAY

"Trustworthy, friendly and helpful – with a reputation for offering wonderful places and discerning visitors."

JULIA NAISMITH, HOLLYTREE COTTAGE

"Sawday's. Is there any other?"

SONIA HODGSON, HORRY MILL

② Hotel  Highland ①

③ **Kilcamb Lodge Hotel & Restaurant**

④ Another beautiful West Coast setting with Loch Sunart at the end of the garden and Glas Bheinn rising beyond. Kilcamb – a barracks during the Jacobite uprising – has a bit of everything: a drawing room with an open fire; an elegant dining room for good food; a cool little brasserie that's recently been refurbished; a handful of lovely bedrooms in warm country-house style. There's a 12-acre garden that rolls down to the sea, where you can spot otters and seals. Ducks and geese fly over, if you're lucky you'll see eagles. Back inside, there's a stained-glass window on the landing, fresh flowers in the drawing room, driftwood lamps and good books. You can eat in the restaurant or the brasserie, either a five-course tasting menu or something simpler, perhaps a plate of seafood, Highland lamb, iced whisky parfait. Bedrooms have warm colours, some with a contemporary feel, others a smart country-house style. All have good bathrooms, crisp linen and comfy beds. Day trips to Mull are easy to arrange. Don't miss Ardnamuchan or Senna Bay at the end of the road.

⑤ Rooms — 2 doubles: £190–£275
6 twin/doubles: £250–£335.
2 suites for 2: £290–£415.
Price includes dinner for 2.

⑥ Meals — Lunch from £7.50. Afternoon tea from £5.50. 3-course dinner included; non-residents about £40.
Tasting menu £55.

⑦ Closed — Jan. Limited opening Nov & Feb.

⑧ Directions — From Fort William A82 south for 10 miles to Corran for ferry across to Ardgour, then A861 to Strontian. Hotel west of village on left.

**David & Sally Ruthven-Fox**
Kilcamb Lodge Hotel & Restaurant
Strontian,
Acharacle, PH36 4HY

Tel — +44 (0)1967 402257
Email — enquiries@kilcamblodge.co.uk
Web — www.kilcamblodge.co.uk

⑩  ⑨ Entry 261  Map 8

# WHY BECOME A MEMBER?

Becoming a part of our 'family' of Special Places is like being awarded a Michelin star. Our stamp of approval will tell guests that you offer a truly special experience and you will benefit from our experience, reputation and support.

## A CURATED COLLECTION

Our site presents a relatively small and careful selection of Special Places which helps us to stand out like a brilliantly shining beacon.

## INSPECT AND RE-INSPECT

Our inspectors have an eagle-eye for the special, but absolutely no check-lists. They visit every member, see every bedroom and bathroom and, on the lucky days, eat the food.

## QUALITY, NOT QUANTITY

We don't pretend (or want) to be in the same business as the sites that handle zillions of bookings a day. Using our name ensures that you attract the right kind of guests for you.

## VARIETY

From country-house hotels to city pads and funky fincas to blissful B&Bs, we genuinely delight in the individuality of our Special Places.

## LOYALTY

Nearly half of our members have been with us for five years or more. We must be doing something right!

*The friendly crew*

## GET IN TOUCH WITH OUR MEMBERSHIP TEAM...

+44 (0)117 204 7810
members@sawdays.co.uk

## ...OR APPLY ONLINE

sawdays.co.uk/joinus